TRANSCENDING
SORROW AND SUFFERING
(TRUST - TEST - TASTE)

TRANSCENDING
SORROW AND SUFFERING
(TRUST - TEST - TASTE)

COL. BISHAN SINGH

PARTRIDGE
A Penguin Random House Company

To order additional copies of this book, contact
Partridge India
000 800 10062 62
orders.india@partridgepublishing.com

www.partridgepublishing.com/india

CONTENTS

DEDICATED

The book is dedicated with love, reverence and gratitude to my parents, uncle-aunty and in-laws for empowering me with self esteem to continue relentlessly in completing the mission of writing this book, their blessings have been with me throughout my journey for attaining the grand success in my venture.

ACKNOWLEDGEMENT

Infact everything belongs to 'That' (Ultimate Truth-Supreme). Only ego belongs to us which our mind creates. The whole universe is learning school as such I am thankful to all that exists and lives which has contributed in some way or the other in completing my mission of writing this book. However specifically and particularly I am grateful to my family, friends and all others who always wished good luck to me for my success in this venture.

I am greatly thankful to my global fame publishers, Partridge (A Penguin Random House Company) for recognizing my work, also for publishing and marketing the book widely world over.

I place on record a special thanks for Farrina Gailey my consultant guide and Gemma Ramas publishing services associate both of them helped and directed me rightly and promptly for the publication of the book.

I have grateful thanks and gratitude for Anirudh singh (nephew) for designing an impressive and appealing front cover of the book. Jatan kanwar (wife) and Bharat singh (son) have earned and are entitled for my special thanks for editing, structuring and typing the script in a commendable manner. My sincere thanks flow affectionately for Dushiyant pratap singh (grandson) for clicking my befitting photograph for the back cover of the book, also for helping in typing the script.

ABOUT THE AUTHOR

The author Colonel. (Retd) Bishan Singh, Sena Medal comes from rural common middle class family of village Bhagwanpura, sub division Nawa, of Naguar division, Rajasthan (India). He graduated from Birla science college Pilani Rajasthan. He was commissioned as an officer into Grenadiers Regiment of Indian Army. He retired from the army after a meritorious service of twenty seven years. He was decorated with gallantry award of Sena Medal (army medal) in the year 1967 while fighting against Chinese in a skirmish at Nathula pass, Sikkim, India for displaying undaunted courage in the face of the enemy and was seriously wounded. He took active part in Indo-Pak wars of 1965 and 1971 respectively. The book is the outcome of almost twenty five years of research in the spiritual field. This is author's inner quest and interest to read, learn and experience the charm of spiritual living which made life festive with celebration, transcending sorrow and sufferings.

INTRODUCTION

Aim

The aim of writing this book is to inspire and awake people who are keen and earnest to go beyond sorrow and suffering. Everyman is born with possibility and potential to grow and evolve internally from within one's own self. It is not the privilege of the selected few only. However in spite of equal opportunity for all, very few persons have attained the true nature of their divinity. It is so because others lack the will, determination and earnestness, besides this they remain mostly mind oriented and least self (atma) conscious.

Mission

The mission of the book is to guide people for self transformation so that they become self disciplined and self controlled at their own from within, bringing peace, harmony and order in the society. When individuals are inspired to attain spirituality through non wavering, stable and silent mind only then, joy, peace and choiceless love are reflected in actions in the outer world, dissolving all distinctions and duality. When this happens it leads you to a blissful living free of disturbance and restlessness.

In this context I have a detached and universal desire that this book must reach the maximum hands world over so that people have easy reach to read it and improve according to their attitude, outlook, interest and earnestness.

Essence of the book

The core factor is the mind which creates and causes suffering because mind has nature and tendency to distort and imagine truth due to its limited nature bound by time and space. When you see things through mind things are seen partially with division and separation from the supreme self. When you see God through mind you see him only in temples and churches but beyond mind he is everywhere.

Mind creates nonself ego on the periphery against the soul at the center which causes duality and distinction. Mind being subjective, personal and private keeps weaving imaginary and illusory world every moment like it happens during a dream. Dream dissolves on waking up and ego dissolves on becoming aware of your supreme nature (divine). It can be attained by going beyond mind (dropping mind).

One full chapter is devoted to techniques for dropping mind through which you can attain thoughtlessness dissolving sorrow and suffering. You remain liberated and free when you go beyond mind. Consciousness is enriched and becomes pure when contents of mind (desire, fear, greed, jealousy, imagination and memory etc) are dropped. Wisdom happens when your mind becomes empty, clear and pure linking you to your divine self.

You need a non-wavering mind, which is totally peaceful to experience silence, joy and ecstasy of your divine nature dissolving miseries, chaos and disorder in life. The supreme self is focused as an embodied self inside all of us which is shinning peacefully and endlessly. We must actualize our essence of divine nature by purifying mind. This is the essence of ancient wisdom and an eternal truth which transformed man from human nature to divine nature. It needs great effort but most rewarding and paying. The light of awareness of the supreme is reflected through consciousness (chetna) in the pure mind. Awareness is centered in the consciousness, consciousness is centered in the mind and mind is centered in the body.

Body is created by nature (God). Guidance and inspiration comes through inner soul (sat guru), provided you become worthy of its blessings on attaining purity of mind. Outer guru (worldly teacher) who is trustworthy becomes our mile stone to guide us towards the journey to the divine source. Infact the whole universe is a learning school for self improvement provided you are alert, attentive, aware and earnest. Reading of scriptures and books containing spiritual matter are equally inspirational to guide you towards self transformation. Such books are only pointers and indicators to guide you for your spiritual attainment and an attempt to explain the inexplicable. If you do not experience from within your own self then the books will not help you much because they will only remain a concept and an idea in the absence of personal experience. The inner and outer gurus including books can only guide you up to the abyss but jumping into it is entirely your own affair which depends on your inner courage, will and determination.

Self (atma) is the common factor at the root of all experience. Experience becomes ego oriented when things are seen through mind. Beyond mind, ego dissolves and you attain egolessness. You must understand that a saint can sin and a sinner can be sanctified, both the possibilities exist. You have the option to become a saint or a sinner. You can become super human or you can go down to a sub human state. The worship of the self leads you to discover the truth of your being which is real and true transformation. Whenever you are egoless (without mind) the divine is present, whenever you are with ego (with mind) divine is absent.

Burdened mind is hindrance to deeper journey to your being (soul). Mind is burdened by learning, knowledge, information and negative thinking which make you selfish and personal. Knowledge, learning and information are essential for your outer growth, making you informative, knowledgeable and scholarly, but you remain spiritually empty. You must attain spiritual richness for attaining eternal virtues, for inner growth and evolvement. Mind by nature is noisy and restless due to endless flow of thoughts. You have to attain the state of thoughtlessness to make mind peaceful. Controlling mind with grit and determination is just not possible. All techniques given in chapter thirteen are aimed to make you thoughtless. Unless that happens craving of mind persists, making it restless and causing sorrow and suffering.

Words and thoughts make mind restless, disturbed and noisy. Nothing ever begins and ends in the supreme reality. Things which have beginning and end are false, unreal, transient and perishable. Thinking and feeling cannot transform you. In fact you have to translate these into actions for attainment of the truth.

Goal of life

The goal of life is to attain our true nature of the supreme self (divine self). This can be done by dropping mind through, awareness, meditation and witnessing. It happens when you enrich your consciousness by making it free of its contents and avoiding its localization. Make mind clear and empty, through techniques given in chapter thirteen of the book. Without inner transformation you will remain only on the outer periphery, which will disconnect you from your inner self.

Title of the book

The book is titled "Transcending Sorrow And Suffering" (Trust-Test-Taste). It is a possibility to transform from human nature to divine nature. You are born with potential to actualize your essence of your being (supreme self–divine) provided you are deeply earnest.

Ignorance does not know your true nature of divinity, also it means attachment to false and perishable things of the world. When you go beyond mind wisdom happens, reflecting insight and understanding for journey to the soul. Trust, Test and Taste means that you must realize and understand, that unknown truth and reality of your supreme self can be known only through total trust and surrender. There is no scope of any doubt. Doubt is the basis for scientific research but trust is the basis for knowing your true nature.

Anything that is not your experience remains a concept and cannot be a reality and truth. Great souls attained divinity through total trust. If they could, you too can. You also possess equal potential, but only lack earnestness. The enlightened souls in the past, translated trust into test by experiencing internally from within their own self and reached eternity. If they could test through experiencing, you can also. Having attained divinity you can taste the charm of love, peace, joy by living a trouble free life, because you transcend sorrow and suffering.

All social evils (rape-murder-dowry deaths etc) are caused by desire and sick mind. Mind becomes sick due to its contents. All this happens due to ignorance which screens your wisdom. With wisdom you become discriminative, self-disciplined and self controlled, dissolving ignorance. When individuals improve, society improves because totality of individuals is society.

Brief details of chapters

The book contains fourteen chapters which have unique significance and importance in their own way. The chapters are interlinked in some way or the other. These chapters cumulatively contribute in transcending sorrows and sufferings. At places some important points of similar nature appear again and again mainly to amplify and highlight the significance and essence of the point so that understanding becomes easier and reading becomes comfortable free of strain and stress without burdening your mind. The chapters deal with different aspects of life that reflect both the eternal dimensions and the transient and perishable scenario. The chapters briefly cover all factors from the uncaused divine source to the creation of the manifested world, till the dissolution of creation.

The brief details of chapters are given as under:-

Chapter – 1 Our Real Nature (Supreme Truth- Divine)

When we realize, understand and experience our real nature of divinity then the sorrows and sufferings end because real nature reflects oneness of our being. Supreme truth or the divine is the source of all that exists and lives. It creates all and contains everything in seed form but it is not contained and created by anything. It is eternal, uncaused, independent, unsupported, all pervading and enveloping. It is still and motionless and makes all motions possible. Reaching there, silence and salvation happens and you experience ecstasy, peace and love.

It is known by different names – supreme God (parameshwara), supreme self (paramatma), pure being, pure existence, ultimate truth, reality, divinity and pure awareness. Awareness is light of the divine which reveals everything but itself remain unaware about things it reveals, as it is formless and beyond time and space. Things are identified when they are embodied. The light of awareness is the divine light and is motionless. It becomes spiritual energy known as consciousness (with motion) to reveal the universe. The spiritual energy (consciousness) when centers in the mind illumines it to cognize, perceive and identify things.

Chapter – 2 Manifested Nature (Spiritual And Physical)

Acquired nature comes to us with manifested world (consciousness). Pure consciousness is cosmic and spiritual as ocean of love where sorrows and sufferings do not exist. Conditioned consciousness by mind becomes particular, narrow and selfish which generates sorrows and sufferings. Pure consciousness is spiritual and conditioned consciousness is physical. Consciousness is motion which is self vibrant and dynamic. Its movement begins from the static base of the supreme divine. This movement continues to create manifested world till its dissolution. On dissolution of creation, everything returns to the source of the divine where all movement ends. The creation is caused mainly by two energies (divine and spiritual). Divine is static and spiritual is motion. Consciousness has two aspects one is unmanifested (spiritual) and other is manifested (physical). Unmanifested is pure consciousness and is called higher nature, super god, cosmic (universal) and spiritual self. Higher nature is unconditioned, formless and without attributes (harmony-passion-pervert) satva-rajas and tamas.

Manifested is lower nature with form and three attributes. It is a conditioned consciousness. It is the embodied God, the embodied self (antaratma) and is physical. The conditioned consciousness illumines the mind which recognizes and identifies things. Pure consciousness is a link between the supreme and the matter. Pure consciousness becomes conditioned through mind and without mind it maintains its purity. Dynamism is in the consciousness and not in the mind. Consciousness reflects knowingness. Consciousness in the mind reflects intellect and in the heart it reflects feeling of love. Beyond intellect and feeling consciousness remains totally pure. Divine truth is beyond pure consciousness

Chapter – 3 God-Personified Reality(Divine-Spiritual-Physical Energy)

God is form of energy which has three aspects. With divine energy you transcend sorrows and sufferings as you go beyond mind by living a life of divinity. Spiritual energy is cosmic beyond duality and distinction, it dissolves sorrow and suffering because it is free of disturbing contents of mind's negativity. Physical energy (conditioned) experience sorrows and sufferings because it becomes narrow, limited and separated, which cause sorrows and sufferings.

The divine truth and the eternal reality is personified as the God for worship. God has three aspects which are categorized differently according to their power of influence. Supreme God (parameshwara) belongs to the source and has power which is absolutely total, whole and perfect. It is the foundational base of all and is motionless, pure being and pure existence. Light of awareness originates from the Supreme God. God can exist without the light but light cannot exist without the God. Next comes the super God (maheshwara), which is pure consciousness. It is the spiritual God and has power over the whole universe. The power of this cosmic God is limited to universe only. Finally comes the embodied God (ishwara) which acts through forms like the sun, the moon, the planets, the stars, men, animals and plants etc. Its power remains restricted to forms only. It is a conditioned consciousness.

God is not a person but energy which is divine, spiritual and physical. Divine energy is whole, total and perfect. Spiritual energy is cosmic and physical energy is limited to form. You have potential to evolve internally and transform, from physical to divine depending on your earnestness. The energy of God is neutral. It neither helps you nor does it harm you. Help and harm is your minds creation. When mind becomes opaque with desire, fear, memory and imagination then suffering and sorrow are experienced. Transparent mind is free of desire and fear and is reflective of pure energy, where you experience joy, peace and love.

Chapter – 4 Religion (Real And Unreal)

Real religion leads us to our divine nature transcending sorrows and sufferings. The unreal religion is a belief which we follow as a concept given by the enlightened souls. It is not our own experience as such unreal and false.

Religion has two aspects, true religion and conceptual religion. Religion is the law of being. Water has religion to cool and fire is to burn and give heat. Tiger's religion is to kill for food and cow's religion is to eat grass and give milk. Whatever is living and existing has its own religion for survival. Without that creations cease. Religion of man is to attain his pure being of supreme divine nature, by dropping mind. When you know, realize and experience your true religion you renounce attachment to body and mind and become self (atma) conscious. True religion is the one which is attained through personal experience from within your own self. On attaining that duality and rituals drop and dissolve.

Conceptual religion, you follow without your own experience. You only worship and follow a thought, idea and concept given by the enlightened souls which they gained through their personal experience of the truth. Hindus, Christians, Islams, Jews and many more follow the conceptual religion which is not their own experience but is experience of great souls which they follow blindly. Lord Krishna, Buddha, Mahavira, Christ and Mohammed were enlightened souls. To understand them you have to transform from human to divine. Following their teachings and reading spiritual literature (Gita-Bible-Quran) may be inspirational but these cannot transform you unless you are earnest to experience the truth of religion through your own experience. Religiousness is in relation to purity of mind.

Chapter – 5 Nature-Temperament (Swabhava)

Man has three kinds of nature. One is the supreme divine nature, which is nature of your true being. It belongs to the supreme self. Solace, silence and salvation are experienced on attaining that. Next is the nature that comes through consciousness, having two aspects. Pure consciousness which is cosmic, spiritual and formless without any attributes (nirakara and niraguna), forms the higher nature beyond duality. The other aspect is that of lower nature, which is conditioned consciousness with form and attributes (saguna-sakara), like harmony, passion and perversion (Satva-Rajas-Tamas) and is physically bound by forms. Duality is experienced in lower nature (good-bad, sin-virtue, and negative-positive).

Society evolves its norms and conventions based on the lower nature. Moral and ethical values originate through this nature. Lower nature is temporary and perishable because it appears with form and disappears when the form dies. Norms, conventions and moral values are product of society as such do not apply everywhere for all time. These keep changing from time to time, place to place and society to society.

The next nature is the nature of cultivation that comes through society, parents, family, friends, education, learning, information and knowledge. Preferably you should live with the nature of yourself (atma). Next best is to live with the nature that comes to you at the time of your birth in the form of the three attributes (harmony-passion-pervert), which make your temperament (swabhava). These attributes remain with all that live and exists. The differentiation is in the dominance of the attributes in different proportions which each form possess. Next comes the nature of learning and cultivation. If you fail to listen to the voice of the soul and lower nature then live life with cultivated nature.

Chapter – 6 Law Of Action (karma)

The aim of action (karma) is to move closer to your inner self. Actions leading to yourself (atma) are righteous actions. Actions which take you away from your soul are wrong actions which happen due to ignorance that causes sufferings and sorrow. Mainly there are three types of actions. One is inaction which means cessation of all actions reflecting attainment of your divine nature or supreme self, which is still and motionless. All actions originate from there. You experience silence and peace when you attain state of inaction. Next is desire oriented actions where you experience anger, greed, jealousy, hate, obsession, fear and duality. Such actions make you selfish and personal and become cause of suffering.

Lastly come the routine and prescribed actions. Routine actions are praying, bathing, walking, working, exercising, learning, entertainment, meeting people, sleeping and social commitments. Prescribed actions are undertaken on auspicious occasions. Sacrifice (yagya) is important aspect of prescribed action. See details of sacrifice actions in the main chapter. Never give up actions of gift-austerity and sacrifice (daan-tapa-yagya). Daan is for human welfare, Tapa is for purification of mind and Yagya is inner evolvement to attain your true nature of divinity.

Chapter – 7 Reality Of The Present (Beyond Past And Future)

The present moment reflects reality because it is free of conditioning by past and future. Past and future is product of mind. Anything that is seen through mind becomes impure due to contents of the mind. Mind appears and disappears as such transient, perishable and unreal. Mind dies with the death of the body and reappears when new body comes up. Present is the only time when you can become thoughtless and get directly linked to the reality of the supreme self because mind stops interfering when you become thoughtless. Past is memory, future is imagination and the present is the reality. It is mind that divides time into past-present and future but for this, time is indivisible. Past is dead memories and future is about unborn imagination as such live in the present reality for joy love and peace.

Chapter – 8 Mind And Body (Liberation And bondage)

Body and mind are matter. Body is gross matter and mind is subtle matter. Mind is a thought content, it desires, thinks, imagines and memorizes past events of pleasure and shuns painful events. The contents of mind are desire, fear, anger, greed etc which make mind opaque and restless. Opaqueness of mind reflects ignorance about your true nature of the divine. It blocks the vision of the reality and the ultimate truth. Consequently you remain attached to false and unreal things of the world. All this happens when you become mind oriented. Mind creates a separate non self ego center on the periphery and as such remains unaware of the inner center of the self, which reflects peace, silence and joy.

Mind is limited and bound by time and space as such you cannot discover through limited mind your true nature of the being which is limitless and formless. Mind has tendency to divide whole into parts (limitless to limit). When you seek solutions through mind it will remain partial only and not total and perfect.

Heaven and hell are not geographical but creation of the mind. Hell is experienced when mind is disturbed and restless and heaven when mind is peaceful. Mind becomes steady, quiet, peaceful and silent only when you create transparency by dropping contents of mind.

See main chapter thirteen for dropping mind. Body and mind have close relationship as these affect each other. For harmonious living, balance between body and mind should be maintained. Body should neither be tortured nor pampered. Toiling and torturing of body is neither hard work nor sacred work. Hard work reflects sincere and concentrated work and for this body needs to be at ease. Sacred work needs silent mind, when mind becomes silent the body gets totally relaxed.

Body strives and struggles as such you must strive without seeking and struggle without greed. All problems are problems related to the body like food, clothing, house, family, friends, fame, name, honour, status, prestige, security and survival. All these dissolve when you become aware and realize that you are not the body and mind but you are the supreme divine, which remains unaffected by happenings of events caused by body and mind. Mind conscious leads to bondage, attachment and involvement which make you a selfish person. Liberation is from an ego oriented person. Liberation reflects impersonality, selflessness and universality with deep feeling of love for all

Chapter – 9 Trust Your Soul

Trusting soul reflects self confidence. It means confidence in yourself (atma). We are generally governed by mind and there by ignore the eternal power of the soul and suffer. We must aim at becoming self conscious for a peaceful and harmonious living. All great souls who appeared on the earth, lived life trusting their own self (atma) and that is why they were equated to God. Godliness happens when you attain your true being by trusting your soul.

Confidence at physical level contains duality and contradiction. But confidence in divine dissolves duality which takes you beyond sorrow and suffering. Confidence seen through mind is fragmenting and physical. But beyond mind confidence reflects spirituality, divinity and beyond consciousness, it is divine. When you trust yourself, you become thoughtless, desireless and fearless. Real transformation occurs when you attain divinity.

Transformation entails transcending human nature to achieve your divine nature, going from mind to no mind state. Surrendering and trusting yourself is sure way to success. Your attitude and outlook changes. You become saintly, devotional and render selfless service with love. Trusting self is trusting god. Without body you cannot be killed, means when you attain divinity body loses its importance for you. You lose attachment and concerned for your body. Without possessions you cannot be robbed and without mind you cannot be deceived.

Chapter – 10 Be Simple and Natural (Purity Within And Without)

Simple and natural living means inner and outer purity, nothing to hide and suppress, also not showing outside what you are not inside.

We show honesty outside but remain dishonest inside. Sufi saint of India, 'kabir' is a leading example of simple and natural living. He attained his divine nature through weaving only. He made the work of weaving meditative turning it into total meditation. In total meditation you become thoughtless because your concentration is on one single thought only and other thoughts drop automatically and mind dissolves. Simple and natural living becomes harmonious and peaceful as no contradiction remains between inner and outer. With inner and outer harmony, you experience a trouble free life. You need not be a simpleton in the name of simplicity. A simpleton is foolish, lacks sharp intellect and has poor reflexes.

Chapter – 11 Wisdom (Dissolution Of Ignorance)

Wisdom is power of discrimination about right and wrong, attained by enriching consciousness. When you attain pure consciousness, mind becomes pure, clear and empty dropping all its contents (desire, fear, anger, greed etc). When mind drops, you go beyond mind and then wisdom happens which gives you understanding and insight of right judgment. There is difference between wisdom and intellect. Wisdom is insight to reach your inner self and intellect is sight for outer world. Intellect belongs to the mind and wisdom happens beyond mind. Intellect is contradictory but wisdom reflects single mindedness. Ignorance means not knowing your true nature (divine) and attachment to false and unreal things of the world which are transient and perishable. Mind is mother of ignorance and intellect.

We remain indifferent and unconcerned about the needs, problems and sufferings of other people because of our selfish attitude which is due to ignorance. Sharing, giving and sacrificing attitude develops only with wisdom. Wisdom is transformative and liberating. Ignorance is binding and suffering. Nature gives no guarantee of trouble free life at the time of your birth. Good and bad will always alternate endlessly. You have no control over happenings of nature. Wise man as such accepts life as it comes whether it brings joy or sorrow. Wisdom flowers when humanity is benefited. Knowing is wisdom and believing is ignorance. Inferiority complex comes through ignorance. Wisdom dissolves both ignorance and complex and makes you self confident and fearless.

Chapter – 12 Living Life

The important aspect of living life is to know and realize difference between what to live and how to live. What to live is living worldly life through mind and how to live is spiritual and divine life, which happens beyond mind. Life is a mystery as such you cannot shape life like shaping of a career. Mystery of life is known by living life as it comes without any choice. In breathing in and breathing out if you choose only breathing in, ignoring the breathing out life will end. Accept life as it comes with festive mood, making life a celebration.

Nothing is eternal in this world as such when you remain worldly you will experience duality, but beyond mind all is divine as duality dissolves and you experience silence and peace. Mind is analysis and beyond mind it is synthesis. Analysis happens to things which have form and are limited. Mind picks up limited things and divides and separates you from your divine nature. Formless things unite as all distinctions dissolve there. Spirituality is cosmic not particular and divine is whole, total, complete and perfect. Spirituality is limited to the universe which is higher and greater to the physical world. Higher and greater to the universe is the supreme divine, the abode of both physical and spiritual world.

Inner growth and evolvement are the core essence for living life at spiritual and physical level. Spiritual is a link between physical and divine. Enrich your consciousness (spiritual), to attain divinity to go beyond sorrow and suffering. Learn from nature about living life harmoniously. In nature things are opposite but are never in opposition. Harmony in life happens when your inner and outer do not differ, which happens when you live a simple and natural life without contradiction. One, who lives a happy life, shall die a happy death. One who lives a worried and restless life will die a painful death.

Live life honestly, truthfully with self confidence and self discipline. To transform life from suffering and sorrow (human nature) to divine nature you have to be self knowing, self surrendering and self less in all your doings. You are not body and mind but your nature is divine so do not identify with events that comes through mind and disturb you. Beyond mind disturbance dissolves.

Chapter – 13 Change Of Mind Set

Transformation of mind from human to divine is essential for dissolving evilness, of the mind which results into suffering and sorrow. Transformation entails going beyond mind. Unless you attain that total solution to social problem will not be possible through mind.

Mind is narrow and limited and as such provides partial solutions. In partial solution, problems keep coming again and again. Problems lie low for some time when man of will, wisdom and power are born but at the end of their period, the cycle of misery starts again. Mindset reflects fixed thoughts, concepts, ideas, beliefs, doctrines and ego. To believe or not to believe, possibly will not change your mind set. Transformation of mind set happens only when mind is dropped through techniques given in the main chapter.

Transformation is possible when you live with the present reality, because mind drops. Past (memory) and future (imagination) are the nourishment for mind to exists. This nourishment of mind stops when you live in the present. Transformation is from inner to outer. Outer (physical) cannot reach your inner self as it acts on periphery only, however inner can always influence the outer. Various techniques to drop mind are explained in the main chapter.

Chapter – 14 Answers To Important Questions

This chapter covers answers to important questions, with a purpose to bring clarity and understanding to reader's mind which will facilitate grasping of the matter with ease and comfort.

Conclusion

If you read the book with patience, open mind and deliberations, you are sure to procure the seed of spirituality by the time you finish reading the book. Sow the spiritual seed through inner evolvement. The seed will sprout with your experience from within, and blossom into tree of divinity as you mature spiritually. But without your personal experience it may die without sprouting.

Even if you are unable to procure the spiritual seed, you need not get disappointed. The reading of the book will definitely make you feel the need for transformation and increase your interest to attain eternal peace and joy. The very single thought of transformation every moment will dissolve other thoughts, making mind clear and empty. With this you will gradually mature spiritually and sooner or later realize about self improvement. It is like seeds thrown in the ground, which sprout at their own when the right season comes.

In the end I suggest that you should be earnest, determined, sincere and honest for self transformation. It will definitely bear fruit one day through patience.

CHAPTER 1

Our Real Nature (Supreme Truth- Divine)

When we realize, understand and experience our real nature of divinity through purity of mind then the sorrows and sufferings end spontaneously and automatically because we become one with our being of oneness, which is a state beyond mind. Our real nature is eternal and uncaused. It is by itself love, peace, joy, harmony, pure, powerful and wise.

The real and divine world signifies our real nature. It is absolute and ultimate truth. It is the foundational base of all that exists and lives. It is total, whole, complete and perfect. It is pure awareness, pure being, eternity, supreme God (parmeshwara), supreme self (paramatma). It is true and real nature of man also the true religion which man aspires to discover. The goal of life is to attain our true nature. The supreme divine contains everything in seed form and creates all but is not contained and created by anything. It is causeless, formless, limitless, unknown and unseen, through mind.

The manifested nature reflects seen and manifested world which is experienced through the mind. Anything that is experienced in the manifested world has its own cause. Awareness is the light of the supreme divine which reveals all but remain unaware as to what it reveals. It is the consciousness (chetna) which identifies things with the support of awareness. Awareness is centered in the consciousness, consciousness is centered in the mind and mind is centered in the body. Awareness is absolute and consciousness is relative.

Imagination and distortion of truth is due to the mind which makes truth a concept. Inner world (unseen-unknown world) is real world as it is eternal and the outer world (seen-known world) is unreal world (manifested world). It is transient and perishable which appears and disappears and as such false. The unreal world is the world of imagination which is weaved through subjective mind every moment.

Truth is known through inner personal experience. The real world is beyond time and space. Anything that is bound by time and space has form like our body and anything that has form exists for specific period of time and then perishes. Time is linked to mind and space is linked to body (form). It is body that bounds space, otherwise space is limitless. Mind breaks and divides time into past, present and future, otherwise time always remains whole, total and indivisive, that is why the supreme is known as timeless. The real world is independent, self existent, unsupported, uncaused, all pervading and enveloping. It reflects infinite space and deep silence. Salvation and emancipation are attained on reaching there.

The reality is experienced through present living, because past and future remain absent in the present. Past and future (memory and imagination) are nourishment for mind to survive. Pleasure and pain are experienced through mind, beyond mind pleasure and pain dissolve and you reach the reality of life (divine).

You always desire pleasure but shun things which cause pain. Past and future are hindrance to your journey to the divine world. Anything that dies becomes greater and higher. Our body on death merges back with the five elements which are universal. Breath merges with the universal air (pran-vital breath), individual consciousness becomes universal consciousness. Embodied self becomes supreme self. Form becomes formless, limited becomes unlimited.

Nothing changes in the real world. All changes happen only in the manifested world where nothing stays. The law of nature is creation, preservation and destruction regardless of any form. Truth is factual and real. It is oneness, beyond duality. Duality is product of the mind because mind imagines separation from the supreme self and creates false non self (ego). Ego gives the sense of pseudo entity of false doership.

Body and mind are only instruments through which supreme self is actualized with the support of vital breath (pran) and consciousness (chetna). Awareness is light of the supreme self it creates an aura around the supreme self. Knowingness of things happens through consciousness when it enters the form (body). Consciousness moves from the supreme self as spiritual energy. Form is vitalized, sustained and kept alive with life through vital breath. It is grosser form of consciousness. Body and mind are material (matter). Body is gross matter and mind is subtle matter. Actions take place through the body and thinking, desiring and imagination through the mind.

Form becomes live and functional with beingness as body, knowingness as mind and pure bliss as supreme self. Beingness is existence, knowingness is knowledge and bliss is undisturbed state of being. These are called Sat-Chit and Ananda. All remain dormant and unmanifested in the supreme self as pure being, pure awareness and bliss. Supreme self, consciousness and vital breath appear together in a form and make matter active and live.

Sunlight reveals worldly things but remains unaware about things it reveals. When consciousness centers in the mind only then, things are perceived and cognized and make identification and distinction possible. When you attain spirituality (pure consciousness) you transcend all distinctions because of universality. Supreme self is light, consciousness is love and pran is life. Light, love and life are a form of energy. The energy at the source of the supreme self is known as divine energy also known as divine God (parmeshwara). The energy of consciousness is known as spiritual energy. It is beyond physical energy and below divine energy. Divine energy is static and spiritual energy is motion, through them process of creation begins.

There are three aspects of reality, physical, spiritual and divine. Spirituality is unmanifested energy, physical energy is manifested energy and divine energy is beyond both. The real world is the final abode of all. When dissolution happens then all return to the source of the supreme.

The real world is absolute truth. Truth cannot be conceptualized, verbalized and metalized as it is formless and beyond mind. Anything that contacts the truth becomes truth itself as truth is pure and purifies all which touches it. The real world is whole and total with oneness. On reaching there all search for knowledge ends, you then desire nothing, want nothing, expect nothing, have nothing and imagine nothing but give everything through love and service. Remembering and forgetting end and non self (ego) dissolves.

The real world itself is static, still and motionless but makes motion possible. Without static base motion is not possible. Axle of a wheel is motionless but the wheel based on it moves. River flows on the motionless river bed. Transport moves on the static base of the earth. Action happens through stability of inaction. Action reflects movement and inaction reflects stillness.

The goal of life is to move from action to inaction. The manifested world is full of action and the real world is totally actionless. Actualization of inaction is possible through action only. Action is disturbance and restlessness that happens through body and mind. Body's action is objective and mind's action is subjective. Actions become impure when identified with mind otherwise actions remain as pure as inaction of the self.

Identification means involvement and interest with physical and mental events which cause sorrow and suffering. Things do not happen as you want them to happen because life is unpredictable. To make actions pure do not involve, but remain a pure witness watching actions happen at their own. When you witness actions without participation they pass away and do not bind you to the worldly life. You remain free and liberated.

Some say world is a cycle of creation and dissolution. Some say, it has existed and will continue existing while some others say it is the result of the big bang. All are concepts no one can analyze as to how the world came into existence. All are ideas, doctrines, theories and opinions. It is accidental, a phenomenon and a process of nature with no definite solutions.

However to understand the existence of the world we have to understand it through hypothesis. Science to reach understandable conclusion, accepts and assumes 'X-factor' for reaching a solution. In spirituality total faith and trust are taken as hypothesis to know and experience the truth of the supreme self. Faith is steadiness of mind and heart, which results in willingness and earnestness.

One thing is definite and certain that the real world is uncaused and has existed at its own eternally. The unreal world is transient and perishable. It appears and disappears from time to time. The real world reflects purity and silence which is attained by nonwavering mind. Real is supreme self and unreal is nonself created through mind. Real and unreal is in relation to both with mind and without mind or physical and non physical.

Physical world contains sun, planets, moons, stars, mountains, jungles, rivers, etc. Real and unreal world are signified with different names like unlimited-limited, formless-form, divine-matter, universal-particular, self-nonself, wisdom-ignorance, inaction-action, intution-tution, light-darkness, spiritual-physical and many more.

To reach the real world you must trust, test and taste. It means that you must trust that there is eternal real world because great souls in the past attained truth through total trust. Once you trust, then you must test truth by experiencing yourself from within as great souls had experienced in the past and attained emancipation (Buddha,

Mahavira and Christ etc) the last stage is taste which means live your life that way and experience joy, peace, and harmony in life.

In real world all are one and one is all. When you experience reality, your actions become pure and mind stops interfering. When you see things without distortion and imagination then seeing becomes whole. Without mind seeing, hearing, feeling and doing, become total and whole. Whole is holy because you see things as they are without opinion, likes and dislikes. When this happens then you do not see the outer structure of a thing but see only the inner consciousness flowing between you and the thing that you see.

Such seeing reflects wholeness, unity divinity, spirituality and universality. When you concentrate on the form (body) then division, separation and distinction is experienced in life. So your concentration and attention should be on the divine (awareness) and spiritual (pure consciousness) which flow equally in all regardless of the form, whether it is that of an insect or a saint.

To be Supreme Being you have to be 'That', there is no other way out. You cannot mentalise and verbalize the supreme self because it is beyond mind. Mind cannot pick up things which are formless and limitless. There is no way out to eternalize the mind, the only way is to drop mind to know your supreme nature. (See chapter thirteen for dropping mind).

Once you realize and experience the ecstasy of the real world then you cease caring for the physical world which is temporary and perishable. It does not mean that you disown the world but it only means that the world doesn't disturb you because you do not identify with the events that are projected through the mind. You transcend mind through witnessing. (See chapter thirteen for witnessing).

Awareness is to know about your pure being and realization is to know about false and perishable things. Self (atma) realization is beyond mind and remembrance of the worldly things is with mind. The process of merging with the real world of eternity happens like ice turning into water, water to vapor which dissolves in the air and finally disappears into space. Similarly physical transforms to spiritual (universal) and finally merges into the divine eternity which is beyond universal.

Knowledge and information are meaningless for spiritual and divine evolvement because knowledge and information divide and fragment consciousness. You need empty and clear mind, free of desire, fear and other negativities. The experience of the real world (supreme) is a happening which happens when you drop mind through personal experience from within. You cannot attain divinity through doing and effort. Effort and doing are required for achievement in the manifested world.

Vital breath (pran) contains awareness, consciousness and matter. It works with their support but remains dominant as life force in the body. Similarly consciousness also has all three aspects but remains dominant in knowingness. Likewise matter contains supreme self, consciousness and vital breath but has no instrument to express the supreme. All remain dormant in matter. However matter becomes a medium to actualize the supreme.

Realized man remains detached from unreal and perishable things. He understands and is aware of his true nature of pure being and as such remains undisturbed by events that happen through body and mind. When you are disturbed and restless it reflects you are still governed by the mind and not the self (atma). A wiseman transcends sorrow and suffering because he goes beyond mind. Sorrow and suffering are products of mind but beyond mind it is all divine reflecting, love, peace, joy and harmony.

Reality (supreme) is objectivity. It means you see things as they are without imagination and distortion through the mind. You see false as false and do not imagine false as real and real as false. Consciousness and vital breath are two important aspects of the supreme, which are eternal but have temporary existence because these disappear when body dies and reappear when new body is born.

The supreme is beyond the cycle of appearance and disappearance. This cycle of coming and going, beginning and ending happens in the process and phenomenon of nature's manifestation. But the supreme is beyond nature so it remains unaffected. However the supreme makes appearance and disappearance possible with its support because it is the abode of all and everything originates from there.

The real world is unknown and unseen but gives birth to the known and seen world through awareness, consciousness, vital breath and matter (five elements and three attributes). Reflection of supreme is focused as self (atma) in the body through consciousness. The self peacefully and endlessly shines inside us as our true spiritual teacher (sat guru) to guide us. True transformation happens when you discover your divine nature of the supreme with that human nature dissolves. It means that human nature will not disturb you because you cease caring for disturbance, having realized that you are not body and mind. You will instantly erase memories of the past and reject thoughts which cause disturbance.

Reality (supreme being) cannot be proved through mind because mind is limited and truth (supreme) is unlimited and formless. Beyond mind you need not prove reality because you become yourself the reality. Proof is needed for false and unreal things which are created through mind. Finding real in the unreal is wisdom and seeing false in the real is ignorance.

The reality is infinite space, peace and silence where all activities and search for knowledge ends because the supreme is the culmination where all things return on dissolution of creation. Reality is beyond objective (physical) and subjective (spiritual) worlds. The reality is obscured by the mind. It is like the sun which is temporarily screened by the clouds but its effect and influence is not reduced on earth. Reality is beyond physical existence because existence is possible when bound by time and space, which exists for sometime in a space bound by body and then perishes.

Existence has beginning and end, birth and death, it appears and disappears and it comes and goes, as such false, unreal and perishable. There is no death to the reality and there is no eternity to the unreal and false. Reality imparts divinity to all which comes in its contact through pure mind.

Awareness is neither virtuous nor sinful because it is beyond mind which creates duality. We are aware of our thinking, feeling and doing but remain unaware of our pure being (divinity–reality). Awareness is our true being and worldly being is false and unreal. Unconsciousness (ignorance) can only be transformed through awareness. For awareness you have to concentrate not on the cause outside but on the source inside. Science is more concerned with the objective world outside and religion is more concerned with the source inside.

Cause reflects environment outside and the source is connected with your real being (ultimate truth). Use your own body as a device for awareness. Do all actions with awareness that you are the supreme truth and not merely body and mind. When you become totally and wholly aware of your pure being then mind drops automatically, linking you to your source (being).

Total awareness is attained when there is no conditioning of awareness through any thinking and feeling. It happens when you become witness to all the happenings that take place around you without participation and opinion. When you involve thinking (mind) and feeling (heart) then the light of awareness is conditioned and does not reflect fully through your mind and heart.

Awareness first throws you out of ignorance and later takes you beyond worldly knowledge which obscures your being. Awareness implies remembrance of self (atma). Whatever you do outside, do it totally with continuous remembering every moment of your being inside. This process will help you centering into your inner self because other thoughts will drop except the thought of your own being. When this happens you are exploded into the reality which transforms you totally. You will be enlightened, become blissful and silent. Presence of your being will be experienced in all your actions and doings, dissolving all the negativities and polar opposites of the false world.

Once you are awakened into awareness you will remain aware every time everywhere like when your mind becomes conscious about certain objects, people and things, it remains so throughout your life. It does not then relegate from that state of conscious mind. You cannot move back to unconsciousness when you become totally aware. With awareness you progress but you cannot regress. It is just like an egg which has become a hen, now the hen cannot move back to be an egg again. A seed which has grown into a tree cannot regress and become a seed again.

Life always moves forward into the future never in the past. You have to bring awareness to every cell of the body, to your total being so that gap between conscious and unconscious is eliminated. Man cannot transform unless inner cells of the body are changed through total awareness and not through physical surgery. Through physical surgery you can stop the instinct of anger and sex from indulgence and suppression but you cannot stop the current of inner energy which gives you urge to express instinct.

If you change the hormones of sex and anger a man may become impotent to express them but sexuality and anger will remain like the electric current which is expressed through a bulb. When you break the bulb, expression of electricity is stopped but energy continuous to exist. You may change hormones of a violent and aggressive dog to make him docile but the energy of aggressiveness and violence continues. It can never be killed, only the medium of expression is killed or changed.

As a man you may become silent and peaceful like 'Buddha' by changing some of your hormones but these are all unnatural and artificial, causing imbalance and disharmony in hormones which may create inner complexities and make you sick and diseased. So never resort to such artificial things but instead be aware and transform your cells of your body, through inner evolvement.

Truth (real world) is inner light you experience during meditation with different colors. But when you attain silence all colors disappear except the white color. However it is said that when you attain total silence even this white light disappears and you experience emptiness, void and salvation which is the base and source of the origin of this light. Silence is the culmination of attainment of your supreme God (parameshwara). This state is called 'Nirvana' (salvation) by 'Buddha'. Salvation and bliss are states where being remains totally undisturbed, still, motionless full of ecstasy with complete inaction.

The light of awareness (pure being) is the divine light known as divine energy. It needs no medium to travel because it is absolute being with constant velocity. There is no change in its velocity from the beginning to the end (creation to dissolution). Pure being is also known as pure existence as it is the base of the light of awareness (divine life). This light is aura of the pure existence (truth and reality). Pure being, the source of the light can exist without this light but the light cannot exist without the source of the pure being.

Light of awareness is a link between the real world and the physical world. The first creation is this light which originates from the ultimate and absolute truth. Matter comes last in the chain of creation and reflects condensed light. It means light of truth is contained in all that exists and lives, the only difference is of subtleness, grossness and density. Consciousness (chetna) is super subtle aspect of this light, vital breath (pran) is subtle aspect of this light and matter is dense form of the light. The same light is known by different names according to their functions and states of purity.

When light grows life happens, which means process of manifestation begins. When life grows love happens which means life is sustained when you experience universal love of brotherhood, unifying all that exist and lives. Without love there is disintegration, division, separation which ruins the sustenance of life.

Light is eternity, life is vital breath and love is pure consciousness. When love rises devotion and prayer happens. When love falls desire happens. It means love is higher growth to spirituality and desire is lower growth for physical existence. Prayer is culmination of love which means you have reached a state of total love. It is higher stage of love where you experience deep feeling of love of oneness between the devotee and the deity. The devotee and the deity become one without distinction. It also means devotee merges with the deity and both become one and that is the aim of life to achieve the divine through devotion (bhakti).

Love reflects macro aspect of oneness with your deity and light reflects micro aspect of oneness with your pure being. Both the devotee (bhakta) and the man of knowledge (gyani) reach the same goal of oneness with eternity. Bhakta reaches through total expansion of his love outside through total surrender and Gyani reaches his being through the path of 'will' negating all that exists outside.

Macro aspect means deepening, widening and enriching your consciousness to make it pure to an extent that it becomes whole, total and complete. Micro is subtlest of the subtle where you negate, disown and discard all that exists outside as false and unreal which covers your true being. You reach the truth dissolving your identity as a seeker and you merge with the sought (ultimate reality). 'Buddha' and 'Mahavira' took path of self knowing (gyan). 'Meera' and 'Chaitanya' took the path of devotional love. Seeker is the one who seeks to attain the truth. Sought (pure being) is the culmination of the seeking where seeker and sought become one.

'Sat' is unreal world and 'Tat' is real world, both combined (tat-sat) become 'Satya'. Our world becomes 'Satya' with the touch of reality because truth purifies all that touches it. 'Sat' has no independent existence without the support of 'Tat'. 'Tat' is uncaused, eternal and has independent existence. 'Sat' is existence and 'Tat' is pure being (pure existence).

The unknown is the supreme truth and the known is the factual truth. Supreme truth is one, single and indivisible but factual truth is multiple, divisible, transient and perishable. Science is for the known world (objective), whereas true religion is for the unknown world (real world). Do not be a scholar, be a lover. Intellect cannot satisfy feelings of love that come through the heart with pure feeling, peace, prayer and devotion. If a man is hungry he needs food and not a book on cooking. In view of this when you deal with the world you need logic and reason to survive and earn your living. Spirituality may not give you food but it gives you contentment, patience, tolerance and spiritual wealth which help in maintaining peace and harmony in the world through eternal virtues that you experience after attaining spirituality.

Consequently you must maintain balance and harmony between physical and spiritual existence. Attaining real world (your true nature) does not mean that you lose the world and develop distaste for it. It only means that your doings turn into noble happenings for the welfare and uplift of humanity. You become selfless and impersonal with deep feeling of love and service to all.

Your very presence fills the atmosphere with love and serenity without any movement and action by you. It is like a flower which fills the space with fragrance without making any movement and action. A candle light fills the space with light without candle moving anywhere and it remains immobile and inactive. Enlightened man (liberated soul) has an aura of light around his head which reflects his purity and makes the atmosphere pure all around like the fragrance of the flower which is felt all around.

It is said that full life is better than long life. Full life means attainment of your real divine self. Having reached eternity you achieve the goal of your life. Living life then becomes a joy, love and peace. You become sharing, giving, loving and sacrificing. Long life otherwise is dragging, painful with stress and strain causing sorrow and suffering. We denote real world as the supreme self (paramatma) and embodied self as the self (atma), but understand clearly that the self reflects both individual and universal self and beyond these is the supreme self. Consequently wherever self is referred it should be understood in relation to different aspects of self in the context where it is referred to.

It is like different ornaments which are created from one single source of gold. The names and forms of ornament may differ but the base and source of all remains the same. The reality has three aspects known, unknown and unknowable. Known and unknown, have been covered earlier in this chapter. The unknowable means that if you want to bring it under the domain of knowing you can know it through your earnestness. It is a matter of actualizing your essence (true being) through knowing, feeling, realizing and experiencing. It remains unknowable if not actualized.

The unknown real world is a mystery which cannot be solved through intellect and feeling. The mystery can be confronted by living it through being existential, through your totality with body, mind and spirit as a whole. Doubt is the method of science, feeling is the method of love and being is the method of trust and faith. Faith is not belief, belief is rational and belongs to the known world. If you trust your own self then you evolve and if you distrust then you remain closed and stagnate.

If seed remains closed and does not open and grow then seed can never become a tree. The totality of reality functions through silence and not through parts of intellect and feelings which condition it through mind. Silence reflects your true being. Just be one with your being.

The words of scriptures are only indicators and pointers to the reality but are not actually reality by themselves. The scriptures talk about the soul that we do not conceive them rightly because we try to understand them intellectually and not through our being. We miss the inner reality of the scriptures when we focus our attention to the words only.

Right response through totality (our being) reveals the real world because right response is free of distortion and imagination. Right response can only happen when mind becomes nonwavering and still. It means dropping of mind. Response maintains its originality of purity as it comes through your being, it is like a response that is reflected back as an echo free of any distortion when a flute is played from the hill top of a valley.

Commentary is a mental product which is dead, being of physical nature. Response is live as it comes directly from your being with no conditioning by any medium in-between and that is why the response maintains its purity throughout as whole and perfect. In our day to day behaviour we comment and react but do not rightly respond in totality as a pure act of wholeness. We miss holiness without wholeness.

Just be silent and passive and let whatsoever happen echo in you. It is certain your echo from your being will be live, pure and innocent free of effort, strain and excitement. The inner divine light is the light which mystics experience either through love (surrender) or through will and effort (knowing).

The moment you enter the inner light, the source of life, you enter deathlessness. To be centered in the inner illumination of the light is the real and true bath needed for worship. The physical bath which we take before worship cleans outer body only but you remain impure and unclean internally without the bath of the inner light. Everything dies except the light as such we should endeavor to reach that immortal light. Unless you are bathed in pure light you are not ready to enter the divine temple of your being. Bathing here implies purifying your consciousness to take you to the divine life.

Pure consciousness means dissolving the dirt of all 'Karmas' (actions) including your ego. When ego disappears you become pure and clean to enter the divine temple of your being. Inner illumination of light is known as 'That' (supreme truth). The Indian Meta physics divides existence into two aspects of reality 'This' and 'That', 'This' reflects manifested world and 'That' is real world, the eternal source of all existence. 'This' is a projected expression of 'That' but is unreal because it appears and disappears.

Science talks about 'This' and religion deals with 'That'. 'This' is known, seen and perceived by senses, intellect and mind, but 'That' is known by being to be. It means merging yourself with your being. You can know your center (soul) here and now because that is the reflection of your being, which is all pervading and enveloping.

Reality cannot be metalized because it exists beyond mind as such you cannot label reality in any way, it is to be experienced only. Mind cannot function without labeling. Reality has no name and if we call the reality as God then we have labeled and named it for our understanding. When you are thinking then you are with logic and reason and not with your being. Non thinking, non desiring and non wavering mind always remain with your being.

There are three states of mind ignorance, knowledge and blissfulness. In ignorance you are blissful because you are not aware. In knowledge you are aware of worldly things but you are not blissful whereas in your being you are both aware and blissful. Your aim of life is to go beyond ignorance and knowledge to attain eternity to be blissful and aware.

There are two ways to become whole and perfect. One is to become totally unconscious (animalistic) and be governed by natural instincts which nature provide (desire, fear, anger, greed, jealousy, sex, hunger, sleep and thirst etc). The other is to transcend unconsciousness through awareness. You have to bring light of awareness to every cell of the body so that gap between conscious and unconscious is eliminated. Man cannot transform unless inner cells change through total light of awareness.

CHAPTER 2

Manifested Nature (Spiritual and Physical)

Acquired nature has two aspects spiritual and physical. It comes with manifested world (consciousness). When consciousness remains pure free of contents, it becomes cosmic and spiritual as ocean of love and pure feeling reflecting unity and harmony between all that lives and exists. Sorrows and sufferings do not exists because pure consciousness reflects a no mind state beyond all negativities. When consciousness is conditioned by mind it becomes particular, narrow and selfish generating sorrows and sufferings. However you are born with capabilities to transform from particular (physical) to universal (spiritual) through earnestness. The acquired nature comes to us in two ways one is through nature (consciousness) in the form of three attributes, harmony, passion and perversion (satva - rajas and tamas) at the time of birth. The other way is through learning, knowledge, culturing and cultivation by society.

Unmanifested and manifested are two aspects of consciousness (chetna). Pure consciousness reflects unmanifested and conditioned consciousness means manifestation. Origin of consciousness begins from the static base of the supreme and ultimate truth, known as pure being which is uncaused. Whenever form comes up, consciousness appears as natural phenomenon. Consciousness is motion and supreme truth is motionless and static.

Motionless static base and motion of consciousness combined cause creations. In all manifestations these two basic elements (static-motion) remain together. Without these manifestation is not possible. It is also called (stithi- gati).

Pure consciousness creates the cosmic world (universal and spiritual world) which is beyond physical and particular. Pure consciousness is formless (nirakara) and without attributes (niraguna). When form comes up vital breath (pran) and consciousness appear and these disappear when form dies. Form conditions consciousness and becomes manifested. The manifested consciousness has form (sakara) with three attributes (guna) – harmony, passion and pervert (satva–rajas–tamas).

In fact all is consciousness because grosser form of it is vital breath and dense form of it is matter. All five elements and three attributes are created and caused through consciousness, as such it is called nature. It is not possible to grasp unlimited and formless reality without condition. Consciousness is self vibrant, dynamic and live. It is mother of creation and that is why it is known as great (mahan). In fact creation is in the very nature of consciousness. Consciousness remains dormant at its source (truth–reality). It has inbuilt movement in itself. It becomes dominant in a particular and individual form, which becomes medium to express it. Creation cannot happen in formless, limitless, boundless and infinite space. Creation can take place only when there is a form.

However the supreme truth has two aspects motion and stillness, inaction and action, these combined cause all creations. Absolute and ultimate truth is causeless and motionless. Embodied consciousness is inner self (anteratma), it stays with man till he dies. The inner self is the true guide as such we should seek its guidance by knowing, realizing and experiencing it. Christ, Mohammad, Buddha, Kabira and Mahavira actualized their inner self from within their own self and attained Godhood. Pure consciousness is universal and spiritual, free of distinctions with deep feeling of love for all. It is like the five elements (space–air–heat–water–earth) which make no distinction between a sinner and a saint.

Consciousness remains same in all regardless of any form, whether it is the form of an insect or a saint. Both experience same consciousness but only appearance differs. Water remains water regardless of the container in which it is kept. Consciousness being universal is free and liberating. It is not Hindu consciousness, Christian consciousness or any other religion's consciousness. Consciousness flows equally through them without any distinction. Universal consciousness when it appears in an individual form gets conditioned. When it identifies with form through mind then it becomes narrow, bound, limited, individual, particular, personal and selfish that causes sorrow and suffering.

There are three possible ways to attain eternity. One is the knowledge of the supreme, by remaining aware every moment about your true nature (pure being). The constant noble thought of the supreme will subside other thoughts which disturbs and cause restlessness. When all thoughts subside then you become desireless and thoughtless which reflects purity, clarity and emptiness of mind.

The second way is devotional and it is attained when surrender is total and complete (egolessness). When mind is dropped, ego dissolves automatically at its own. Ego is a false, unreal, transient and perishable. Mind has nature to create non self ego center for physical living. Non self center works on the outer periphery. It blocks your inner growth and evolvement to spirituality because of mind's limited and narrow vision.

The last way to reach eternity is through selfless service and actions, which make you holy and sacred. Your selfless work becomes meditative purifying your mind (see chapter thirteen for meditative work). Whatever way you follow (self knowledge – self surrender – self less work), dropping of mind is an important aspect to discover the truth.

The realization will awake and open your window of wisdom. You must shift your focus of attention from mind conscious to self (atma) conscious. Impure mind reflects movements, disturbance, restlessness, worry, tension and disorder, causing sorrow and suffering. Opaque mind (impure mind) blocks the vision of the soul. You can see the bottom of a pond in clear water when there is no disturbance on the surface of the water, your sight penetrates to the bottom uninterrupted but when disturbance is caused vision is hindered.

The five elements are created with the combination of space (static) and air (motion). With the movement of air in the space, friction is produced that causes heat, culmination of heat gives birth to water, all combined elements create the earth. Matter is dense form of consciousness, water is liquid form and heat is gaseous form. Air is vital breath (pran) which moves in the space. Space is foundational base which supports movement. Space and air are two basic elements that set the process of creation rolling.

There are many concepts and theories about the existence of the physical world. These remain concepts only and are not the reality and truth. Do not get much concerned about these. Concentrate on the present reality for self improvement which will be more beneficial than getting entangled in concepts.

Consciousness first appears in space which is known as satva (harmony-spiritual). The origin of consciousness is from infinite space of silence of the supreme (static). When consciousness moves, it retains static space of the supreme divine within, for continuity of movement that makes creation possible. From infinite space, consciousness appears with specific (form) space. This space compared to infinite space is insignificant. Consciousness actualizes through form, without form consciousness remains universal beyond duality. Specific space is taken as form for consciousness to appear which is known as universal space (cosmic). It is also known as spiritual world beyond material and physical dissolving distinctions.

The consciousness gets bound by form but it does not lose its spiritual energy. Like water remains water regardless of any container that holds it. When consciousness is identified with mind then it becomes bound and makes you attached to physical things, otherwise it always maintain its purity. Impure mind is the culprit which pollutes consciousness because it fragments and localizes consciousness dividing its power of energy.

Duality reflects two aspects, one is action and the other is inaction. Self (atma) is stable and denotes inaction, whereas body and mind are unstable and reflect action. Duality exists in the physical world because of the non-self, ego center which is created by mind as an imaginary center on the periphery. Anything that works on periphery is gross in nature and has no power of penetration to go deeper to your inner self (center).

Pure mind reflects nonwavering mind which means coolness, peace, steadiness, wisdom, clear understanding, confidence and enthusiasm. Impure mind is ignorance, bondage, perversion, disturbance, misunderstanding, anger, desire, greed, fear and jealousy. Pure and impure mind together reflect both positive and negative aspects of life which alternate endlessly.

True nature (divine) is our essence of life, we must actualize the essence of our being (supreme) for living a trouble free life beyond sorrow and suffering. It happens when you enrich your consciousness by making it free of contents. All things become live and joyful with consciousness. It provides us the sense of being (presence) knowing about all that exists and lives. The consciousness inherits the power of being and knowing through pure awareness, reflecting light of truth and reality. Awareness only reveals but consciousness when conditioned by mind illumines it, only then, it is possible to identify and cognize things that exist around us. Mind reduces formless to form, unseen to seen, unlimited to limited and whole to part.

Without mind consciousness remains pure and unconditioned. Pure consciousness is as good as awareness. You cannot identify things with pure consciousness because it is formless, universal and not conditioned to form and particular entity to recognize. Consciousness has two aspects pure and impure. Pure reflects universality signifying freedom and liberation of the self from attachment to the false and perishable and impure reflects particular and physical denoting bondage, ignorance and attachment to sensuous things.

In fact when the reality is expressed through consciousness it becomes pure witness because you see things as it is and not through distortion and imagination of mind. Conditioned consciousness is participation and involvement and not a witnessing. Witnessing is a direct reflection of reality through pure consciousness. However you can be a pure witness if you do not participate and involve with endless flow of thoughts. But just watch thoughts without opinion, judgment, interest and participation. The thoughts will subside finding no nourishment and patronage for their survival. It will lead to thoughtlessness.

Thoughtlessness reflects pure, empty and clear mind which means dissolving of mind or dropping of mind. So witnessing (pure consciousness) is the best and reliable method to discover your true nature of pure being which we all are, but remain unaware due to ignorance. Ignorance means lack of realization about your true nature, also absence of realization about false, unreal, transient and perishable things which have more attraction and attachment for us due to temporary pleasure we experience with their association and possession.

Consciousness does not shine by itself but it shines through the light of awareness which is beyond consciousness and belongs to the supreme truth. Experience is always through the conditioned consciousness (mind). Any experience that comes through mind is temporary because existence of mind itself is temporary, it appears and disappears. For eternal experience you have to attain your divine nature which in fact is the real experience.

Space is bound by rooms of a building, when the building collapses some rooms are ruined and some remain intact, but can you say this about the space, it is ruined or intact. Space remains space regardless of the state of the building. Space of the ruined rooms becomes free and universal and space of intact room remains bound and particular.

Consciousness remains pure regardless of the form in which it appears. When form dies consciousness disappears and become universal. Consciousness becomes impure when identified with mind. Consciousness has three aspects, waking, dream and deep sleep, (conscious, subconscious and unconscious). Nothing happens to the life, all happens to the form. Infact life becomes live, affirmative and aware only through consciousness. Without consciousness we remain only a bag of bones signifying lifelessness.

Pure consciousness does not give you any status and power. It gives you freedom from false and unreal living of hypocritic life. It dissolves ignorance, bondage and attachment to worldly life. When you go beyond consciousness you reach a state where you do not experience duality. This state is known as 'samadhi' (oneness).

Gross, subtle and casual bodies are forms of consciousness. In gross (body) it works as vital breath (pran). It illumines subtle body (mind), which gives us sense of being and knowing. Universal consciousness (spiritual) is known as casual body because it causes creation of body. Gross, subtle and casual body disappears when body dies and reappears when new body is formed. It is again a concept that new body carries old memories of unfulfilled desires to suffer in this life for its bad karmas of the past life. The real fact is that all concepts are false and untrue because these are not based on your own experience but are known through the experience of others.

You yourself are the supreme truth that is your true and eternal nature. Some people remember incidents of their past life. It is not your experience but someone else's experience. Such happenings are exceptional in nature as some woman deliver five children at a time, some children are born with defective organs, and some are born mentally retarded. All these are exceptions and exceptions do not make a rule. We should go by the rule of averages. We cannot analyze and predict the happenings of nature. It is better we accept life as it comes. Even one knows and remembers incidents of past life, it will in no way help to improve and transform you. It can only load and burden your mind with memories of past life.

So focus your attention on purification of your mind through thoughtlessness. (See chapter thirteen for becoming thoughtless). Gross, subtle and casual bodies are in relation to the physical existence in this life. Linking these to next life is a concept. However some aspects in this context are given in chapter fourteen, under answer to question five. 'Chit' is consciousness and 'chitta' is mind. Movement and rest are in relation to the state of mind. Restlessness of mind reflects movement and peaceful mind is nonwavering mind full of rest without any disturbance. Physical body reflects being, mental body reflects knowingness and casual body reflects pure consciousness. The self entails inner self, universal self and supreme self. Inner self is embodied self, universal self is spiritual self and supreme self is divine self.

Truth remains truth regardless of name and form. Sun light remains sun light regardless of the thing and objects it reveals. Some people ask as to what we gain by attaining spirituality and divinity. We do not gain any status and power but we certainly gain purity of mind, wisdom, understanding and insight to the inner world which transform us from human nature to divine nature, transcending sorrow and suffering. When you attain your pure being then silence and salvation is experienced.

Liberation is of the self from false and imposed ideas, concepts and imagination which accepts real as unreal and false as true. Self makes perception and cognizance possible through consciousness. Mind is both habitual (non-self) and spiritual (self). It is all in relation to the purity of mind. Self reflects eternity and mind is transient, temporary and perishable. In self awareness you learn about your true nature and realize what you are not. It means that you are not a body and mind but you are the master and ruler of these.

You own a house and live in it does not mean that you are a house, you are the master of the house. If you focus your attention on the house then the house becomes important than the master. But when you shift the focus of attention from the house to the master (self) then the reality is known and experienced. There is no specific path to take you to the self because everything is within yourself. If you are dead earnest, you can discover from within your own self.

In self realization the first thing that happens is that restlessness and disturbance subsides and you experience patience and tolerance. Self realization means realization of the falsity of worldly things and knowing about your divine nature. Patience and tolerance reflect maturity of inner growth. Whatever happens, happens to the body and mind, you remain unaffected because you are not the body and mind but the supreme being.

All disturbances are at physical level, (surface) as waves on the surface of the ocean remains disturbed. The physical events are unpredictable and come in endless series which are beyond your control. It is better to accept life as it comes. If you become body and mind conscious, then you will remain disturbed and restless.

The real transformation is from sorrow and suffering to joy, peace and harmony. When consciousness deepens and widens mind automatically drops. The responsibility of enlightenment is entirely yours. It is your inner quest and you alone can discover and none else can do for you. It is here and now, means it is in the present and everywhere because the consciousness is all pervading and enveloping.

Life has two dimensions, one is horizontal movement and another is vertical movement. Vertical movement has two aspects one is moving upward and another is moving downwards to the inner self. Upward vertical movement is the peak of expansion that is reached through love and devotion. When expansion becomes total and whole you reach eternity. This is known as path of devotion (bhakti). The downward vertical movement is contraction, signifying the movement to the source (soul) through pure knowing. Pure knowing is when there is no interference of the mind, as such you are linked to your pure being. One is the beginning (downward) and another is the end (upward). Both movements take you to the eternity (deathlessness).

Horizontal movement of life (human life) is a routine movement which leads you to the cycle of birth and death with sorrow and suffering. Death is the enemy of love because love cannot flower without vertical upward movement. All fears are basically linked to fear of death. Fear dissolves on attaining deathlessness. Fearless mind is total love without any distinction, it means pure consciousness. At physical level we pretend love and appear lovable but real love needs no pretention because every cell of your body becomes love. Physical love suffers from duality (love-hate) but cosmic love is beyond duality where only love exists, you do not experience polar opposites.

Love is your being and not an act. Light and love are opposed to death as they belong to our very being which is deathless and immortal. To counter death be aware and watchful totally and constantly about your being to reach immortality. The manifested world is governed by the consciousness. Without knowing, cognizance, perception and identification world becomes lifeless for you. Mind becomes dynamic with the dynamism of consciousness. Mind is otherwise defunct. The world without consciousness is a dead world.

Consciousness is the medium to actualize your essence of pure being. Seed has two possibilities, one is to die and grow into a tree and other is to die as a seed without growing into a tree. Death of a seed without growth is negative death. Positive death of a seed entails growth. Man has also two possibilities, one possibility is to remain as man without internal evolvement and other possibility is to actualize his essence of divine nature through pure consciousness.

The growth and evolvement of man implies transformation, it means to die on a particular level as conditioned consciousness and to be reborn as an enlightened soul with pure consciousness (born with human nature to be reborn as divine nature). Flowering of consciousness means deepening and widening of consciousness. Flower is the crown of a plant which adds beauty and charm. Man attains and actualizes his essence of his pure being through flowering of his consciousness. Flowering of consciousness is the light of awareness which dissolves darkness of ignorance and awakens your wisdom and understanding.

We should always endeavour to awaken and make people aware about their divine nature so that man's transcends sorrow and suffering. The comfort and convenience oriented mind is to be dropped and that is the real renunciation (sanyas). This can happen through the light of awareness (pure consciousness). Darkness of ignorance is absence of knowledge of light. Unconsciousness can be won over by consciousness. When we become super conscious then we focus our attention on inner self, transcending the outer that causes sorrow and suffering.

All vices (desire, anger, fear, greed and jealousy) are dissolved when you become fully aware of your pure being. The vices originate from the source of unconsciousness which has natural instincts and social learning stored. When you avoid indulgence and suppression through pure witnessing (pure consciousness) the energy goes back to its source and remains unspent. The energy is wasted through vices and it is conserved when vices are dissolved, linking you to your inner self.

There are two births for a man. One birth is routine physical birth through your mother's womb and the other birth is when you are transformed from the womb of unconsciousness to super consciousness. This is special and real birth which takes you to your divine self. That is how, in India an internally evolved person is called twice born (dwij). Brahmin means who knows the ultimate Brahma (supreme) through second birth. It can be attained by any one and not only by a person of Brahmin caste.

Only one part of man is conscious and nine parts remain unconscious which governs our life. The irony of fate is that you go on thinking about what you are not and you go on deceiving yourself about what you are. You are divine by nature in the center but remain ego oriented on the periphery (surface). 'Buddha' says that only awareness can make you a man otherwise your behaviour remains animalistic, governed by unconsciousness (delusion-ignorance). Buddhahood means the awakened one who is fully aware and has attained super consciousness transcending unconsciousness.

Yoga is concerned with enrichment of consciousness for unity with all that exists and lives. Presently we all are unevolved as such unconsciousness persists. Unconsciousness has two aspects, one is biological another is sociological. All instincts are biological (desire, fear, hunger, anger, greed, sleep and sex). Social aspects include cultivation and culturing which comes through society as taboos.

Whatever comes through society becomes your conscience that guides you for right action according to the norms of the society. Right doing is when you follow norms and conventions of the society. Conscience is habitual and cultivated through society but the consciousness is your nature of being which you attain on transcending society. When you attain pure consciousness, you become blissful inside and remain compassionate outside. When your consciousness flowers fully only then you are accepted to enter the temple of the divine.

Man can be at peace in two ways, one is to become totally unaware like animals and the other is to transcend ignorance (unconsciousness) and become part of the divine being. Man operates between these two alternatives either to exist and live unconsciously or transform and attain super consciousness. Ignorance is blissful because you are not aware of the problems. Problems are subjective because these are created by the mind. Unless mind is transformed (impure to pure) problems will persist.

Real and total solution of problems comes through inner religion of yourself. Objective problems are solved through physical science of outer dimension. Knowledge is a sweet fruit because it gives you power but it becomes bitter when it creates problem due to your entangle meant with the world through mind. The manifested world (nature) is innocent beyond good and bad. We corrupt its innocence (purity), through mind. It is our projection and interpretation which corrupts nature and produces many concepts of guilt, sin and morality.

We condemn sex and anger etc, because we have learnt condemnation of these through society which makes us aware of guilt, sin and fear. Whatever we condemn through mind has origin in our unconsciousness (biological instincts and sociological cultivation), these remain stored in the unconsciousness. Unless you attain super consciousness, your instinctive nature will keep appearing and continue causing problems.

We are divided between conscious and unconscious. Conscious is the product of society (ego-false-imaginary) and unconscious is natural instincts which come to us from nature at the time of birth. The feeling of guilt is through ego and not through true religion which is your real being beyond ego. The religion that comes through a concept and thought is religion of the society which exploits your ego by making you guilty, fearful and sinful, so that you follow the norms and conventions of the society.

Society divides your face into two parts, private and public face. Public face is maintained to follow social conventions. Natural living is real living. Living through society is cultivated and artificial living. Tiger kills for hunger without any sense of ego (doership) but man becomes violent and kills without hunger to satisfy his ego for dominance. Killing by a tiger is a natural phenomenon but not the killing by man.

Knowledge (worldly) gives you ego, comparison and judgment. We must endeavour to go beyond ego by enriching consciousness. When consciousness spreads fully evolution stops. Evolution is required to dissolve unconsciousness, signifying moving from darkness to light. Evolution stops when you attain pure consciousness because you become universal and spiritual and then you make no distinction between things which exists and lives. The purpose of evolution is to create pure consciousness and that is the culmination of evolution.

The internal evolution is the growth to reach your divine self. Science can give you only things, it can give you moons and planets but true religion gives you your being (inner self). Man is free to be or not to be. Animals have no choice to grow or not to grow because they remain under the domain of nature which has programmed their lives. Consciousness grows when your ego dissolves. Whenever you transcend natural instincts unconsciousness dissolves.

Manifested world happens through duality of polar opposites (positive-negative, male-female). Man and woman create humanity. Man alone is not humanity, nor is woman alone humanity. One pure element (truth- reality) cannot create anything. The same phenomenon of male and female, positive and negative happens in the inner being of man as is seen in the outer world. Sun is the inner male (positive) and moon is the inner female (negative). Outer sun and outer moon have physical dimension but the inner sun and moon reflect spirituality and enlightenment. Everything exists through duality in the manifested world. Sun and moon are used in Indian symbology. The sun is positive, hot, active and vibrant energy. The moon is cool, silent, still inactive and negative.

Harmony and balancing of sun and moon is salvation. The balancing means centering to your being where you attain, silence and peace. Imbalance between sun and moon cause action movement and creation (manifestation). Awareness creates both sun and moon. When you become aware of whatever is happening in you, the inner most unconscious activity become enlightened in you. All cells become conscious and your whole being is filled with light.

The sun in its deepest center is the coldest spot in existence. Reality exists in polarity, hot and cold. Life and death are two positive and negative realities. You are alive with a death center. When awareness penetrates to every cell of body, cells becomes heated and warm and starts spreading heat towards periphery making your being cooler and cooler inside. A stage comes when heat turns into light. It happens when heat is totally dispersed.

The process of cold and hot is an unending phenomenon which alternates. When periphery is cold the center becomes hot and when center becomes cold, periphery becomes hot. Heat turns into light when it spreads and that is a stage of enlightenment. But inside coolness is created when complete heat is turned into light.

The sun releases energy in two ways unconsciously and consciously. Unconscious energy is rooted through sex, anger, greed etc but consciously it is transformed into light making you wise and enlightened. When you become enlightened outside you become cooler inside. More you become aware the more the heat is transformed into light. When your total energy has become light you experience full moon inside. That is the state of salvation and silence where you transcend polarities (duality). At this stage you are beyond life and death and this is the stage known as deathlessness.

Heat first turns into flame and then to light. A flame signifies revolutionary aspect. When you are at flames stage you become revolutionary, which has two aspects positive and negative. Gandhi was revolutionary in a positive sense and Hitler was revolutionary in a negative sense. But beyond flame when you become light you attain enlightenment and salvation.

The sun and moon in the outer world sustain life on earth. The sun and moon of inner world transform yours human nature to divine nature. The sun and moon reflects cycle of movement of energy from cold to heat and heat to cold. When heat of sun reaches climax it turns into cold. When cold becomes dense at the center it radiates heat. This is the phenomenon and process of nature which continues endlessly, consequently manifestation is actualized. Heat and cold are outer and inner movement of energy. Sun's inner movement is cold and outer movement is hot. Moon's inner movement is hot and outer movement is cold.

When you attain full moon you reach inner reality the eternal reality. The goal of life is to transform heat into light. Observation and witnessing makes heat diffused and turn into light. The energy of anger and sex is transformed into light when you simply observe them without indulgence and suppression. Egyptians and Tibetans preserved the enlightened bodies of their great souls through the principle of inner transformation.

Existence as mentioned earlier is possible through duality only. Two great culture which influence the world – Indian and Greek. Greek approach is logical, intellectual and verbal. Indian culture is experiment from within to move towards your inner self, transcending thinking, mentalisation and verbalization. Indian culture is 'to be' with your being dissolving all projections, imaginations, attachment and illusions which cause sorrow and sufferings. 'To be' means peace, silence and salvation.

The Greek mind being scientific and intellectual thinks in abstract terms, as their thinking remains mind oriented. Hindu mind is soul oriented and moves beyond mind to experience the truth from within. Science gives you fact about objective world, religion gives you life which is beyond matter (objective), mind (subjective). Emphasis of religion is on feeling, experiencing, understanding and realization. Science is manifested world which deals with physical aspect of reality. Religion deals with spiritual and divine aspect of reality.

Be one with existence without knowing objects through labeling (name-form). See tree or a flower as being and not through conditioned form and name. To make your seeing whole and total ignore thinking and feeling so that pure consciousness flows between you and the object you see. With this process seer and seen becomes one, dissolving the appearance and outer structure. Approach things not through mind but through being which is free of condition, labeling and categorization.

CHAPTER 3

GOD - Personified Reality
(Divine-Spiritual-Physical Energy)

God is form of energy which has three aspects. If you remain with your divine energy then sorrows and sufferings cannot enter your domain to disturb and make you restless. Spiritual energy is cosmic beyond duality and distinction with no sign of sorrow and suffering because there exist only purity of love and pure feeling negating impurities of the mind which create problems of misery and chaos while living life. You experience sorrow and suffering when you permit your physical energy to flow through lower aspects of your physical entity with a selfish attitude. Energy flowing in any form remains neutral. It is up to you as to how you make use of these through your psyche. If psyche is opaque with its content then it will make you ignorant but transparent psyche with purity in its entirety will make you wise and understanding. Spiritual and physical energy disappear with the death of the body and these reappear when new body is formed. Divine energy remains eternal and unchanged as a foundational base to the other two energies.

God is not physical in appearance but is spiritual and divine energy. It is the supreme (pure being). At the source it is known as Supreme God (Parameshwara) and is the static base for all that exists and lives. In fact all existence is rooted in the reality of the God. It is all pervading and enveloping. Consciousness originates from the supreme God. It is known as super God (Maheshwara) reflecting pure consciousness. The conditioned consciousness is known as God (ishwara). In fact the supreme God is the light of awareness, which revels the world but itself remains unaware because of the oneness entity.

Awareness is the aura of the supreme God. It is like the Sun which is the base of rays that reveals the world. Light of awareness is single and indivisible, changeless and eternal. At universal level it reveals the universe through the process of manifestation. Supreme God is one but super God (consciousness-maheshwara are many). All are rooted in the supreme God (parameshwara). Super God (maheshwara) manifests its own universe. The God (ishwara) reveals the embodied God as soul.

The supreme God is divine, pure being, light of awareness, eternal, total, whole, complete and perfect. Super God is spiritual, pure knowing, universal, pure feeling and pure love and is a link between God (ishwara) and supreme God (parameshwara). God (ishwara) is individual, particular, bound and conditioned consciousness. The conditioned consciousness is temporary and perishable because when body dies, bounded consciousness disappears and becomes universal consciousness. Understand very clearly that super God (maheshwara) and God (ishwara) carry all the potential of supreme God (parameshwara). Both are reflection of the supreme God (parameshwara), the supreme is expressed through these. These remain dormant in the supreme and become active when process of manifestation begins. Consciousness (super God) is dynamic and self vibrant.

Supreme God is a static base for movement of consciousness. Super God is being and knowing at cosmic level-spiritual level. God (ishwara) is actualization at physical level. You are the supreme yourself as divine. You have all the potential to dissolve God and super God to discover the supreme God, by going beyond mind. The experience of God is through the empty, pure and clear mind. The experience of God means experiencing and knowing your true nature (supreme God), by becoming 'to be'. Pure mind reflects transparency and opaque mind reflects ignorance.

The light of supreme God is known as supreme self (paramatma). The light of super self is consciousness (anteratma) known as knowingness. The light of embodied self is the light of God which helps us identify things of the world. Supreme God, super God and God have same power and potential but their power of influence differs. It is mind which divides and categorizes different Gods. Pure mind sees whole God, impure mind experiences limited God and between whole and limited God is cosmic God (pure consciousness). Supreme God reflects bliss, peace and love. Cosmic God (super God) reflects deep feeling of love without distinction and duality. On attaining it through devotion you become spiritual with an attitude of compassion.

God reflects embodied God which means God in all that lives and exists and not only in man. The difference is that the man has potential to actualize it but animals and others have no possibility to actualize it. God is manifested through mind and body, which are instruments to express reflection of God and self. When mind is pure the reflection of God and self (atma) also becomes pure and holy. You must understand that God and self always remain together, because God is the base to sustain the self (atma) as light of awareness. God can exist without light but self (light of awareness) cannot exist without the support of God. God is existence and pure being, self is light of awareness which becomes consciousness (knowingness). It is the conditioned consciousness which is called God at the physical level. Identification of worldly things happens through the God which supports consciousness for cognizance.

The light of awareness of supreme self becomes consciousness in the process of creation. Consciousness is grosser form of light of awareness, grosser to consciousness is the conditioned consciousness. Conditioned consciousness (God) has three aspects. One is mind center through which logic and reason is produced. Second is heart center which reflects feeling, love and compassion. Lastly is the navel center which is the abode of self (atma), it is also known as life center. The light of awareness reflects both the supreme self and the supreme God, whereas pure consciousness reflects super God and cosmic self. You must understand that God and self always remain pure regardless of forms. Mind is the main factor to pollute and make these impure, when identifies with it.

There is no physical appearance of God. It is all imagination and illusory created by mind. Mind endlessly weaves its own illusory world which is not reality and truth but a distortion of truth. When you see God through mind you see him in temples only and beyond mind he is everywhere. It is your inner quest to experience from within, which can lead you to him, through awareness, witnessing, meditation and attention. (See chapter thirteen for all these).

The supreme God cannot be worshipped directly, as he is formless and timeless. To worship him you have to personify him as imagined God of form as a medium. God is not what you have imagined through your thought and concept but God is pure awareness and pure consciousness.

In spirituality stress is on inner growth of each individual. No one else can evolve for you nor anyone can purify your mind. You have to do it yourself. Lord Krishna could not produce hundreds of Krishna's to eliminate evil and sins from the earth. God does not involve in miracles and magical stunts, which are product of imagination of mind. They reflect a weak mind loaded and burdened with contents of beliefs, ideas, concepts, customs, traditions and rituals.

No God can eliminate sins from the earth nor can he bless you with virtues because he is beyond sin and virtues (duality). Sin and virtues are created by mind and God is beyond mind where there is no duality. The great enlightened souls become an ideal example to inspire and guide you to the unknown abyss but to jump into it is your inner courage which you have to grow from within your own self.

God helps those who help themselves, the light of awareness is always available. You should make your mind reflective (pure) so that light of awareness is received through your pure mind, which will give you wisdom, insight and understanding to make your living virtuous and holy. Christ, Krishna, Buddha and many other great souls actualized their essence of truth (God) through their own earnestness.

We all can attain the Godly status as we are born with the potential and possibility for inner growth but we are not earnest, keen, interested, willing, honest, sincere and truthful. We remain unsuccessful, disappointed, rejected with delusion and ignorance. If the room is dimly lit, you cannot clearly identify between a nail and a needle but identification becomes easier when room is flooded with light. Likewise mind is flooded with light of awareness, you can effectively discriminate between right and wrong. Right is needful and necessary and wrong is unnecessary and needless.

When you attain Godhood, each cell of your body is potensized with love, peace and joy. It is mind which creates divine and devil, God and no God. When you attain divinity then you see divinity everywhere and in everybody. Every moment is auspicious and pure, every man is good and divine. It is so because same pure consciousness and divinity (supreme God and cosmic God) flows in all. If you focus your attention on consciousness (cosmic God) you see unity in all that lives and exists. When you focus your attention on outer appearance and form then you experience division and separation from God and that becomes cause of your sorrow and sufferings.

God does not choose path for your physical and spiritual living. God is non-interfering. It is you who have to purify your mind for transformation from physical to spiritual. God does not eliminate evilness from the society, evilness is to be won over by individuals themselves. Great souls appear on earth to inspire and awaken people from darkness of ignorance to light of God (wisdom). It is like when you awake a person from sleep his dreams dissolve. When man is awakened into wisdom, ignorance dissolves. The enlightened souls can only awake you for attaining inner self but they cannot possibly transform you because that happens through you and not through anybody else. It is an individual exercise.

To remove darkness of a room, you may worship and pray to God endlessly, remain hungry, spent sleepless night, follow strictly religious rituals, customs, traditions and beliefs which could be torturous and cruel to execute but still darkness will not go unless you open the door of the room. The moment you do that room will be flooded with light and darkness will disappear instantly. Similarly to dispel darkness of ignorance, you have to empty and clear the mind of its contents so that the light of awareness enters your mind and make you wise to dissolve the ignorance.

Positive mind reflects Godliness, negative mind reflects sorrow and suffering. Mind becomes positive with inner evolvement reflecting light of God and negative mind reflect denial of God, reflecting non use of Godly energy (divine and spiritual). Beyond positivity and negativity is the supreme God reflecting oneness beyond duality. Supreme God (reality) is neither created nor contained by anything and is causeless.

When we say God is love, joy and peace, it gives you an impression as if God is a physical entity but it is not so. It only means that when you attain Godliness you become lovable, joyful and peaceful because these are contained by God in seed form which could be actualized by any man through the light of God which is received through pure mind. Man becomes medium to express Godliness as had happened in the past through Buddha, Christ and Mohammad. Supreme God is the abode of all that lives and exists. On dissolution of creation everything returns to that abode, where you experience silence and salvation. Sacred and holy eternal virtues of love, peace and joy sprout from the Godly state of your being. It means these virtues are expressed through your behavior, when actualized.

Cosmic God (super God) is a symbol of love. It is spiritual, universal and beyond duality. The love that you experience in the world is false because it contains polar opposites (love-hate), which keep alternating. But universal love is open and free of duality. It synthesizes. Universal love is indivisive, selfless and impersonal. God is joy, when you attain Godhood, you reach the undisturbed stage of your pure being, where only peace and ecstasy are experienced.

Attaining supreme God means that you lose your worldly sense of attachment and concern for sensuous things. It means your vision, wisdom and understanding become cosmic and divine. Peace and love are your nature. You needlessly identify with mind which causes disturbance to your peace and make you restless. Total peace reflects Godliness. Real peace happens not through becalmed mind but it happens by going beyond mind.

Understand clearly that wherever the word God is referred it applies to different types of God as mentioned earlier. So link it according to the relevant contexts. You have to be aware, awake, know, realize and experience your own God from within. God is absolute, ultimate, supreme and universal. He makes no distinction between black-white, literate-illiterate, ignorant-wise, rich-poor, male-female, young-old. It means that man who attains Godhood also makes no distinction because his vision and understanding deepens and widens as he transcends duality.

God cannot help you directly but you get helped indirectly as you have the inbuilt potential to harness its energy. God's power of energy is utilized profitably when mind is pure and non-wavering. The power of energy of God remains unutilized when mind becomes impure. The divine and spiritual energy are equally available to all but only selected few take the benefit to actualize it into action and attain enlightenment and salvation.

If you want to know and experience God then you have to be 'That' by attaining totality and wholeness by dropping mind (see chapter thirteen for dropping mind). With mind you can only experience the world and not the God, beyond mind God is everywhere. Universal God is a witness to the whole universe manifested and unmanifested. It means when you attain spirituality you become one with existence and witness it as such through pure consciousness.

All sorrows and sufferings happen when you drift away from divine and spiritual energy of the God. Heaven and hell is in relation to going closer to God or drifting away from God. God has nothing to do with these it is beyond both- hell and heaven. It only provides light of awareness which you can wisely utilize according to the quality of your psyche. In this light you can plan murder or you may render selfless service with love, for the common good of all.

Awareness, the light of supreme self (supreme God) and consciousness (cosmic God) always remain pure, nothing can contaminate and dilute their purity. Dilution and impurity happen when these are identified with mind. As a matter of fact God (consciousness) remains pure in spite of fragmentation and localization through the mind.

The fate of the body is death and the fate of the world is dissolution. But fate of God is eternal existence where nothing changes ever because on reaching there one becomes deathless. Anything that has beginning and end, appearance and disappearance, coming and going, birth and death is false and unreal. In the divine world nothing ever begins or dies as such it is real and the ultimate truth.

God neither makes you suffer nor saves you from suffering because it is neutral energy. Suffering and non-suffering is your own doing when you misuse his energy through your mind and suffer. God is not a person as explained earlier but a reality personified as God for worship. God is non-interfering, neither it appreciates nor reprimands you. Most of the energy of God is scattered in petty things and wasted through mind. Without mind the divine and spiritual energy of the God is available to be utilized for the benefit of the humanity as had been done in the past by enlightened souls.

Man wastes God's energy mainly through indulgence and suppression to live an unnatural life of hypocrisy. The energy has tendency that it moves in circulation, if you can maintain the circular movement of energy then you can conserve the energy as is happening in nature. The energy in nature is never conditioned and fragmented because there is no mind to do so as such total energy continues its circular movement without any interference. You can also do this by total and complete witnessing of event without participation, involvement and conditioning, avoiding indulgence and suppression. If you do that then there will be no break in the circular movement of the energy, that will give you tremendous energy which can be utilized for the common good of all.

It is a natural phenomenon that divine and spiritual energy of God are automatically replenished when the circular movement of energy is maintained, as it happens in nature. Like sea water that comes through rains and rivers slowly evaporates back to the sky, forms rain cloud, false on earth as rain and makes rivers flow with water which ultimately merges with the ocean. This process of water replacement endlessly continues in nature. It is up to you as to which direction you want to direct the Gods energy – physical or spiritual. God's energy becomes physical when used through mind, beyond mind it is divine and spiritual.

Sex is a creative energy which you can direct through physical channel with mind and beyond mind the sex energy becomes divine and spiritual. Likewise desire, fear, anger, greed and jealousy becomes negative when used through mind and beyond mind this energy can be transformed to spiritual and divine energy. The indulgence and suppression through mind blocks the vision of God as such you experience sorrow and suffering. To experience God follow one of the techniques dedicatedly and sincerely, given in chapter thirteen. Out of these techniques you chose the technique which suits your nature, temperament and attitude. However witnessing is the easiest way to reach God.

When you realize that your true nature is the supreme God and not the body and mind which are only instruments through which the reality is expressed. Physical and mental events affect body and mind and not your true nature of God, as such it should not become a cause of worry and tension. The world is reflection of God as everything in the world is divine because the supreme God contains everything in seed form before the process of creation starts. Anything that originates from supreme God has to be divine. If you want to see God then see God through the world, his creation, which has three aspects - supreme God, super God (cosmic) and God (embodied), all these work in cooperation and with complete coordination to sustain life in the universe.

Godliness is to be realized, known, experienced and lived. It is not thinking and feeling but it is translating into action for inner evolvement to reach divinity. Godliness is to be lived and not talked. Trust and faith are essential factors for realizing and experiencing the unknown God. Faith and trust means willingness and determination to try. This happens with steady, pure and clear mind with charitable and clean heart, besides these sanctified and selfless actions are also essential.

You cannot attain God by effort, learning, doing, practice and training these are required for worldly growth. Experience of God is a natural happening, which happens when you go beyond mind. You are religious or not do not depend on how much God fearing you are but it all depends on the state of purity of mind. If your mind is impure then you are an atheist and non religious. If you have pure mind, charitable heart and sanctified actions then you have to fear no God because without mind you are God. Knowing and experiencing God happens from within your own self and needs no help from outside but in doing you need external help. Doing is physical, happening is natural and spiritual. Doing happens from the surface (body and mind) and happening happens through the center (self).

The aim of worship and prayer is to make your thinking, feeling and action pure because when you concentrate on prayer other thoughts subside and your prayer becomes meditative. But if you do not concentrate on prayer then the prayer turns into ashes. Prayer is your being (self), it is culmination of love. Through prayer you can reach eternity. Love is spiritual (pure consciousness) and step short to prayer (supreme God-your being). Love is between devotee and deity and when devotee and deity merge with deep feeling of oneness then it becomes a prayer. It is not the prayer which we do at physical level as a habitual and routine with a burdened and worried mind. Real prayer happens when mind is clear and empty. Till then it only remains a show.

Real transformation from sorrow and suffering to peace and love happens through true prayers. You cannot attain Godhood instantly. Instant precedes long preparation. Fruit falls suddenly but ripening takes time. Godly man (man of pure mind) is not afraid of death because he realizes his eternal true nature of deathlessness as such he becomes fearless. Death happens to body and mind and not to God and self (atma). Godly man experiences fearlessness as his mind is already dead, means he has dropped mind which causes fear.

God knows you when you know yourself. Knowing yourself means growing and evolving from within for attaining spirituality. It is up to you to either know the God through internal evolvement or disown him through mind orientation. God is an idea, concept, thought that come to you from outer world through elders, family, friends, society, custom, traditions, education, learning, information and knowledge. It is not your experience of God as great souls had experienced in the past, as such for you the God remains a concept without your own experience.

The God is always available in the present and not in the past and future because present reality cannot be conditioned and remains pure linking you directly to God because past and future dissolve in the present. Past and future are product of mind as such in the present mind also dissolves. 'AUM' is a sound symbol of God. It signifies Sat-Chit-Anand (Pure being-Knowledge-Bliss). 'A' – reflects mind center, 'U' – reflects heart center and 'M' – reflects navel center. It also means 'A' is waking state. 'U' is dreaming state and 'M' is deep sleep (AUM). There are three ways to experience God – self knowing (gyan), self surrender (bhakti) and selfless work (karma). Saints attain Godhood through self knowing, devotee attain through surrendering of ego and man of action through self less action (Karma). All paths which lead to God needs enrichment of consciousness through pure mind, but for this God remain unknown and hidden.

Although God is always present with you regardless of purity and impurity of your mind, but its actualization can only happen through internal evolvement. Fearlessness is the experience of God because you cease caring for the body, as you realize that your true nature is the supreme God and not the body and mind. Death happens to body and mind and not to your true self.

If you draw out water from a well with a bucket with many holes in the bottom of it, then you cannot fetch water. Similarly if you want to experience God through fractured consciousness (disturbed mind with desire and fear) then you cannot experience God and will confront frustration and disappointment because you need total and whole focused consciousness to attain Godhood.

As explained earlier prayer is total silence (non wavering mind) because when you merge with the supreme God, silence automatically happens. Prayer in the physical sense is request to demand favour but in divine sense it is your entry to the kingdom of the supreme God. 'Sadhna' (spiritual practice) is a determined way for spiritual growth. 'Sadhna' does not mean punishing and torturing your body nor does it mean disowning of the world. 'Sadhna' only means enriching your consciousness for purification of mind.

God is Satyam, Shivam and Sunderam (truth, consciousness-beautiful). Supreme God is Satyam, universal God is Shivam and the world they create is Sundram. Shivam is male aspect, it is pure consciousness and female aspect (Parvati) is grosser aspect of consciousness–vital breath (pran). Shankara is conditioned consciousness which appears and disappears with the body. It denotes death and destruction. God is nature and nature cannot exists without the support of supreme God. The process and phenomenon of nature is creation, preservation and destruction. Creation is consciousness (cosmic God), preservation is vital breath (pran) and destruction is form (matter). Creation is Shiva (consciousness), Parvati is vital breath which reflects preservation and destruction is Shankara (matter), because it is matter which is destroyed.

This can be seen in different context. 'Brahma' is a personified God which Hindus believe as a creator, like wise "Vishnu" is preservator and "Mahesh" is destroyer. They reflect supreme God, super God and God (divine – spiritual – physical). It is also known as awareness, knowingness and beingness. All these are created to understand the different types of energy that originates from the supreme God (divine, spiritual and physical energy). You cannot stop the process of nature as you cannot stop the crop growing, you have to accept it as it comes because you have no control over the happenings of nature which happens unpredictably and accidentally.

God expresses his power of energy through the medium of man's mind. If man's mind is opaque with darkness of ignorance then the power of God is diminished. However pure and transparent mind reflects full power of God. We generally have a habit to find some excuse and blame others (person, fate, God, past actions) for our sorrow and sufferings. But in fact it is our own wrong doing that we suffer in life. So instead of blaming others concentrate on self improvement from within. God is beyond distinctions and is not involved in magical and miracle stunts. God is neither involved in granting grace or disgrace. Petrol as an energy moves a vehicle when it is used through mechanism. If a vehicle meets with an accident due to bad driving, then it is not the petrol energy responsible for the injuries you sustain.

God is a mystery. Mystery is beyond any analysis, prediction, expectation and certainty as such we should accept and live what nature brings to us – joy or sorrow. If you feel the presence of divine everywhere through your clear mind and pure heart then you need not visit Mecca, Kashi and Kailash because divinity is not specific, it is cosmic. Sugar is physical and material but sweetness of sugar is formless and universal. When you say you are God it only means that everything that exists and live is divine provided you actualize the divinity through your internal growth.

You cannot attain Godhood by toiling and torturing the body, Godhood is attained by dropping mind other than that nothing helps you to discover your inner God. When good things happen in life you thank God for his goodness and when bad things happen you blame God that he is annoyed and granted disgrace to you but it is not so it is only illusory and imaginary. Good and bad actions reflect inner harmony and disharmony. God is not a person but a presence in the core of your being (body). The crux of the whole thing is that you don't have to move to jungle and caves to search God, you can find God sitting at home provided you purify your mind. Jungle and caves in no way can help you in purification of your mind except torturing your body and causing other discomfort and inconveniences.

The Godliness comes to the seeker when he matures spiritually. The waves of Godliness come to the seeker from the divine center of God at its own just like water waves touching the bank, bank does not move anywhere, waves come to it. Seeker need not move anywhere, the divine waves will strike him when he is ready. Ordinarily seeker try to go towards the divine but until divine comes to you through your spiritual maturity, you may just be in a illusionary dream. You will go on searching, but you will never find him. When your invitation (invocation) is valid and total, he is there. Total and valid means when you attain silence through non-wavering mind.

When we begin any worship and prayer especially in yagya (sacrifice), we invoke the deities, call and invite them. How can you pray unless you have invited? How can you surrender unless you have invoked. Invocation has a deeper meaning. It means inner silence. Invocation becomes total when all outside actions cease. This is the entry point to enter kingdom of God, so unless you achieve silence how can you invite the divine with a disturbed and noisy mind. Innocence reflects purity and that is true invocation (silence).

All those who pray in temples, churches and mosques are really not praying, they are praying to avoid loss of life and wealth because they always remain fearful of death. Praying in temples cannot guard you from death and other losses, but experiencing your own self will make you deathless and fearless because that is yours true and eternal nature (supreme God). Death happens to body and mind and not to your being. If you are experiencing existence through the medium of body and mind, it is the world but if you are experiencing the existence of God with innocence and silence it is the divine. A still mind can lead you to the kingdom of God. Still mind means non-wavering mind without thought, desire and fear.

We generally believe that if you make your body still, mind becomes still. It is not true, in fact contrary is true. If mind becomes still then body automatically becomes still. You may imitate better posture physically then Buddha but spiritually the physical posture that you create is defunct and dead because it is cultivated and is not natural happening with inner transformation. Buddha was still and steady mentally even when he was involved in activity, there was no turmoil inside, there was total silence. Without stillness of mind you cannot discover divine God because noisy mind works only on periphery and lacks deeper penetration to your inner self (center).

Grace of God is not a help but just it is a law of nature. The moment you enter the gravitational zone (grace) of divine the law begins to work in your favour. It is like water evaporates on reaching certain degree of temperature because of the law of evaporation. On crossing gravitational zone of earth you automatically transcend gravitational pull of the earth as a law of gravitation.

Divine grace happens as a law of divine nature when you attain purity of mind. One reality has been divided into two polar opposites (divine–devil, positive–negative). Devil is another name of divine because divine God is centered in the devil. It is like hate is centered in love and love is centered in hate, death is centered in life and life is centered in death, that is how you experience duality in the world. Until you reach your divine source of God you will continue experiencing polar opposites in this world.

On the periphery it is devil governed by mind and at the source (center), the reality of divine God exists. Existence is oneness in nature. Seeker is the sought that means divinity is centered in the seeker and when the seeker actualizes the divinity it becomes sought because seeker and sought merges. When great enlightened souls, saints and sages say that 'I am God' and 'I am That' it means everything is God and everything is 'That'. Try to be total in your doings so that your doing become Godly. Partial doing means wavering of mind which becomes hindrance to realize God. Thinking about God will not take you to God, only experiencing can do that. Thinking is an intellectual exercise. God takes over when mind stops.

CHAPTER 4

RELIGION (Real And Unreal)

Real religion is one which takes us to our divine nature transcending sorrows and sufferings it happens through purified mind. When we realize, understand and experience our real nature from within our own self as was experienced by great souls in the past (Christ-Buddha-Mohammad etc). The unreal religion is a belief which we follow as a concept given to us by the enlightened souls. It is not our own experience as such when we follow and depend on the experience of others it becomes false and unreal which cannot lead us to eternity of reality and truth

True religion is about knowing your supreme nature. It is a journey from beingness to pure being, form to formless, matter to eternity and human nature to divine nature. True religion of the pure being is eternal, it never changes. However religion of the body and mind is transient and perishable. True religion happens through your own inner experience. Experience through body and mind is unreal and false religion, as mind dies with the death of the body. The religion which is born through a thought becomes a conceptual religion, as it is created and cultivated by the society, it lacks personal experience from within.

When you try to understand real (true) religion, through intellect, then you understand the religion only partially as a concept and not wholly as eternity. Intellect remains limited because of minds limitation as such the true religion which is limitless and formless cannot be experienced through the limited intellect which has form. To understand formless you have to transform from form to formless, limit to limitless.

Mind imagines and distorts true religion as such true religion understood through mind becomes a concept and not a reality. True and real (supreme) never dies and unreal and false (mind) never stays. True religion is silence, salvation and liberation but conceptual religion is particular, bondage, disturbance, sorrow and suffering.

Reality and truth reflect presence of the divine religion every moment and everywhere. All originates from the divine religion. Conceptual religion is ego oriented and true religion is beyond ego. When conceptual religion is present the true religion remains absent and when true religion is present the conceptual religion dissolves.

Man of wisdom realizes that the true religion is all pervading and enveloping but ignorant remains unaware, he follows and believes whatever others tell. Wise man who knows true religion becomes a witness to all that happens around him, knower and observer (Gyata and Drashta). Ignorant who follows only conceptual religion remains only enjoyer and doer (Bhogta and Karta).

True religion was experienced by Krishna, Christ, Buddha, Mahavira, Mohammad and many other great souls. Based on their experience of the true religion, their followers felt satisfied with the concept given to them by these enlightened souls but they never experienced in life the true religion at their own, as such it remains only a distortion, imagination and a falsity but certainly not the reality.

All scriptures contain truthful experiences of great souls about true religion. But scriptures are not the truth but explain about truth which was experienced by other great souls, as such scriptures remain concept only. Reading scriptures can inspire you but cannot transform you unless you translate inspiration into action through your own inner experience. Hindu, Christian, Islam, Buddhism and Jainism and many more religions are conceptual. It is so because you follow these without your own personal inner experience.

You cannot jump directly from physical living with human nature to divine nature (true religion). Spirituality is a link between physical and divine. Those who are deeply earnest can attain true religion in one life. Conceptual religion causes conflict, confusion, chaos and contradiction. Such false religions divide, separate societies and cause disharmony and destruction.

True religion unites and synthesizes, promoting love and brotherhood universally. There is no Hindu consciousness or Christian consciousness. It is only pure consciousness. Conditioned consciousness centered in the mind creates concepts and thought of false religion. Religion has two aspects one is religion of the supreme self (true) and the other is religion of the mind (false). One is real and eternal and the other is unreal and perishable.

The religion of self is experienced from within internally and the religion of the mind is experienced from without externally. People are mistaken in their understanding of the true religion because the religion of self talks about the inner aspects, whereas we try to understand the inner realities through mind which works at surface level only. One is physical, outer and remains restricted to periphery and the other is spiritual, inner, divine and remains at the center.

To understand your religion of self you have to transform from physical to spiritual by dropping mind till then everything remains meaningless. The religion of mind reflects outer world and the religion of self (true) reflects inner world. You cannot enter inner world without distillation of the impurities of mind. The religion of the mind being physical and gross lacks deeper penetration to the subtle aspects of inner self.

The experience of truth by great souls is similar but their expression in action is different. Christ expressed his experience of true religion through love and service, Buddha through silence and salvation,

Mahavira through nonviolence and austerity, Mohammad through brotherhood and simplicity (oneness of purity inside outside), Meera through dance and surrendering of ego.

Religion is the law of being. Religion of water is to cool and religion of fire is to burn and give heat, likewise every being has its own religion to exist and sustain. The entity of existence collapses once religion dies. Religion sustains life, without true religion existence extincts. Your actions become sacred and holy when you experience true religion. Peace and love become your true religion. You cannot exist for a moment and die instantly without the support of your true religion. The goal of life is to discover your true religion to sustain and live a harmonious life with divine and spiritual virtues.

Nature is a happening that happens as a process independently beyond man's doing. True religion is supreme nature, conceptual religion is a thought and a belief man follows. Spiritual religion is cosmic and universal reflecting pure consciousness. The religion of nature has two aspects one is religion of physical self (swadharma) and the other is the nature of physical self (Swabhava). Details in this context are covered in chapter five.

The cultivated and created religion comes to us through society and learning. The true religion (supreme nature) is beyond religion of physical self and religion of nature, these dissolves when you attain your true religion. Religion of physical self differs in every man.

It is advised by Lord Krishna that one should live one's life with one's own temperament (religion of nature), as received from nature in the form of three attributes (harmony-passion-pervert). This only applies while living in the world till one has attained and evolved spiritually from inside. On attaining your true religion of divinity the religion of nature (swabhava) dissolve and stop interfering in your behaviour. It means you transform from human nature to divine nature.

Physical self as explained earlier has different nature and temperament but the spiritual self (atma) has only one nature of divinity. Spiritual self is single minded and indivisive but physical self governed by mind is multi minded. The religion of nature appears and disappears it dies with the death of the body and it reappears when new body comes up, similarly the cultivated and cultured religion is also temporary and perishable which comes and goes. But the true religion is eternal where nothing changes.

It is the cultivated religion which comes to us through society, divides society into higher and lower for selfish reasons. Infact higher and lower should be in relation to the purity of the mind and not by birth in a particular community. A man born in a created lower family may be wiser, have sharper intellect to grow externally and internally to reach higher status of spirituality then a man born in a ruler family (higher class) with ignorance and impurities of mind. If such a prince with low intellect takes over the rule of the kingdom in a traditional way, he is sure to ruin the kingdom.

We do not stop believing in false traditions and customs and continue patronizing higher and lower caste system, instead of eliminating this social evil from the society. We know and realize that no two men are born alike. Each is born with different temperament and nature. But in one sense we all are born equal because we are all divine and have potential and possibilities to grow to eternity.

The creation of higher and lower is created by the mind. The lowest of the low can rise high and the highest of the high can fall low depending on the state of purity of mind. 'Vyas ji', the writer of the Vedas and Puranas belong to the so called created low caste. Likewise 'Vidhur' of the epic Mahabharata fame also belonged to a low birth. 'Valmiki' the author of the epic Ramayana was also not a Brahmin (upper caste). This reflects that regardless of low birth one can evolve and reach to higher status of divinity and spirituality.

Some may argue that animals and birds have higher and lower breeds so why do not we accept this reality for man. In animals higher and lower breed is related to their physical form and intellect which differs as such they are categories into lower and higher breeds. Animals have no scope to grow internally because they are born actualized and programmed by nature as such. They do not have possibility and potential for self improvement and transformation, which happens through the purification of the mind. As such they remain as they are born however to some extent they can be cultured and cultivated but certainly they cannot be converted.

Man on the other hand has to actualize his essence of true religion by growing from within. In this context every man has equal opportunity to grow and experience his true religion, regardless of his birth in higher or lower class. Higher and lower dissolve when you attain total purity of mind, it has nothing to do with your birth in lower or higher class, these are all created class. To move closer to the self (atma) is religion and moving away from it is ego (nonself) created by mind. Those who remain mind conscious become religiously (spiritually) empty.

Self experiencing and awareness is the religion of the divine where as logic and reason is the religion of the mind (nonself). Conscious mind is outer religion to deal with the objective world. Spirituality is inner religion which leads you to divine religion (true religion). Religiousness is not reflected by the fact that how much you worship, pray and visit Temples and Churches but religiousness is known through your inner purity and inner silence which you attain through non wavering mind.

When you see religion through mind (concept and thought) you see in temple, idols, and scriptures but beyond mind the religion is cosmic and divine. People who fear God are considered more religious but it is not so because religion of your supreme self (supreme God) make you fearless because on attaining your true religion there is no other to fear from as all becomes one. Conceptual religion and morality are designed to instill fear and guilt feeling in you by elders, society, priests and pundits so that you follow norms and conventions of the society, Churches and Temples, and you remain open for exploitation by them.

The non realization of your true religion causes sorrow and suffering in life. The true religion is a salvation and liberation but the conceptual religion created through mind is bondage and misery. Religion is your true nature it cannot be created and imposed from outside. You are born with it, you live with it and you die with it.

Religion is generally linked to morality but these are two different things. Religion is your true nature of eternity and morality is the product of the society, which creates moral and ethical values to be followed while living with the society. Moral values are product of mind and religion is product of divine. Moral value that come through mind do not apply everywhere for all time, changing from time to time and place to place with different societies. Religion is inner growth to discover the divinity and morality is the set values for outer behaviour. Morality is physical and true religion is divine.

Man may appear moralistic outwardly what he may not be internally reflecting hypocrisy. In true religion you are one inside outside, free of split personality but morality is contradictory, transient and perishable because it originates from the mind. Real and true eternal virtues come through the divine self and not through nonself (ego). Craving is the product of religion of mind. Where ever you go mind remains with you as such craving stays regardless of your going anywhere. The religion of mind is dissolved when you attain your religion of true being. It means you have to transform from nonself (ego) to egolessness (self), from conceptual religion to true religion to dissolve and kill craving without that nothing else will help you.

With realization of true religion you accept life as it comes, without shaping it. Religion is not ritual, rituals reflect dead religion because these originates through impure mind. Rituals are beliefs which have transient nature. No transformation is possible through rituals because rituals being physical in nature are gross and work on surface level only.

The philosophy of rituals is that anything done at physical level can transform you internally but it is not so. It is vice versa. Internal transformation happens when outer activities subside. On knowing your true religion you automatically become self controlled, self disciplined and self inspired and then you need not impose these from outside.

Religiousness needs no scriptures it needs only purity of your mind. True religion awakens people from falsity of the world which has temporary existence. In India philosophy means 'Darshan' (seeing). It means seeing and experiencing through inner vision (insight) your true religion. 'darshan' is whole and total but philosophy is partial and physical. Philosophy is through intellect, logic and reason.

Anything that comes through mind is partial, imperfect and incomplete. Religion of physical science make you outwardly rich, where as science of true religion makes you divinely rich. Physical science has no potential to transform you but divine science has. If you want to know matter then be a scientist and if you want to know love then be like Meera, Chaitanya (Indian devotee of God). However, if you want to know your true self (divine self) then be like Christ, Buddha, Mohammad and Kabir. Religion of physical science deals with 'How', philosophy deals with 'Why' and religion deals with experiencing your true being.

Religion of your true self will make you master of your mind. It means you will go beyond mind and it will no more disturb and interfere in your affairs. Realization must be firm and strong to dissolve sensuous things which attract and make you attached.

Conceptual religion survives when you remain fear, sin and guilt oriented. A fearful man surrenders his independence and blindly follows what society, priests and pundits say. Fear is product of ignorance about your true nature, which leads you to sorrow and suffering. It means living an impure and a nonreligious life.

Ignorance is dissolved through wisdom as had happened in the past with Buddha, Mahavira, Christ and many others who by their self improvement transcended fear and with that they went beyond the norms and conventions of the society, temples and churches. However they only followed eternal divine virtues, which never changes like social norms and conventions.

Man of true religion attains enormous inner power and strength of tolerance and patience. He remains cool and steady even under grave harassment, physical and mental torture. Christ maintained his cool when he was being crucified. Indian Sufi mystic 'Kabir' maintained his cool and calmness and remained un-ruffled when he was trampled by elephant to death. He was continuously composing divine couplets (dohas), unmindful of imminent death. No one understood those great souls when they were alive. They are worshiped as God after their death.

It is seen that people generally link and understand nonviolence in relation to the habit of vegetarian eating. But if you happen to be born in a nonvegetarian family you will become nonvegetarian by a family habit. But the eating habit has nothing to do with violence, nonviolence and true religion. Eating is a physical aspect where as nonviolence is peace and love that originates from divinity on purifying your mind.

It is mainly the state of purity of your mind which reflects violence and nonviolence, eating has nothing to do with these. You may be a vegetarian with impure mind that can make you violent. On the other hand you may be non-vegetarian with pure mind that reflects nonviolence. Some say if you eat non-vegetarian food you become violent and aggressive but it is not so. However non-vegetarian food can affect your physical health. For most of us body is more important than the spiritual self, not realizing that the fate of body is death which can happen any moment. Therefore there seems no sense to attach to the body at the cost of the soul. Attachment to body is ignorance and detachment from body and sensuous things is wisdom.

In the absence of love and your true religion you become violent and aggressive because of your selfish and personal interests, as had happened in the past with 'Ravana' of epic Ramayana era, 'Hitler', and 'Chengiz Khan'. They were stone hearted people who killed mercilessly many innocent people for satisfying there ego.

When total and complete nonviolence is attained on experiencing your true religion, then you do not hurt and cheat anyone in thought, speech, feeling and action. It is the killer who is hurt and suffers and not the killed. The killed loses all sensation of pain and suffering with his death. However the normal man definitely feel pain and suffering during killing, till he is completely dead but the one who has experienced his true religion (true nature) does not feel the pinch of killing because he transcends his mind.

Suffering and pain happen through mind only beyond mind sorrow and suffering dissolves. We want peace in the world but where are the peaceful people? All endeavour to bring peace in the world are superficial at physical level (surface). Restless and disturbed mind cannot bring eternal peace. It can only bring partial be-calmness, which is not a total peace. Partial peace contains duality (peace and disturbance) which keep alternating endlessly.

Real peace happens through true religion which remains undisturbed always and everywhere. To help the world you have to go beyond the need of help yourself by knowing and experiencing your true religion. If few individuals attain their true religion it can sweeten and improve the atmosphere. But things don't happen as you wish and plan because we lack earnestness, will, determination and willingness.

Nonviolence reflects religiousness and violence reflects non religiousness. We commit violence in many ways inadvertently and hurt people directly and indirectly. Needless display of wealth in marriages and birthdays hurt people indirectly who are not privileged to celebrate such occasions. Children of rich family wear and carry expensive things to school which affects and hurt other children who are deprived of such things, this is committing violence indirectly. Interfering in the affairs of other, causing disturbance in their independence is also a form of violence. In a family as an elder you order a particular type of food, you like the most, without caring for the taste of others and you force others to eat that food which you like, that too is a form of violence. Disturbing others by visiting at odd hours and interfering in personal life hurts people which you do not realize and understand. Forcing people to attend your function regardless of inconvenience to others and their inability to attend your function also amounts to committing violence on others.

We commit violence on our self also when we kill our mood, interest, happiness and nature by suppressing to appear what we are not and live a hypocritic life as a split personality. The outer chaos and disturbance reflect inner disharmony. Inner disharmony is caused by mind which remains engaged in desire, fear, greed etc. These cause worry, tension, anxiety, anguish, conflict, contradiction, sorrow and suffering.

If you check and control your child then he may feel hurt but this hurt is essential to discipline him so it is not violence but certainly a right religious attitude. Surgical operation is done by a doctor to cure a patient and not to hurt him. The motive of doctor is welfare of the patient as such doctor's action to operate on the patient is an act of nonviolence, the pure intention and motive is religiousness.

True nonviolence happened to 'Lord Mahavira' of 'Jaina' religion who attained true religion. He lost complete sense of his body (existence) and moved naked without any sense of outer nakedness. This nakedness was inner nakedness which is attained when you reach your true religion. It reflects inner purity (inner nakedness) where you conceal nothing and show nothing. For lord 'Mahavira', identification with physical and mental events had suspended. He purified his mind and became total innocent (pure) by going beyond mind and transforming himself from non-religiousness to religiousness. Nonviolence was a happening to him on reaching his true religion it was not created by doing effort and cultivation.

When you act with cultivated nonviolence then you have chance to commit violence any time in reaction to others actions. The act of nonviolence that we see these days implies non use of weapon and temporary physical control on thought, speech and action which should not hurt anyone and appear violent. Such nonviolent acts remain physically controlled from outside to achieve temporally the aim for common good of all, but this is not the real nonviolence. The real nonviolence is inner happening which comes through self discipline and self control.

The act of nonviolence that we exhibit outside is governed by reason and logic a product of mind. Anything that comes through mind is false, temporary, created and perishable. Mind provides only partial solutions and not total and perfect solutions. 'Mahatma Gandhi' man of will and wisdom came on the Indian scene to achieve independence through physical nonviolence but the cycle of miseries started again after his death because the nonviolence that 'Gandhi' gave to the world was a physical nonviolence and not a inner nonviolence which happens at its own on attaining your true religion. So we can say the nonviolence that came to us from 'Gandhi' was physical but certainly not spiritual and divine which is beyond mind.

All great enlightened souls who reached their true religion (supreme nature) never aimed at mass movement. True nonviolence is evolved from within your own self, it is a happening and an individual exercise. This principle does not apply to individuals who involve and participate in mass movements without inner self improvement. They only follow and participate in such movements on call given by some wise man as was done by 'Mahatma Gandhi'.

The aim of true religion is to transform you from physical nonviolence to spiritual and divine nonviolence which gives you perfect and complete religiousness in your behaviour and conduct. When individuals improve internally, the society which is totality of individuals will automatically improve. To transform society as a whole entity is not possible. The improvement in society has to come through individuals separately.

When a religion dies it becomes a ritual. Rituals are nothing except a routine time pass of a dead tradition. Rituals mean belief, that something done outwardly can create inner revolution. Transformation happens on knowing, realizing and experiencing you inner being and not through rituals performed outwardly. Inner is basic and outer is secondary. The outer always follows the inner, but never the vice versa. Ritual is born because of this fallacy.

You may imitate posture and silence without inner attainment but that will lack originality and liveliness like plastic flowers bear no fragrance. A pure man will always be moral and ethical, in his conduct and behaviour. He cannot ever become immoral. Where as a man who appears moralistic actually may not necessary be pure internally and as such he can always switch over to immorality. Some details in this aspect are explained earlier in this chapter.

Values set by certain societies have been on wrong beliefs like untouchability, child marriage, committing sati and many more like these. You cannot call such acts and traditions ethical and moral. Any person who opposes them was victimized. The great souls in the past had to pay a heavy price for objecting the blind beliefs that ruined the society. They were genuinely keen for reforming the society against such beliefs but none cared for them and they were killed. 'Christ' was crucified, 'Kabir' was trampled by elephant, 'Meera' and 'Socrates' were poisoned.

True morality originates from your true religion of your inner being. The morality that we pretend to exhibit outside is to conceal what we are not. The outer morality which we show is false. Self styled moral people of society are like water bubble which comes up for a moment and dissolves, leaving no impact of their existence. Purity of religion means innocence, maintaining complete harmony inside outside. It reflects a non-wavering mind still and steady, full of silence and bliss. Death and desire are happenings of the future as such make us fearful because future is uncertain and insecured. To become deathless, fearless and desireless you must experience your true religion through nonwavering mind. When you live with the present reality avoiding past and future, you automatically attain deathlessness, because the present reflects reality of your true religion.

One can be religious without any God and one can be non religious with all the Gods of the world. To survive in the materialistic world, you have to depend on science. But for peace, joy, love and harmony, true religion is essential. However balance of both can bring cheers in life. You should not choose between religion and science because they have their own significance in their fields.

When you chose only religion, ignoring science then you remain economically and technologically poor and backward. When you choose exclusively science then you remain spiritually empty. The best way is to live life with harmony between science and religion, because both are significant and important.

CHAPTER 5

NATURE-TEMPERAMENT (Swabhava)

To understand the dynamics of nature, it is essential that we know the background as to how nature and allied things are created (also refer to chapter two in this context). Nature here means broadly, temperament, tendency, attitude and interest. Lord Krishna called it religion of physical self (swadharama) and in Jaina religion it is called nature of physical self (swabhava). Self here is physical self, signifying body and mind and not the spiritual self (supreme self). Supreme self is beyond temperament and tendency. The supreme self is reflected as self (atma) in the body through consciousness known as inner self (antaratma). This inner self is always shining eternally inside to guide us as a spiritual teacher. It is always liberated and free but it becomes embodied when conditioned by mind.

The basic nature of man is divine, supreme, real, absolute and ultimate truth. All that exists in life is rooted in the supreme divine in seed form. The goal of life is to attain eternity of your supreme being transcending the relative physical and spiritual nature.

Nature (consciousness) is self vibrant and dynamic which begins its movement from the motionless base of the absolute nature (supreme truth). The nature is created with the combination of divine absolute energy and spiritual (consciousness) relative energy. The creation continues till it reaches the state of matter. Infact divine energy makes consciousness dynamic for movement. Movement reflects creation.

It is all the play of consciousness. Higher and lower nature are two aspects of consciousness.

We are basically governed by three natures, supreme nature, higher nature and lower nature (divine nature, spiritual nature and physical nature). The nature, tendency, temperament and attitude are all formed through lower nature, which come to us at the time of birth. Higher nature is formless and without attributes lower nature is with form and with attributes

The three attribute that we receive from nature remain with us till our death and govern our behaviour and conduct while living life. Everything that exists and lives possesses these attributes in different degrees and as such temperament, tendency and behaviour differ. Man is known by his predominant attribute that he displays during his conduct, whether he is harmonious, passionate or pervert. You are born with potential and possibility to transcend these attributes and attain divinity that should be the goal of life.

All creations are in relation to subtle, grosser and dense form of consciousness. Space reflects satva (harmony) attribute and down the chain the remaining elements form other two attributes, rajas and tamas (passion-pervert). The consciousness illumines the mind but mind works according to the attributes it receives from the nature. Also what he learns from the society as a cultivated nature. Man has no control over these attributes (harmony, passion and pervert) which comes to him accidentally which is beyond analysis. It is meaningless and reasonless to concentrate on happenings of past life.

Anything which happens unpredictably and unexpectedly become an accidental happening there are belief systems which have been drummed into our mind by society, that we suffer in this life due to our bad actions (karmas) of past life and accordingly we receive three attributes (harmony-passion-pervert) from nature. We follow these concepts unknowingly but we understand clearly that our actions of past life are dead events as such we do not have any control over them except accepting them as they come in our life bringing either joy or sorrow. Instead of wasting time and energy in remembering past happenings, it is better to concentrate to improve the present happenings. It is only a concept which is not true because concepts are imaginary which distorts truth.

Concepts are product of mind as such anything that comes through mind is false and unreal and not the truth. However concepts only load and burden mind but these cannot transform you. Concentrate mainly on self improvement rather than knowing and believing these concepts. Consciousness is localized by mind which fragments and divides it and reduces its universal power to particular. Nature of mind is to desire, fear, think, memorize, imagine, worry and tension etc. When you identify events with mind then suffering and bondage are experienced. Our endeavour should be to transcend the nature of conscious mind making it single minded to penetrate into our inner self.

When consciousness illumines mind it starts creating and weaving imaginary world of its own which is subjective, personal and private about which none knows and none can help. In dream you suffer agony but none knows about it and none can help.

Body and mind are product of five elements. These elements also create three attributes which reflects temperament and tendency. Space reflects harmony, air passion and earth perversion, besides this element of heat and water also contribute in making three attributes and that is how we find some people cool and passive and some other are aggressive and hot. All this is a process and phenomenon of nature beyond any analysis and explanation.

Logic and reason originates from the head center (mind). Feelings, emotions and love come under the domain of the heart center. Self (atma) reflects the navel center (life center). There are seven dynamic centers of energy in the body but only three centers are significant (mind center, heart center and navel center). Mind center is gross, heart center is subtle and navel center is subtlest of the subtle. Heart center is the link between navel center and mind center. Mind center reflects outer world and navel center is the inner world. The self always remain beyond mind and heart as such it remains free and liberated. Nothing can condition the self's effect and influence like clouds may screen sun light but cannot stop its effect.

Bondage is the product of conscious mind which cause disappointment, chaos and confusion. Belief, concepts, ideas, thoughts, doctrines, false traditions, customs and social norms harden bondage to sensuous things of the world, which cause sorrow and suffering in life. The three attributes that we talked about earlier are in relation to the purity of mind.

Contents of the conditioned consciousness can be dissolved in two ways- external and internal. External is actualized through physical control which remains partial and temporary. External control reflects control of mind, which cannot be totally controlled through outer factors. The self control and self discipline happens through inner evolvement by dropping mind and in that state outer control becomes meaningless. The temperament and tendency that comes to us through nature can only be eliminated through inner transformation and there is no other way out to dissolve them.

We are never total in our doings through mind (temperament and tendency). We always remain partial, incomplete and imperfect because of the limited nature of mind. We always work in a routine, mechanical and habitual way through the mind. With habitual and routine way of working we become insensitive and unconcerned about problems of others because of our personal and selfish attitude. When mechanism of mind is broken we become selfless and impersonal with concern for good of all. We become compassionate and sensitive to problems of others and then we cannot see suffering of people.

Differentiation is nature and that is how temperament and tendency (swabhava) of every individual differ. Some are intellectual, wise, lovable and selfless. Some are emotional, talented and disciplined. Some are lazy, inert, ignorant and selfish, likewise there are many more tendencies and temperament that each man inherits from nature.

No one can know as to how nature creates five elements and three attributes at its own. It should be accepted as phenomenon of nature, beyond our understanding and control, as such we should live life as it comes because these happen beyond the reach of mind.

We can study and analyze things that happen through the mind. Mind can only analyze things which are limited and have form but anything that happens beyond mind is formless and limitless about which we remain unknown and unaware, as such that cannot be analyzed. We should concentrate on self transformation by transcending the attributes of nature instead of getting involved in the process and phenomenon of nature. Knowing about physical facts and analysis of these may give you information and make you knowledgeable but concepts, doctrines, ideas and thoughts cannot transform you from human nature to divine nature. You must understand the falsity of unreal and untrue things of the world as such be aware and ignore these, so that ignorance and attachment to worldly things are dissolved.

Life comes to the body through vital breath (pran) which vitalizes the body. Perception and cognizance comes through mind when it is illumined by consciousness. When consciousness identifies with the body and mind it becomes bondage. Beyond body and mind is freedom and liberation reflecting universality. In the body self is centered around navel. Pure consciousness is centered in the heart and conditioned consciousness exists in the mind. Mind center is essential for survival in the world, heart center is needed for peace and universal love in living life. Life center (navel center) is the very existence of being without its support nothing can exist at its own because mind and heart have no independent existence.

No one can plan nor have control over the three attribute that come to us through the nature, we have to live with them until we transcend them through inner transformation. The swadharama (religion of self) and swabhava (religion of nature) are same and reflect physical self and not spiritual self. Nature is the law of being. Nature is differentiation as such existence has different nature. Variety provides charm and beauty to creation only when living is harmonious, free of opposition, comparison and contradiction.

Nature is a mystery which is beyond our understanding, the best way to understand mystery is to live with mystery as it comes. You should not impose your interest, taste, temperament and nature on others nor you should copy and imitate others because you are born with different nature. If you do so then it will become an artificial and contradictory living, thereby you will lose harmonious living. When you copy and imitate others contrary to your nature than it will not bring cheers and joy for you in life.

A father may be a professional by nature and may have become a famous doctor. He expects his son to become a doctor against his nature and potential. The son has poetic and literally mind and want to pursue his interest in life against the desire of his father. The mismatch of interest between father and son will cause infighting in the family. Now the son has to choose between the profession of his father or his own interest of poetry. In such cases imposition of father's desire will be harmful. The son can never be happy and successful in life.

Profession will earn him living and poetry will satisfy his feelings and love for nature. Profession is material and poetry is spiritual. You must find a balance to do a job for earning or pursue your talent. You can develop your interest in your leisure time. If you want to avoid job then you should transform internally so that you transcend the requirement of worldly jobs and enter the kingdom of divine where problems of the world dissolve.

If you carefully notice the behaviour that you exhibit during the day, you will find that your temperament keeps changing because of natures changing phenomenon. Sometimes you have pure feeling of divine sometime you feel universal love and at times you feel disturbed through desire and fear, caused by your lower nature. Sometime you are cool, steady, mature, wise and remain undisturbed with worldly events. The next moment you become violent, aggressive, hurting and dishonest in your behaviour. At times you feel compassionate, concerned, sympathetic with selfless and impersonal attitude.

When you notice and record your behavior of whole day you will realize and understand that the attribute which remains dominant during the day, reflects your nature and temperament. Go deeper and observe your behaviour daily, weekly, monthly and likewise go on adding observations of your behaviour during different periods and decide by yourself the nature (swabhava) that belong to you.

The behaviour and conduct remains contradictory while living a physical life, but your behaviour become spiritual and cosmic when governed by higher nature (pure consciousness), dissolving distinctions. When you attain your nature of spirituality, spiritual virtues start reflecting in all your action making you honest, lovable, and compassionate with an attitude of universal brotherhood.

When you discover your real nature of supreme self then physical and spiritual aspects dissolve. On attaining that stage rulers and kings fall at your feet in reverence and people feed and serve you with love, dissolving all your worries and concerned for earning your living. You cannot control your temperament with grit and determination, it can only be transcended by inner transformation till then you have to confront and live with the temperament and tendency which nature has given you at the time of your birth.

You cannot shape life because it is unpredictable and formless. You may try to shape your career according to your nature because shaping is possible for things which are bound by time and space. However you can only make an effort to shape your career but the happening of success to your expectation remains uncertain and unpredictable. Doing is in your hand but not the happening as such you cannot predict the result which remains uncertain and unknown because result is a happening governed by outer factors beyond your control.

In the spiritual world when you evolve internally, willingly and earnestly then transformation is certain to happen as outer factors of distinction and duality do not interfere. These dissolve on your becoming universal. But in the physical world outcome of result of your hard work in your favour remains uncertain as outer factors matter more than the sincerity and hard work. Life is happening and career making is doing. Doing is through mind (lower nature) happening is beyond mind (higher nature).

To understand nature (swabhava) you must first understand that your behaviour and conduct is governed by three different natures (supreme nature, universal nature and physical nature). To live life peacefully and joyfully you must listen to the voice of your true nature (inner self). The voice of self can be heard when mind becomes non-wavering and attains silence and stillness.

We are screaming inside and outside so much that the voice of soul remains unheard. The next voice is the voice of nature that comes to us in the form of attributes. If you live your life according to your inherited nature you will find life become harmonious and peaceful but if you act contrary to your nature (swabhava) then living life becomes burdened with stress and strain. Your life becomes uncomfortable and boring if you work against your nature and attitude.

When you act through the voice of your soul then your actions become sacred, noble and holy. The divine aura of an evolved soul can extend to many miles around depending on the degree of attainment of inner purity. Spiritual aura (pure consciousness) is shorter than the divine aura (supreme). Spiritual aura is the aura of the self and divine aura is the aura of the supreme God. When you attain the supreme real being then the distinction of self and God merges into pure being. Aura here implies the area of influence of supreme and cosmic nature where serenity, peace and happiness prevail, making the atmosphere sweetened and fearless.

However the temperament (swabhava) is temporary and transient and not eternal. Swabhava is to the body and mind and true nature is beyond body and mind reflecting divinity. Higher and lower nature, dissolve on discovering your divine nature. The great enlightened souls who attained their supreme nature are worshiped till today. Those who only followed them, not experiencing their own self have been forgotten because they followed a concept and a thought given by the enlightened souls and did not take action for inner transformation from within their own self.

Experience is reality and concept is falsity. If you ignore the voice of your soul then the next best thing is to stick to your 'swabhava' which has come to you from nature in the form of attributes. It may be called your second voice. It is better to die with your 'swadharama' than to imitate 'swabhava' (nature) of others, which may not suit your temperament and attitude. If you do that then you invite miseries in your life because your living becomes contradictory to your nature. You should be with the nature you are born with, no matter it may affect you adversely in worldly life but in the long run you will realize that you have been benefitted.

It is certain whatever you sow, so shall you reap. If you are wicked you will be punished sooner or later, if you are wise you will be rewarded sooner or later. You cannot hide wickedness (negative nature) by culturing and cultivation. You may conceal it for some time to mislead and misguide people. Wicked people will get retribution for their wrong doings by nature. No one can escape this law of nature. It had happened in the past with wicked Ravana and Hitler who could not escape from punishment. Such nature continues till one is governed by lower nature. It is beyond once control to dissolve born nature. However in the center of wickedness divinity prevails, which one can actualize by transcending it through inner transformation.

'Arjuna' a warrior and a brave fighter of the epic 'Mahabharata', under delusion and ignorance started behaving contrary to his born nature of a warrior and refused to fight the sacred and holy war. Ignorance had clouded his wisdom and he tried to give up his 'swadharma'. At that time Lord Krishna awakened him into his true nature with his divine guidance. Lord Krishna did not transform Arjuna but only awakened him because transformation happens from within your own self no one else from outside can transform you. Arjuna was already an evolved individual so he needed timely push and guidance to wake him from the sleep of ignorance. It is like an imaginary and illusory dream which dissolves on waking up.

The third voice that affects our behavior is the voice of cultivation that comes to us through society, learning, education, parents and family etc. If you fail to listen to the voice of the soul and to the voice of the nature (swabhava) then the last best way is to live life with cultivated and cultured nature. If you are reserved and serious type be that, if you are jovial and talkative type, be that but do not copy, imitate and follow traits which you do not posses. If you do that then you will tumble in life and suffer sorrow and suffering. You have the capability to transcend natural attributes, provided you are willing and earnest. When inner transformation happens, the attributes stop interfering in your behaviour and conduct.

You should understand that your being (divine) wants to express through you as a good and a bad man as such be that, till you are totally transformed. If you remain what you actually are without a covering and concealment then it is easier to identify your real character so that people deal with you accordingly. Everyone has equal opportunity to transform his human nature to divine nature but they do not do so because of their ignorance which screens their wisdom, willingness and earnestness.

Our aim should be to try and awake such people through guidance and rightful punishment so that they are awakened for self improvement. Unless total transformation is attained the attributes of nature will keep interfering in your behavior and conduct.

'Valmiki' who wrote the epic 'Ramayana' was a dacoit initially and robbed many people but later he realized and transformed into a saint. When you are governed by the self everything is set right and straight. Man has choice either to remain subhuman or evolve to eternity (divine-real being). Man dies differently according to his inner evolvement and attainment. Some die a happy and peaceful death whereas some die a miserable death.

We are anti sex (celibate) at surface but remain sexually inside. This is a hypocritic living. Your aim should be to dissolve such cravings from your mind through awareness and transcending such nature. There is no point, fighting instincts of sex and anger because fight will give nourishment to these to flourish. External and physical control to neutralize anger, sex, greed, fear etc is meaningless because imposed control remains partial because of its physical and gross nature. Total control and discipline to neutralize the instincts happen through inner transformation. Instincts will keep interfering in your physical life when you are governed by mind but beyond mind there remains no trace of these due to inner transformation. Whenever you imitate and copy others you will realize and experience that you remain awkward in your behavior because you remain unnatural in living your life.

You may imitate anger as actors do in movies but this anger is different than the happening of anger that comes through nature (swabhava). You cannot possibly create natural anger, hate, fear, greed, jealousy, coolness and sadness etc. These are instinctive and happen at their own like sleep, hunger and digestion etc.

Spiritual literature say that wealth is sin because the enlightened souls have experienced the distastefulness of wealth and its evilness, as such they have declared wealth a sinful aspect of life. On attaining your true nature you will also feel so. But if a man is born with a passion for wealth, he will never realize this fact without experiencing the evilness of wealth by himself and he will feel that there is nothing wrong in wealth unless, he suffers in life with the ill effects of wealth.

No doubt wealth by itself is not sinful but your mind makes it so when you become obsessed and attached to wealth blindly to earn it through wrong means and utilize it for wrong activities. There is nothing wrong to earn wealth with rightful means without greed and temptation. The wrong is in your selfish and personal attitude.

If you are an ascetic by nature (swabhava) then be so and do not try to become worldly, because harmony with your nature will be disturbed and cause misery in your life. If you are worldly then do not try to act and imitate ascetic. This dual existence (ascetic-worldly) will cause confusion and contradiction. Be with your nature.

Personality has two aspects one is outer and other is inner. Outer aspect is called personality which is governed by mind (ego). The inner aspect is known as individuality which happens through inner transformation as that makes you egoless. The individuality is a change of identity from human nature to spiritual nature. Personality means your bearing, thinking, desiring and behaving reflecting manners and etiquettes. Personality is the product of ego as such you become sensitive to name, fame, pride, honour, status, prestige and good will.

Learning, information and knowledge become part of your personality. You use intellect, reason and logic to develop your personality. It is cultivated and cultured by parents, family, friends, society, learning and education etc. Man of personality is mind conscious and not self conscious. Personality functions at physical level with selfish and personal attitude. Individuality reflects inner transformation from human nature to divine nature. You attain separate identity as an individual when you mature and experience your true nature. Buddha had attained an individual identity on discovering Buddhahood (divinity).

On attaining individuality you become egoless, selfless, impersonal, desireless and fearless. You do not identify with physical and mental events. Everyman has his own individuality in relation to his inner purity. It has nothing to do with his worldly greatness and talent because genius and talented man experience duality of the world. Spirituality and divinity are culmination of individuality which gives you eternal identity as an individual. It had happened in the past with great enlightened souls (Christ-Buddha-Mahavira-Mohammad).

When you identify with body and mind you become a person governed by ego that gives you a sense of pseudo entity of a doer, separate from the reality. It is so because ego reflects non self center on the surface opposite to inner self at the center. The doership happens due to ignorance and unawareness. As a matter of fact the real doer is the consciousness.

Body and mind are only instruments which are dynamized by the consciousness. Body and mind have no separate and independent existence without the support of your being. Life becomes active and live when consciousness enters the form otherwise the form remains dead and lifeless. You may have light of awareness to reveal, you may have vital breath to vitalize the body but unless consciousness comes into play you remain a bag of bones only. With consciousness charm and joy comes in living life, without it you are as good as dead.

It means personality is unreal as it appears and disappears with the death of the body and mind but the individual identity remains eternal because that is the real transformation from physical matter to eternity. Personality and individuality are differentiated through one's nature (temperament and tendency). It is up to you whether you live life as a person or evolve to individuality. Nobody would have remembered great enlightened souls till today if they had died as a person without internal growth and evolvement which transformed them to become divine, sacred, holy and noble. Their thoughts pervade the world even today as an inspirational guide.

Mahatma Gandhi died long ago but his thoughts pervade the earth even today as an inspirational guide for the posterity. Hitler had own individuality which was negative, damaging and remained at physical level without inner transformation. As such no one remembers Hitler today for his destruction and atrocities. The individuality of Buddha and Christ was spiritual, divine and eternal and will be remembered till the dissolution of creation.

Personality and individuality should be in harmony, which means outer (personality) and inner (individuality) should be in complete coordination and tune. Be a person while dealing with the world and be an individual while evolving internally. To reach your true nature of divine you have to transcend personality (ego) and individuality (spiritual). A person is himself responsible for whatever wrong happens in his life. Physical nature reflects personality, spiritual nature reflects individuality and divinity is abode of silence and salvation beyond physical and spiritual.

Frankly speaking there is nothing wrong with the world, your attitude and outlook with your nature (swadharama) made the world wrongful. The outer disturbance and chaos reflect inner disharmony so to see harmony outside in the world maintain purity of harmony inside.

The physical world that we see outside in term of planets, stars, mountains, jungles, rivers, flora and fauna do not disturb our life in any way but the disturbance is caused by illusory and imaginary world that we weave through our mind. Life on earth is sustained by the sun, yet you cannot blame the sun for all that happens on the earth because whatever happens, happens through your own psyche which is cultured and cultivated as such.

The difference in temperament categorizes the man into good, bad and worst. Saint and insect has different nature. Saint has potential to enrich consciousness and evolve but insect remain an insect till death because it lacks capability to evolve. However the same consciousness flows between the saint and the insect. If you focus your attention on appearance and outer structure of others then you commit sin of seeing separation from the reality but if you shift your attention from appearance to the inner flow of the consciousness which flows between the seer and the seen, then you become compassionate, concerned, sympathetic, lovable and deep feeling of oneness as pure consciousness.

The physical world that we see outside has complete harmony in existence, they appear opposite but they are not in opposition. Disharmony is created by man through his mind which remains disturbed and restless due to ignorance and unawareness.

You should neither be impressed by others nor should you try to impress others, it reflects your inferiority complex. We react to comments and criticism of others because of our weak personality (weak mind). This happens that we feel we are body and mind and not the soul. When you identify yourself as body and mind you will remain ignorant and consequently you will react to people's comment and criticism.

When you go beyond mind you ignore all such comments and criticism because you become universal transcending distinction and duality. Lord Mahavira's inner nakedness reflected inner purity which happened through discovering his true nature. He lost complete sense of outer surroundings and reactions of people. He was completely in total silence and peace where reactions dissolve. The same thing happened with Meera, she was totally lost in devotional dance in reverence to Lord Krishna, unmindful of reactions people were expressing outside. You react when you are governed by mind which exists in duality. Beyond mind reactions dissolve.

There are no miracles in life everything is governed by the law of nature. A man of weak mind believes in miracle and magical stunts due to ignorance. His focus remains on the outer periphery which is full of noise and disturbance. He remains unaware of total silence at his center (soul).

Remember all creations happen through creative mind (inner mind). When man evolves and reaches to the center of creation of the consciousness, then creation happens at its own without effort and cultivation as it had happened with 'Edison' who was illiterate but carried out six hundred inventions including the electric bulb. You cannot possibly jump out of the cycle of birth and death that happens in nature, without inner transformation.

You must have experienced that in life goodness always wins over evilness. The victory over evilness is reflected through historical events (Ravana-Hitler and many others). Goodness always wins in the end defeating evilness because goodness has touch of truth and reality. Anything which touches truth becomes truth. We all are divine by nature which we can always actualize by attaining our true nature through inner transformation. However goodness contains wickedness in the center and wickedness contains goodness in the center. It is up to you to remain wicked or transform to goodness.

CHAPTER 6

LAW OF ACTION (Karma)

The law of karma (action) is an important aspect of life. In this world nothing is achieved without action, doing and effort. However everything happens at its own in the spiritual world (inner world). Nothing is attained through action there. Once you become universal then all desires and distinctions dissolve automatically. Sleep, hunger, breathing etc happen at their own, you cannot create or cultivate these. Happening happens in nature at its own as a natural phenomenon.

Worldly actions are self and personal oriented, but the happenings of nature are selfless and impersonal, these are not for particular but are universal without any distinctions. Five elements of nature can be used by anyone, these make no distinction between sinner and saint. While dealing with the world you should be discriminative for right actions for general good of all. In all actions of nature there is complete harmony and peace, there is no confusion, contradiction and chaos.

However the actions that we undertake in the outer world are contradictory, competitive, and comparative with total conflict and clash causing sorrow and suffering. Actions done through outer mind (conscious mind) are binding because you remain ignorant about your true being as such you get attached to false and unreal sensuous things which don't stay with you forever.

Actions through inner mind (pure mind) are liberating as you renounce attachment and emotional involvement. There are two aspect of Karma in life, one is life of attachment and misery and other is life of detachment and bliss. Beyond doing and natural happening is the divine world where all actions end, only inaction prevails. Inaction means stability, motionlessness and stillness, it becomes the foundational base for all that exists and lives in the outer world. All movement and action is possible only through static base of inaction. Wheel moves on static base of axel, river flows on static bed. The world needs action for survival and sustenance but the eternity needs inaction, silence and salvation.

The goal of life is to attain salvation as Buddha had attained his Buddhahood (nirvana). To attain Buddhahood you need to drop action oriented mind and focus your attention on becoming self oriented. Self orientation makes you aware of your true nature every moment, dissolving other thoughts except thought of your true nature. Once you attain this state your mind is automatically emptied from thoughts which disturb the peace of your mind.

The law of karma aims to take you closer to your soul where only silence, peace and bliss prevail. This law signifies that you should not be a doer and an enjoyer (karta ad bhogta) but you should be a knower of your real self and seer of all events as witness (gyata and drashta). Karma (action) is product of desire. Desire originates from a thing which has form and is limited because limited things are imperfect and incomplete. You should always have only one noble desire to become complete and whole. Anything that is bound by time and space is limited because it has beginning and end (birth and death). It stays for a limited time period in a form (body) and then perishes.

Desire is an important aspect of action (karma). We must understand desire in greater detail. The inner actions happen at its own but outer actions actualize through desire. Inner actions remain hidden, secret and unknown. Transformation happens through inner action. Healing process of injury remains hidden and unknown but healing process continues unnoticed. You come to know about your healing only when you experience relief on being cured. The process of transformation happens through inner action and its effect is seen through outer actions. Transformation is from human behaviour to divine behaviour. Beyond inner and outer action is inaction of eternity.

Whatever we are is because of our desires. If we are miserable, if we are ignorant, if we are in darkness, if we are frustrated, it is all because of desires. Desire means something to happen in the future. Desire is for pleasure always, which you have tasted in the past. Mind has tendency to attach to things of pleasure but runs away from thing which cause pain. Desire is never in the present because the present belongs to your being which is devoid of past and future (desirelessness and imagination). When there is no desire for gain or loss then action becomes a play free of anguish, anxiety, stress and strain.

Real wisdom lies in transforming work into play without any desire, expectation and seeking. The world is not the creation of the divine but it is a play (lella). Creation entails desire and divine is desireless. Creation cannot happen without desire. Where ever there is creation there has to be desire along with it. Desire gives birth to man's vices. When your desires are fulfilled you desire more and become greedy. If desires are not met you become frustrated and angry. You feel jealous when others succeed in their desires. Desires for pleasure, tempt and attract you towards attachment to people and things.

When you do not desire the unknown divine comes to you because non desiring mind is clear and empty to receive the eternal divine. Unless you over power mind, you will remain slave and suffer miseries in life. If you do not cooperate with the desiring mind then desires will subside at its own. It is your cooperation to desires which gives dynamism to the desiring mind.

When the conditioned consciousness is localized through mind then it takes shape of desire. Desire is a form of energy. This energy is dissipated when it is used for multiple desires. The energy of desire is the energy of consciousness only in a grosser form. The movement of this energy through desirelessness remains unspent as such conserved.

In desire the energy is used either for indulgence or for suppression. The natural movement of energy is creative, spiritual and desireless. Energy moves not for something but it moves because it is energy and is self vibrant and dynamic by nature. Energy remains neutral, it does not move either to negative or positive channel unless you desire it to move through these channels.

Going out of desiring mind is going into pure consciousness, it means centering to your true being. The moment you are born desires grip you and these keep multiplying as you grow, only the dimensions of desires change. It is a concept that the unfulfilled desire of past life becomes the base for the new birth. You may except the concept or deny it. Your focus should be for transformation from desire to desirelessness and not for entanglement in concepts. Let concepts, idea, thought, theories and beliefs continue you need not get influenced by these and surge ahead to discover your true being, unmindful of concepts.

The life of desire is through body and life of desirelessness is through pure consciousness. What so ever you are, it is because of your own actions. You may change objects for happiness but real happiness comes not by changing objects but by transforming human nature to divine nature. When you reach a state of eternity (inaction) then you need nothing, want nothing, desire nothing and have nothing but have everything as a divine wealth which make you sharing, giving, sacrificing and understanding. You go beyond the need of any help for yourself.

However on attaining that state you can really help the world. Your actions become spiritual and universal when you transcend mind which cause duality and distinctions. Universality and spirituality dissolve all these because you become formless and limitless, free and liberated from bondage of Karma, which make your attitude selfish and personal. Becoming formless means your vision and perception becomes cosmic with deep feeling of love for all that exists and lives.

You realize and understand that the same pure consciousness flows between you and the things that exist outside.

When you become cosmic you become automatically fearless because there is no other to fear from as you become one with your pure consciousness, where all distinctions and contradictions dissolve. Fear happens to body and mind which are limited and has form but not to your true being which is formless and limit less beyond mind.

When you are awakened into your being, all actions cease and you attain a state of inaction where you experience total bliss, peace and silence which is known as salvation and enlightenment (nirvana). At that stage mind become nonwavering, still, steady and peaceful. Saints reached that state of salvation through self knowing (gyan), devotees reached through self surrender ego (bhakti) and man of action reached through selfless service with love. All this is possible when conscious mind becomes super conscious by dropping all its contents through techniques given in chapter thirteen.

Actions which are undertaken for the common good of all are right actions which liberate you from bondage. The actions undertaken for human welfare enriches your consciousness because there remain no distinctions between you and others as pure consciousness. You experience deep feeling of oneness. It is the law of energy that when you desire to act for common good of all then conscious energy deepens, widens and is enriched. But when you desire for personal interest the energy shrinks and become limited. So our aim should be to become unlimited (universal) from limited and particular.

Actions as such are neither good nor bad but these are categorized into sin and virtue through a sick and diseased mind. Sick mind is that which remains disturbed and wavering because of desire, fear, greed, etc. Sick mind is a burdened mind which draws screen to conceal your real self. The actions through your mind take you away from yourself and make you ignorant and blind. But actions beyond mind take you closer to yourself through wisdom and insight.

Your actions should aim to attain wisdom and understanding. All worldly actions are fear oriented. Religion, societies and parents etc make your existence fearful to keep you disciplined and under control. Such imposed discipline and control is unnatural living. Man under fear cannot put his best due to pressure and tension created by society. Wrong actions lead to sorrow and right actions lead to joy. Desire oriented actions make you strive only to seek also to struggle only for greed to grab more. But right actions means striving without seeking and struggle without greed. Why do we become selfish in our attitude while working through mind? This question nibbles everyone to know and understand the cause as to why we are selfish and personal in our motive and not act selflessly.

The selfishness is not our inborn quality because our true nature is the supreme Being which is beyond selfishness. Selfishness is the acquired, cultured and cultivated nature that comes to us from society, parents, friends, family, education and learning. As you know the mind is limited and bound by time and space and disappears with the death of the body as such transient and perishable. Anything which has perishable nature is false and unreal.

All actions through mind make you think and imagine low and narrow due to its limited nature. Mind divides the reality of the whole into parts and imagines separation from it. It is so because mind creates nonself center (ego) on the periphery, opposite to the eternal self at the center.

Karma (action) has three aspects. One is desire orientated actions that lead you to bondage, attachment and fear. Actions done through conscious mind apply to past (memory) and future (imagination), because mind gets its nourishment through memory and imagination. Mind drops while living in the present because present is the reality and is free of past and future. Actions done through total concentration in the present are the right actions because in the present mind has no role to play.

The second aspect of Karma (action) belongs to selfless and impersonal actions. Such actions lead you to freedom, detachment and make you desireless and fearless because you go beyond mind, dissolving all distinctions of polar opposites. These actions take you closer to the self (atma). On knowing and realizing your true self from within, all actions (selfish and selfless) dissolve, only inaction prevails. Such actions are not binding but they are liberating from the nonself (ego). In fact needful, necessary actions for common good of all are rightful actions. Needless and unnecessary actions which are selfish and personal in nature are wrong actions.

Third aspect of Karma (action) is routine and prescribed actions by society and scriptures. Routine actions are undertaken for personal sustenance like bathing, prayer, eating, walking, working and sleeping, etc. Prescribed actions are undertaken on auspicious occasions through rituals (birth, marriage, festivals and sacrifice). Sacrifice means (yagya), signifying transformation from ego to egolessness, form to formlessness, matter to eternity, desire to desirelessness, fear to fearlessness, mind to mindlessness, conditioned consciousness to pure consciousness.

Sacrifice (yagya) is considered a sacred act. Sacrifice is a process of Karma where you surrender to become better and higher by transforming your present identity of human nature to new identity of divine nature. A seed sacrifices and surrenders its identity to sprout and become a tree. This sacrifice is a natural phenomenon of existence. Infant sacrifices in a natural way to transform to youth. Creation happens through sacrifice, without sacrifice creation comes to standstill. Sacrifice works both ways in manifestation and also in attaining eternity. Sacrifice is an internal transformation. Sacrifice that we conduct in the outer world as a traditional routine is physical and is not sacred and spiritual. Physical routine procedures cannot transform you internally because all physical actions end on periphery, like waves end on the surface of the ocean. However in worldly life you cannot achieve anything without hard work. The worldly sacrifice may bring success in earning your living but it cannot enrich you spiritually which happens to be an internal phenomenon. The sacrifice is sacred and an auspicious action only when one is transformed internally otherwise it remains meaningless.

The cultivated sacrifices that we perform as a ritual cannot transform you accept following the traditional routine of performing a sacrifice. Sacrifice is a natural happening at spiritual level through which all existence is sustained. Killing animals in the name of sacrifice are cruel and torturous traditions as such these be ignored. Actions by itself cannot transform you at its own unless you are earnest and determined.

The will and determination is not possible through mind, it happens when you go beyond mind. Will and determination means steady mind and pure heart. Actions of gift, austerity and sacrifice (daan, tapa and yagya) are important actions which you should never give up because these help for your inner evolvement and growth.

'Daan' is mainly for human welfare at physical level, 'Tapa' is for mental purification by exercising restrain through self discipline and self control to dissolve human nature. 'Yagya' is aimed at transformation from human to divine nature. You should be a knower and witness to your action. Knower means knowing your eternal self (atma) so that your total focus remains on that for evolvement. Witnessing means witnessing happenings and actions that take place around you by maintaining neutral attitude without participation and judgment. If you become a doer of action through ego and enjoyer of sensuous things then such actions turn success into failure.

Darkness of ignorance cannot be removed by outer actions of doing, efforts, practice, rituals, prayers, worship, knowledge and devotion etc, so the best and easiest way to dispel darkness is to bring light through inner action of awareness which will dissolve darkness of ignorance. We generally blame Karmas of our past life for our present suffering. We our self are responsible for suffering by our own doing and none else is to be blamed. Blaming others reflect weakness of our mind and inferiority complex. It is so because we want to project false image of our goodness to others. It is nature of mind to find fault in others rather than accepting your own faults.

Mind has habit of working in a contradictory way. You are selfish but you want to appear selfless, which you are not. Such superficial and artificial living bring sorrow and suffering in life. No action is bad if done with noble motive. Actions become impure when conditioned, particularized and identified with mind, beyond mind all actions are divine.

When you see things through mind then you cannot remain single minded because mind has tendency to split single mindedness to make it multi minded. The only way you can dissolve your natural instincts is through actions which totally transforms you from human nature to divine nature. Everyone cannot possibly transform and that is why we continue living our life as it is in complete disorder, confusion and chaos.

All instincts (anger, sex, greed, etc) are forms of energy. You can with righteous action either divert this energy towards divinity or with wrong action use the energy in indulgence and suppression. In the atmosphere there are billions of negative and positive vibrations of energy that are flowing. We catch approximately thirty two thousand vibrations. Our instruments are designed by nature to pick up that much vibration only. Pure, empty and clear mind picks up positive vibration and impure, stuffed and burdened mind pick up mostly negative vibration of duality. Consequently you should undertake actions which purify your mind.

When negative instincts appear, these can be tackled in three ways. First is to suppress so that these do not appear on surface for expression. Suppression eats away lot of energy also it causes inner complexities, which may harm you later physically and mentally. Second way is indulgence. It also dissipates energy but it is better than suppression because indulgence does not cause inner complexities. The third way is that you can recycle the energy through pure and total witnessing so that the energy goes back to the source unspent, thereby you conserve your energy for benefit of humanity.

The suppression and indulgence pushes you to negativity because you lose energy which makes your mind weak and non reflective of your true being. Right action happens when you become self disciplined, self controlled and self confident through purification of your mind. Imposed, control and discipline may work for some time but cannot work everywhere for all time.

It is nature of mind that good and bad, sin and virtue alternate endlessly till you are totally transformed internally by dropping all actions and attaining stability through inaction (nonwavering mind). It is up to you to jump out of the cycle of alternating good and bad by dropping mind. Actions through conscious mind provide you partial solution to the problem and not total solution. For total solution you have to experience your true being where perfect, complete and whole solution is possible. But for that you will keep confronting the cycle of miseries from time to time.

The law of nature is to repeat and rotate the cycle of good and bad alternatively. That is how, Rama-Ravana, Gandhi-Hitler, Devil-Divine keep appearing on the earth from time to time beyond any ones control. Sorrow and suffering are experienced when you work through mind but beyond mind it is total ecstasy and joy.

When you attain divinity then you transcend society and follow your own conventions of divine virtues. You become a blessing to humanity because with your divinity harmony and serenity are experienced all around. If you want to improve and bring order in society then first improve and bring order to yourself by going beyond mind. If you concentrate your actions through mind on physical attainment then do not expect any transformation and continue facing the sorrow, suffering and miseries of life.

The best way against localizing of the consciousness is to develop a sense of witnessing all physical and mental events without participation and opinion. Do not think nor feel anything about events that happen around you only watch and observe. The instincts of anger, sex, greed and jealousy etc will not disturb you when you become total and complete witness to them.

Instincts get nourishment through your interest and involvement. When you stop nourishment to instincts, these stop interfering as such the energy moves back to the source unspent, there by energy is conserved. The conserved energy then can be utilized for action to evolve internally for spiritual growth and maturity. The instincts automatically subside when under witness. Like a thief withdraws when under watch.

Action of pure witnessing is the way to distilise the impurities of the mind. For attaining pure witnessing refer to chapter thirteen. When you are with the world take action through logic and reason and be discriminative between right and wrong action. When you are with yourself concentrate on inner evolvement and transformation till you reach eternity (your true nature). You are punished for your action during your physical existence in this life only, there is no geographical existence of hell and heaven up in the sky, for reward and punishment. Hell and heaven are in relation to your good and bad actions for which you are rewarded and reprimanded.

There are many ways of suffering subjectively and objectively. Mental tension, worry, fear, insecurity, survival, anxiety, anguish, clash, violence, sickness, terminal diseases, hunger, sleeplessness, death of near and dear ones, disowning by society, natural calamities, accidents, frustration, depression, social punishments and many more. So what else you want man to suffer from and in what form. Is this not enough retribution for mans wrong actions. So why do you need created and imaginary departments of hell to mislead and confuse people. You are so much obsessed and restless to see others punished in public view for their wrong actions. You do not stop here but want them to be punished in their next life as well, which is a misnomer and a concept that bears no truth.

No one can plan next birth in this life, it is all illusory and accidental. Did you plan your birth with your mother? You could have been born to any other woman. All is accidental, unpredictable, uncertain, unknown and that is why it is called fate, destiny, and creation of God. It is easier to link with these when you find no definite answers. By the way in what way are we affected whether one is punished in this life or next life for his actions. If one has committed wrong action, he will suffer mentally and physically in his own way. The subjective and internal suffering that one experiences cannot be assessed and known by you. In a dream you suffer agony, none knows about it and none can help you.

So concentrate on improving your own self through right actions rather than believing and accepting meaningless concept which have no touch of reality and truth. Hindus have concept of rebirth, Christians discard this concept. So many concepts are prevalent in the world with definite following of each but none match with one another. They are the cause of creating disharmony and disorder in the world. Once you become independent in all respects you will disown and discard all which has come to you through your cultivation, reflecting forced imposition of discipline and control.

Body is the instrument of action (Karma) one should neither torture nor pamper it. But a balance between the two be maintained. You can produce a rhythmic music from a guitar provided it's strings are neither tight nor loose. Body receives energy for action through food, sleep, work and the five elements which sustain and survive the body. Without the nourishment of work, body becomes inactive. Mind become inactive without knowledge, heart remains empty without love and feeling, soul remains undiscovered without meditation and witnessing.

You cannot dissolve your sins through actions by visiting temples, churches and bathing in sacred rivers. These are dissolved by transforming mind from ego orientation to egolessness through pure, empty and clear mind. Actions are neither good nor bad but your attachment and involvement make it so. The crux of the whole thing is that you should focus your attention on self improvement rather than living life through conscious mind which blocks your transformation.

In law of Karma, there is significance of three important bodies – gross, subtle and casual bodies. Gross body reflects outer physical structure, subtle body reflects subjective mind and casual body is consciousness which becomes the cause of creating five elements and the body. Consciousness appears when body comes up and disappears when body dies, it becomes universal on death of the body.

However it is in your hand, that you can become universal while living life without death of the body provided you spiritually grow from inside. When this happen all distinctions and duality dissolves, only pure love for all exists. A neighbour comes for help to you for taking his son to hospital who is critically ill. You refuse to help him because you are busy with your prayers. Such prayers turn into ashes because you have put self before service. Pure actions are deep feeling of love and service to all without any exception.

There are people who remain steady, cool and unperturbed under grave situations. It reflects maturity, clarity and purity of mind which make you do right actions at right time. The root cause of our worry and unhappiness is due to our obsession and attachment to false and unreal things of the world. These attract us fast because these provide us quick pleasure easily for some time to relieve us from sorrow and suffering. You should undertake actions which take you closer to yourself to experience eternal joy and peace.

Words are only pointers and an indicator which explains about the things but are not the reality. Reality is known through your own experience. The word saint reflects serenity and holiness but real holiness lies not in the word but in the character, conduct and behavior of a person who is labeled as a saint. For example one saint is dedicatedly involved in the service of humanity and the other saint is violent, insulting, hurting, committed to amassing wealth for selfish and personal interest. However the word saint applies equally to both but their characters remain polar opposite. Words are only indicators and not the reality.

Words have power to motivate and demoralize depending on the purity and impurity of your mind. Pure mind can be motivated but impure mind remains ignorant and unaware. Involvement is both physical and mental, beyond these (physical and mental) you become deeply devotional with spiritual maturity, dissolving involvement and obsession. The physical involvement stops when thing is removed from the scene but mental craving continues, till you transcend mind. It does not matter how much you have or you do not have, what matters is your obsession and attachment which is caused due to ignorance and unawareness.

Initially due to ignorance you run after things which gives you temporary pleasure, but later on being aware of your true nature you run away from things and persons because you experience renunciation. You must take actions which detach you from perishable things. Attachment is false and unreal.

A man was deeply attached to his only son and expected that his son will take over his roaring business, when he matures. But unfortunately his son died accidentally. Death is the reality of life, sooner we except better it is but the man was totally shocked and broken and could not reconcile to the fact of life and ignored the business. Consequently the business became loss bearing for want of personal supervision and control. He realized this fact after five years that fate of body is death but by then the business was completely ruined.

We all have tendency to live in the world of imagination and illusion, ignoring the reality of life. Real actions are those which do not invite reactions, this happens when you transcend human nature and experience divine nature as great souls in the past had attained. Once a man came close to Buddha and spate on his face, Buddha did not react but his disciples became furious and wanted to beat the man who did this stupid action but Buddha stopped them. Buddha told them that if the man had done such silly action ten years ago, he would have also reacted like them but now he had gone beyond mind, beyond any reaction because his human nature had dissolved.

Our actions as human beings are not real actions, our actions are only reactions to the action of others. That is why action reaction exists in the world of duality. Real action remains hidden, unknown, unseen and secret. When a seed is sown in the earth, actions of its internal transformation of sprouting and growing continues but it remains unknown till the plant comes out of the earth in the open. Similarly mans internal (spiritual) transformation remain hidden and unknown till it is reflected in his behaviour and conduct outside. As such for real actions we have to evolve internally and become spiritually mature. Understand clearly that your true nature is the supreme self as such you remain unaffected by the happenings of the body and the mind because you are beyond these.

CHAPTER 7

Reality of the Present

Present is the eternal reality and actuality because it is free of past memories and imagination of future worries of unborn events. Past and future cause disturbance to the mind. The present reflects and links us to our supreme nature because the present is clear of events. Anything which is free of events, remain unconditioned. It enriches consciousness that links us to our inner self. Present reflects wholeness, totality and completeness. Present means dissolution of thoughts and desire making mind refined and clear to reflect the light of pure awareness of your being (divine).

The present reflects non-wavering, silent and still mind because minds interference stops. But when unending thoughts flow through the mind, the present becomes polluted and loses it purity and reality. Present reflects liberated mind, without contents of consciousness. Living in the present helps in self evolvement and inner growth.

When the consciousness is localized or conditioned by mind it shrinks and gets fragmented, thereby losing its power of wholeness and totality. Living in the present is an ecstasy and joy because you go beyond mind transcending past and future which makes mind waver and unsteady. When mind drops suffering and sorrow dissolves. It is mind which identifies with events and becomes restless at its own. Without mind's interference your life becomes joyful and peaceful. The reality of the present is obscured by the mind because it carries the memory of the past and has imaginary outlook for uncertain future.

Living in the present reflects that you totally and completely concentrate on work in the present, relegating the past and the future. Anything belonging to past which has relevance in the present becomes part of the present. We learn from past experiences and plan for better future for humanity. We must learn from history and try to shape our future planning accordingly to deal with uncertainties of the future. But all these happen at physical level. The present which we refer here is a silent and a thought free mind which is focused totally on events that are happening in the present, subsiding thoughts of past and future. Time by nature always remains indivisive but it is mind that divides time in different categories– past, future and present. With mind we experience division of time and beyond mind it is timeless.

Present should be kept free from impure thoughts and feelings so that you experience the actuality of the present reality. Anything that has form is bound by time and space and becomes limited, it is so because mind makes it as such. Form cannot transform you to formless, because form reflects disturbance and formless means silence and stillness. Form (body-mind) is governed by memory and imagination but formless is eternity which is attained by living in the present with an attitude of self improvement and transformation. Past and future have transient and perishable nature as such unreal and false. Present reflects single mindedness, avoiding multi mind entity. If you miss living in the present then you really miss the charm of life. Without the present all remains mind oriented which disturbs your peace and joy.

Physical entity has different dimensions then the divine entity of the present. Physical entity of time belongs to the mind and beyond mind it is eternity and divinity. Your goal of life should be to attain divinity of the present rather then getting engaged and remain committed to the unreal physical entity.

All scriptures of the world reflect past happenings of attainment by the enlightened souls. These are helpful for inspiration to put you on spiritual track provided you are willing and determined. But mere reading of scriptures and inspiration through them cannot transform you unless you translate inspiration into real action by self improvement from within your own self.

Transformation happens by knowing and living in the present free of past and future. If you copy, imitate and cultivate false image of enlightened souls to look what you are not, will mean living in hypocrisy. Imitation reflects that you have drifted from the present living. Unless you attain your true being through inner transformation, the understanding of scriptures will remain confused and contradictory. You must understand that a physical and gross thing which works on periphery lacks penetration power to go deeper to your inner self to transform you.

To expect transformation through physical and outer actions remain a misnomer, you will achieve nothing except disappointment and frustration. Present is a spiritual link between physical and divine as such it reflects pure consciousness. Once you attain pure consciousness then attaining divinity becomes easy and comfortable. Mind (past and future) has tendency to pollute and contaminate the purity of the present.

Informative, knowledgeable and scholarly mind is a loaded mind reflecting memory and imagination which becomes barrier to the present living. Present living means erasing of memories and rejecting of thoughts instantly. When you work in the present with total concentration, your work becomes meditative because with deep concentration no other thought can enter your mind except the thought of work in hand. That is why it said that sincere, honest and concentrated work is equated to worship, signifying selflessness and impersonality.

You serve all with love with your dedicated work without any distinction. Your aim of work should be to work for the common good of all. Whatever activities you do during the day (walking, praying, bathing, eating, seeing, hearing, talking, playing and working etc) you must focus your total attention to the activity to avoid other thoughts entering and disturbing your mind. In the absence of other thoughts your attention and concentration on a single thought will make you meditative. We generally ignore this way of concentration and attention and remain burdened with multiple thoughts which enter the mind, there by scattering the energy and breaking the power of concentration.

The fractured consciousness (energy) when identifies with mind, loses its power of concentration by remaining committed to localized and petty engagements through desire. With mind, (past-future) your entry to the divine world remains forbidden, you are permitted to enter the kingdom of God when you attain purity through living in the present.

Impurity is the game that you play while dealing with the world. Experience has two aspects. One is outer experience and other is inner experience. Outer experience ends on the surface and inner experience transforms you from mind to no mind stage to discover your true nature. The outer experience is gained from your personal experience and also you learn from the experience of others. But the inner experience is an experience from within your own self, which is an individual exercise and no one else can help you. The inner experience you have to earn at your own.

'Arjuna' of the epic Mahabharata (India) left the thought of living in the present and associated himself with past memories and future imagination. He got confused and indecisive and refused to fight the sacred war. He had lost his sense of discrimination between right and wrong in the face of war. This is what happens when you get associated with past and future through mind, ignoring the present reality and truth.

Association with past and future causes ignorance, delusion and unawareness whereas the present reflects wisdom, understanding and insight to your inner self. Without attaining the purity of the present, inner world (divine) remains beyond your reach. Purer the things subtlest and powerful it becomes. Divine is the supreme subtle as such most powerful. In the world of matter atom has enormous power as atom is subtlest matter.

Divine experience is living in the present for transformation from matter to the eternity and physical experience is moving from the eternity to the matter which creates duality and distinction. We possibly cannot control happenings of mind but we can certainly control our attitude and outlook. Liveliness comes in life through present living. Present reflects direct link with our true being as it remain unconditioned by mind. Conditioned mind clouds the vision of the divine.

Energy is dissipated, scattered and becomes fractured losing its power of penetration and effect. Energy reflects pure consciousness which is experienced while living in the present without contents of past and future. The conditioned consciousness through mind gives birth to concepts, ideas, thoughts and opinions which we follow blindly and remain frustrated and disappointed.

Inner transformation happens while living in the present through your own experience of the divine truth which always remains whole, total, complete and perfect. But the past and future divides the wholeness and totality into parts when you associate yourself with the doings of the mind. Past and future reflect disintegration, division and separation. Present reflects unity, integrity and oneness reflecting desirelessness, fearlessness and thoughtlessness. There only peace and silence prevails.

Disturbance, restlessness, confusion, conflict, contradiction and clash are the outcome of absence of living in the present. Man matures through inner experience while living in the present. Outer experience through the mind is helpful in earning your living but is meaningless for inner transformation. To maintain the wholeness and totality of the present you need pure mind and a clear heart free of contents.

However pure feeling (unconditioned) is self expressed, it needs no language for communication and expression. Pure feelings are experienced while living with the present. Deep feeling of love is easily picked up by man, animals and birds without any medium of language. Deep feeling of love is a direct flow of consciousness between the man who feels and the object about which he feels. Both become one on realizing that the same consciousness flows between the feeler and the felt.

When this happens then the object about which you feel, dissolves and only consciousness remains which reflects deep feeling of love of oneness. The man's aura of energy around his face is circular and reflects the state of purity of consciousness. The dimension of aura of energy around the face can increase and decrease according to the degree of purity one attains.

Through concentrated focus the circular aura of energy can be straightened and in that state one can attain tremendous power of energy to push back an advancing elephant towards you. A small feeling (bhava) has deep penetrating impact and it can change the attitude and total complex of life. It is like a small burning match stick that can set the whole forest on fire. Feelings (bhava) have deeper impact then reason and logic being the product of heart (pure consciousness), also heart is closer to the life center (soul center) at the navel, as such heart remains under the influence of soul more than the mind center and that is why feeling coming through heart have greater impact and appeal.

If you are gripped by a feeling of fear, it takes tones of energy to dissolve it through the guidance of the spiritual teacher (inner self) also it needs inner transformation from within your own self. On attaining that you become fearless and develop inner courage to handle worldly things. All this happens when you live with the present reality. Anything that originates through present reality makes you self disciplined and self controlled but for this all remains an imposed affair.

There are three worlds, world of divine, world of feeling (bhava) and world of logic and reason (intellect-thought). The world of feeling is a link between the soul and the mind. The world of feeling denotes the pure consciousness which exists in the present free of conditioning. As a matter of fact the soul must control your feeling and feelings must control your thoughts, only then real transformation is actualized.

But if you try to control feelings through thoughts then feelings become contaminated and polluted denying you the possibility of reaching your inner self. It is so, because thoughts always reflect desire which originate through impure mind. Thoughts belong to past and future and are grosser, as such have no penetration power to move deeper to your inner self. Feelings are subtle and have power of penetration to reach to your inner self when totally and completely pure. This is possible when you live with the present reality.

Subtleness reflects wholeness and totality of the supreme reality which is available in the present only. The past and future contaminates and conditions the innocent reality of the present. When you shift your attention from past and future to the present then human behaviour automatically drops because there remains no space for human behaviour to exist in the present. The logic and reason may convince you intellectually but these cannot transform you spiritually from inside, that happen through deep feeling of love of oneness through the heart center.

Heart is the core center (pure consciousness) which can be experienced in the present only. Partial solution comes through intellect but total solution to a problem happens through the present reality. There are two aspects to tackle the social evils that exist in the society (rape, murder, violence, hate etc). One aspect is to use iron hand to control the social evils temporarily with good governance. The other aspect is to awake and make people aware about their spiritual nature so that people become self disciplined and self controlled.

All cannot be awakened to spiritual awareness as it is neither possible nor desirable. When spiritual awareness happens things fall in line at its own. It is not possible to make everyone spiritual as such we have to use physical means to bring order and discipline in the society. However, even if a few individuals in the society attain spirituality and divinity, it will go a long way to improve the atmosphere of the society. Spirituality reflects present living which provides you inner courage to transform internally. The aim of life is to maintain harmony between inner and outer. When you are with yourself then try to transform yourself from within your own inner experience. But while living in the outer world use logic and reason for sustenance of life.

The present is the way to reach eternity because the present remains unconditioned by intellect and feeling (past future). The learning, culturing and cultivation received through mind reflect past and future, making you bound and limited, denying your journey to the supreme self. Mind dies without duality as such for its sustenance polar opposites, duality, past and present must exist. Beyond mind you exist and survive with the present reality.

The biggest problem which cause sorrow and suffering is the craving of the mind, as such to dissolve the craving you have to live with the present reality. Interference by mind stops when you live with the reality of the present. Live moment to moment with the present if you can do that then transformation from human nature to spiritual nature becomes a certainty. When you are with the nature (present) then things happen at their own, peacefully and harmoniously with ease and comfort.

We have learnt from scriptures and elders that wealth is sin, forgiveness is a great virtue and conserving energy (consciousness) is a great divine wealth. These proverbs are meaningless without knowing, understanding and experiencing them by your own self. There is no sin in anything, sin is with your mind which is sick and diseased and longs for greed and grabbing which makes wealth sinful. Association with the past and future, events make your attitude sinful, so to dissolve the sinful attitude you should concentrate living in the present.

Forgiveness is a great virtue, but is it possible by man who is governed by a conscious mind. Beyond mind forgiveness is not required because you become divine dissolving duality and distinctions. Forgiveness applies to the body and mind and not to the soul which is beyond these. Forgiveness through body and mind is physical and not spiritual as such forgiveness ends at surface without any impact and realization deep down.

Forgiveness is a routine procedure governed by your conscience that is created by the society but for this forgiveness has no meaning. It is only a routine ritual which genuinely doesn't appeal your heart it is superficial, physical and gross, it dies on the surface, and beyond surface it has no role. Waves rise and subside on the surface of the ocean these waves have no role to play deeper down to the silence of the ocean. The waves can neither disturb nor can these interfere, the silence that exists beneath the sea. Forgiveness is not possible through mind which does not pardon for mistakes at all, instead it becomes revengeful and reactive to the follies you commit.

It is said by wise people that conservation of energy is the greatest spiritual wealth which you actualize by evolving from within your own self. Energy is conserved when you deepen and widen your consciousness by becoming desireless. However consciousness shrinks when it is localized and fragmented by mind. Shrinkage of consciousness reflects dissipation of energy and enriching and expansion of consciousness (without contents) reflects conservation of energy. Unless you experience by yourself the enrichment of consciousness, the proverb of conserving energy is a great spiritual wealth is meaningless.

Following such proverbs without your own experience cannot bring any change in you (transformation). Knowing about conserving of energy will not help you in any way unless you translate the knowing into action through inner transformation.

It is uncertain whether you will be alive next moment. It is unknown whether sun will rise tomorrow or earth will revolve next moment. So whatever you want to do, do it now in the present moment. Someone comes to you for help and you tell him to come tomorrow as if you are certain that tomorrow will come. If you can help and have the source and means to help then do it in the present moment when he seeks help from you. Do not leave it to future which is uncertain to come.

Make use of the present in a rightful way. We care little when parents are alive but make a great show of repentance by crying painfully when they die. Imagination of future reflects worry and insecurity and memory reflects pain and pleasure (fear and desire), of the past. So to dissolve all these uncertainties, start enjoying the present moment of living life.

Nature has provided inbuilt energy to man to face unpredictable reverses of grave nature. This energy remains dormant but becomes active and effective when fatal and grave situations come up. Mind by nature is fearful because it imagines separation from the reality as it has limited nature, bound by time and space. It remains fearful of the unknown truth. Beyond mind (in the present state) you experience fearlessness because you become universal, whole, total and perfect. There exist no other to fear from only peace and silence prevails undisturbed.

Fear loses control over you when you go beyond mind and reach your true nature. If you continue your association with past and future (mind) then you will continue living life with a fearful atmosphere. You must have experienced that some time in life extreme adverse situations come up suddenly without any warning which shatters and breaks you totally. You get too shocked to confront such unwarranted situations. Your mind stops working means thinking stops completely yet you salvage the situation and win over because when mind stops you move beyond mind and become universally powerful through pure consciousness which opens the door of intuitiveness (reserved energy) to salvage you out of the situation.

Intuitiveness reflects natural action free of thought and feeling, such actions are pure and innocent which make the intuitiveness more powerful, strong and effective to deal with the dangerous situation. However a weak minded man collapses and breaks down because he falls below mind and becomes unconscious which blocks the energy power of intuitiveness. Man of normal mind has potential and possibility to make use of this energy power of intuitiveness. Beyond mind you become yourself total energy which salvage you from awkward situation. Beyond mind reflects strong mindedness which makes you fearless to confront adverse situation.

A weak minded man is he who is extremely ego conscious and is deeply attached to sensuous things and persons. Weak mind reflects conditioning through past and future however the strong mind is which transcends past and future conditioning, reflecting pure consciousness. Normal mind is functional mind which is helpful in physical existence of worldly living. Below mind is unconscious mind which reflects ignorance and unawareness. Above mind is beyond mind reflecting spirituality and divinity which makes you super conscious through which you attain wisdom, understanding and insight.

We must accept present reality of life and live accordingly because there is no way out to shape life to your terms, life is mystery, uncertain and unpredictable as such you have to live life as it happens favourable or otherwise. Real, natural and right actions reflect that you exist in the present, dissolving mind and ignorance. In life doing is in your hand through mind (past-future) and happening happens beyond mind at its own when you live with the present reality.

Socrates, the famous Greek philosopher accepted the present reality of his wife's behaviour. She was cruel, nagging and torturous but Socrates did not identify with her past behaviour nor did he imagine about her future behaviour. He preferred to live with the present happenings ignoring the past and future. He joyfully accepted events without involving mind and showed no reaction to wife's stupid behaviour. Reaction automatically stops when you realize and accept the reality of the present. Reactions happen through mind (past and future). Beyond mind (present) reactions dissolve.

When you enrich your consciousness through living in the present you reach your point of creation (dynamic energy center in the body) on touching that creation happens automatically without effort, cultivation and culturing. 'Kabir' did not make effort through mind to compose deep meaning couplets about the divine truth. Composition of couplets happened at its own when he touched the center of creation. 'Meera' did not create dance, dance happened to her in devotional reverence to Lord Krishna with whom she had deep feeling of love and oneness. Dance of 'Meera' was devotional, spiritual and a happening which happened on dropping mind. 'Meera' became dance herself dissolving mind totally thereby not reacting to comments and criticism that happened around her because she had gone beyond mind through devotional dance.

'Edison' the great scientist was not literate and was a watchman with low intellect but he conducted six hundred inventions at his own on reaching the point of creation through pure consciousness and total devotion and concentration. The electric bulb was his invention as a gift to the humanity. You can never get a thing in life you desire the most because your concentration gets fragmented with desire which dissuades you from dedication and devotion required for focused attention to achieve your aim. With desire you become restless and impatient, relegating action of concentration.

Consequently you fail to achieve things of your desire. Flow with life without getting attached to the desire you want to fulfill the most. We generally live enclosed in our minds which keeps us away from the present. Whatever we see, hear and do is never total because we remain governed by mind which provides partial seeing, hearing and doing.

Unless there is totality of presence of divine all doings remain incomplete and partial. Mind that troubles you and creates different type of problems is a thought content only it has no dynamism of the present reality, it comes through pure consciousness which makes mind live and active.

You are not the mind but you are light of awareness and consciousness beyond mind. Whatever happens to mind cannot affect you in any way because you are the soul and not the body and mind. Soul remains unaffected by the events of the mind. When you miss the present, you miss the being of your reality. The deepest understanding is possible through your being which is experienced in the present. Be total, move totally, and act totally, do not divide yourself. Dissolution of ego is possible through your total being which is experienced while living in the present.

You must understand that present reflects indivisiveness and oneness. It is mind that breaks the cycle of oneness through past and future. In the spiritual sense presence reflects stillness and nonwavering mind. In the physical sense presence that you show remains ego oriented with endless flow of thoughts. When, you are present (with ego) divine remains absent. When divine is present your ego remains absent. Both cannot remain together because in oneness there is no other to exist.

You cease caring for body and mind when you experience divinity by going beyond mind. When we are totally and wholly involved in any act without fragmenting the reality through thought and feeling, only then we attain our true being of the present. Deep involvement in any act with ego (wavering mind) negates the presence of your being. Man's inner personality glitters through experience which he gains with the present reality. The man who lives with his inner mind of present reality, neither blames other persons nor he blames circumstances but accepts that everything is a fare and just decision of the supreme self and he flows with life without any resistance. The past is dead, future is unborn so the real living is in the present which has direct reflection of your true being.

CHAPTER 8

MIND AND BODY (liberation and bondage)

It is rightly said that mind is the gateway to heaven and hell. When mind identifies with sensuous things and gets attached to people, idea, thoughts and concepts, then pain, suffering and sorrow are experienced. Mind creates nonself center (ego) on the periphery which causes ignorance about your true nature of being. When detachment happens on knowing yourself then your human nature drops and divine nature reveals. Hell and heaven are creation of your own mind. Mind is the core factor in life. You create hell through mind when you remain ignorant and unaware about your true nature. You create heaven by knowing, realizing and experiencing your true nature of being where peace, silence and bliss happen. Bondage to false and unreal things dissolves on knowing your pure being, which liberates you from attachment and involvement to worldly things.

Liberation happens when mind is clear and empty of desire and fear (pleasure and pain). Liberation is the way to salvation and bondage is life of sorrow and suffering. We have to know and understand the laws of nature and mind to understand the inner world.

There are seven dynamic centers, (chakras) in our body. These have enormous energy power of their own. Energy of these dynamic centers belongs to pure consciousness (spiritual energy). The spiritual energy has its source in the foundational base of the divine energy which reflects inaction and stillness. The spiritual energy is motion which causes manifestation with the support of the divine energy.

To attain pure consciousness you have to pass through different stages of consciousness which has two aspects outer consciousness (conditioned consciousness) and inner consciousness (pure consciousness) also these are known as outer mind and inner mind.

Stages of outer mind are as under:-

a) Conscious mind

b) Sub conscious mind

c) Unconscious mind

d) Collective conscious mind

e) Collective sub conscious mind

f) Collective unconscious mind

Stages of inner mind are as under:-

a) Center of spontaneous mind (intuitive decision without thinking and feeling – natural decision)

b) Center of concentration (focusing of attention without any thought)

c) Center of wisdom (third eye – discriminative)

d) Concentrated energy (total dense energy – coiled as a serpent)

e) Center of creation (on touching this center new inventions and creations happen at physical level and transformation happens at spiritual level)

f) Center of pure consciousness (duality and distinctions dissolve)

g) Soul (reaching that eternity, peace, silence and salvation happens)

You have the potential and possibility to harness the energy by activating the dynamic centers through techniques given in chapter thirteen. Sometimes miracles do happen through these dynamic centers but you should not stop your inner evolvement at these but go beyond miracles and attain your true being for total transformation. Miracles reflect that you are still governed by mind and not by your soul.

To deepen and widen consciousness you should concentrate mainly on three dynamic centers. Navel center (self-life center), Heart center (feeling and love) and Head center (reason and logic). These centers when developed reflect spontaneity in decision, universal love, wisdom, insight and understanding, self confidence, foresight, enthusiasm and concentration etc.

When you identify events through mind then consciousness is conditioned and localized which becomes a hindrance to attain pure consciousness. Mind has three modes through which the consciousness is expressed or experienced. One is conscious mind which perceives and cognizes things, it is awareness about worldly things and is useful for living in the world. The second is subconscious mind, it stores all learning, its state remains half awake and half sleep. It is cultivated and cultured by society. Third is unconscious mind which again has two aspect one is biological which is instinctive and the other is sociological that comes from the society.

Newly born baby has natural instinct to suck milk from mother's breast. Animals have natural instincts of fear, sleep, hunger, anger and sex, like wise man also have these instincts but man has capability to transcend these through internal transformation.

Unconscious mind is the store house of suppressed thoughts, desires, fear, anger, jealousy etc. To dissolve these, we have to be aware, awake and witness events so that nothing happens unconsciously, mechanically and habitually. The more aware you become of your true nature the less the unconscious mind disturbs you because on knowing your true nature the energy of unconsciousness remains unspent through indulgence and suppression.

Mind has three layers one is conscious mind, it reflects reactions and reflexes that happens moment to moment. A snake is seen and you jump away in reaction. The house is on fire and you run out as a reaction. This is peripheral reaction and is natural. It is a guided response which comes through culturing and cultivation by society. Child reactions are pure and innocent because his reactions are not affected by learning and culturing.

The second layer is that of the subconscious mind. This layer is created by learning through parents, friends, family, education and society. It is called as conscience. The conscience is a particular frame of mind which makes us follow ethical and moral norms and conventions of the society. Conscience is different to consciousness. Conscience belongs to the world and is bound by duality (sin and virtue) whereas consciousness is beyond duality and distinctions.

Every society creates a different type of sub consciousness. Hindus, Christians Jainas etc belong to the subconscious mind. All social evils which are prevalent are caused by subconscious mind, which projects, distorts and perverts your mind. We understand well intellectually, that the problem of untouchability is cruel and unjustified but subconscious mind is colored in such a manner that it becomes our conscience to practice it. Otherwise there seems no logic and reason to follow such corrupted traditions.

There is another control by sub conscious mind which is deep and more dangerous and that is the control on our instinctive nature. The instinctive nature is the third layer reflecting unconscious mind. It is our biological nature we are born with. The sub conscious mind is controlling outward behaviour (conscious mind) and also controlling inward instincts (unconscious mind). The sub conscious mind prompts us to suppress natural instincts which seem to be anti society as sin according to norms of the society.

Sex is energy and a natural instinct but society is anti sex as such wants us to suppress it. Energy by itself always remains pure but your psyche makes it sinful, when you either suppress it or waste it in indulgence through wrong channels.

By witnessing techniques the instinctive energy of sex and anger returns to it source, there by energy is conserved. You should never fight with your subconscious mind instead be a witness to instinctive nature without participation and involvement, it will dissolve. Sub conscious mind has no will of its own. If you order it firmly it will drop. With that all vices and habits will also drop.

Mind dies with the death of the body and it reappears when new body is born as such mind is temporary and unreal. The attachment to false things through mind reflects ignorance and unawareness about your true nature of the supreme, which always remains detached from sensuous things through wisdom.

Wisdom guides us that external things affect body and mind and not the true being. With inner transformation from human nature to divine nature the attitude and outlook changes bringing peace, harmony, joy and love. Unconscious mind is like a deep sleep as such let things not happen in that state of sleep which is total ignorance. Bring things under the domain of conscious mind by being aware so that the unconscious mind stops working mechanically and habitually.

In the life of polarities that we experience in the world you cannot choose any one for living but you have to live life with both negative and positive polarities, until you transcend both through inner transformation. While living in the world accept life with duality regardless of pleasure and pain these bring.

People who had achieved greatness in different fields like religion, science, art and business etc utilized only eight to ten percent of the potential of their conscious mind and rest remained unused. Rama, Krishna, Buddha, Mahavira, Christ and Mohammad have honorable place in religion as enlightened souls. Edison, Newton and Einstein etc were renowned scientists. Picasso, Hussain, Lata Mangeshker, Michael Jackson, William Wordsworth have great place in the field of art music and dance. Tata, Birla, Ford, Ambani and Bill Gates have excelled in the field of business.

The goal of life is to become a full man then a great man. Full man means a fully evolved and enlightened man who has experienced his real being (supreme self). Whereas great man is a talented man, who is head and heart oriented. Full man is divine oriented. A great man experiences polar opposites because he remains spiritually empty and unevolved.

Mind and body are matter (subtle and gross), as such have unreal existence because matter appears and disappears being of perishable nature. Conscious mind is the surface of the ocean of consciousness (chetna). All activities are on the surface like waves of the ocean but deep down in the center (self) all is silent and still.

Mind has two aspects one is transparent and other is opaque. Transparent mind reflects clear and empty mind and opaque mind is a loaded mind which reflects ignorance and unawareness. Body is vitalized by vital breath (pran) to keep it alive with life. Mind is illumined by consciousness to perceive, cognize, identify and to know things through the light of awareness of the soul (supreme).

Awareness is supreme subtle, consciousness is super subtle, pran is subtle and matter is gross and dense form of energy of consciousness. Everything is supreme divine but it is categorized differently in relation to purity. A child's behaviour is innocent and Godly because his mind is free of impurities and he doesn't understand distinction between good and bad. This innocence lacks awareness because of rawness of mind, consequently his mind cannot pick up imprints of good and bad for any reaction. Innocence of a saint is due to awareness which he attains by going beyond mind. Saint transcends his mind and therefore interference by mind stops and he becomes pure inside outside on realizing his true nature of supreme self.

A child is enthusiastic, confident and remains tireless because his energy remains conserved without dissipation in desire, fear, anger and greed etc. Child is governed more by heart (feeling, love and emotion) than the mind (reason and logic). When child grows his mind starts receiving impurities which makes it opaque and that becomes a hindrance to knowing his inner self. Child's heart becomes impure with negative feelings when he identifies with mind.

Conscious mind is not sinful by itself but identification, participation, involvement and interest in physical and mental events make it so. Be a total witness to these events then you remain unaffected by their contamination (see chapter thirteen for witnessing).

There are two aspects of life one is physical and mental and the other is spiritual and divine. These aspects should not be mixed up. Dealing with the world be scientific in approach with logic and reason. Use heart, feeling and love for inner growth to evolve to spirituality and divinity. When you mature spiritually your worldly actions become holy and sacred, that will help humanity in maintaining peace and harmony all around. You will automatically become self disciplined and self controlled. Outer growth is through learning with mind and inner growth is through understanding and realization when you go beyond mind. Effort and practice are required to achieve assigned goals for physical living because nothing comes to you at its own without hard work in the outer world.

However things happen at their own in the inner world. Love, peace, compassion happens when you attain spirituality and universality. You cannot create these by doing and efforts. Growing of hair, nails, digestion, sleep and hunger are natural happenings, you cannot create these through effort.

A meditative mind makes work holy and sacred and that is how work becomes worship. Meditative mind means total concentration and attention on the work in hand, so that other thought subside and stop disturbing your mind. With meditative mind doing becomes happening and not a burden, stress and strain. Burden is experienced when other thoughts interfere and confuse. Be meditative every moment in all your actions (bathing, prayer, eating, walking, playing, working, reading and listening etc). Meditative actions will dissolve imagination, illusion and distortion that happen through conscious mind (impure mind).

You must see things as they are without any opinion, judgment, like and dislikes. These condition your whole seeing which takes you away from the reality. When we see things through mind we generally see false as real and real as false and that becomes cause of contradiction, confusion and chaos.

When you see things through mind then you always see fault in others for your wrong doings because the selfish mind has false sense of pride and attitude that it can do no wrong. Mind is subjective, personal and private, it keeps weaving imaginary and illusory world according to the quality of psyche. No one knows about it and no one can help. It is like you suffer agony in dream, none knows about it and none can help. Dream dissolves on your waking.

Similarly when you know realize and awakened into your reality the illusory world (nonself world) disappear. Becalmed mind is not a peaceful mind, absence of disturbance for a short period is not peace. Eternal peace happens on attaining your supreme nature. Mind has nature to desire success first and happiness later but the law of life is that happiness must precede success because with happy mind you can totally concentrate on the work without any disturbance. It also means that when you are happy and peaceful you become fully meditative in your work subsiding other thoughts, which makes you succeed in life.

The happy and peaceful state of mind inspires and strengthens your spirit for dedicated action with enthusiasm and confidence. Mind has tendency for craving for sensuous things of the world. The aim is to dissolve the craving by evolving internally from within your own self so that you attain your spiritual and divine nature where craving stops interfering. Until you attain divinity the craving will persists regardless of your going to jungles or caves. Where ever you go with your mind craving moves along with it.

Through mind you can know what to live but you do not know how to live. What to live means worldly life and how to live is spiritual and divine life. How to live reflects peaceful, harmonious, selfless, impersonal living with sharing, loving, giving and sacrificing attitude. What to live reflects desire, anger, greed, jealousy, fear, imagination and memory which cause sorrow and suffering.

Enrichment of consciousness reflects pure mind and conditioned consciousness is impure mind which blocks the wisdom and power of discrimination. Purity of mind means simplicity and innocence which reflects purity inside outside. Mind becomes most powerful when it attains purity and start reflecting the light of awareness in its entirety through consciousness.

Awareness (supreme self) dynamises consciousness and consciousness illumines mind which becomes dynamic and active. Some people use power of the mind for displaying miracles (unnatural happenings). Miracles only satisfy your ego as such you should not stop at miracles but aim at attaining your true being (supreme self) for total transformation from ego to egolessness, desire to desirelessness, fear to fearlessness, from matter to eternity.

In spite of so much spiritual literature available, so many temples, churches and mosques existing with so many evolved and enlightened souls of past, still we find that we remain uninspired for self improvement. Our total focus of mind remains on external things of the world, where you look for peace and happiness, but that does not happen because worldly things are transient and perishable. Real peace and happiness comes through your supreme self which you have to discover from within your own self.

Through intellect you can earn your living but it does not give you trust, confidence, integrity, character, discipline, control, compassion, love, peace and joy. These happen when you attain spirituality and divinity through pure and transparent mind.

It is a matter of interest to know as to why do we attach total attention to outer things of the world and least interested to realize and understand our true being (supreme). It is so because our culturing, cultivation and learning has been through mind orientation. Mind follows a cycle of birth and death (appears and disappears), as such it is false and unreal. A very few people have the inner courage and earnestness to jump out of this cycle.

The easier way to live life for those who are governed by mind, is to become part of the cycle of coming and going, beginning and end. We prefer habitual, mechanical and routine way of working and avoid path of will and austerity, which exercises restrain on our habitual doing.

Self improvement is an individual affair which happens when purity of mind (non-wavering mind) is attained. We in the East are neither spiritual nor material as such we get beating on both fronts by remaining spiritually empty and materially non progressive (backward). The West has totally accepted scientific approach of reason and logic which has made them leaders of the materialistic world.

You do not become spiritual by reading, hearing, seeing, writing and with the experience of others but you as an individual have to grow internally for transformation from human nature (desire, fear, pleasure, pain, anger, hate, greed and jealousy etc) to divine nature (bliss, peace, harmony etc). We all have capability to attain Buddhahood through pure mind but we are not earnest and willing to attain that.

It is the mind which divides and categorizes humanity into lower and higher but beyond mind there is no such distinction because you attain universality and spirituality that dissolves duality of living. Outer mind clouds your real nature and keeps you ignorant and unaware about the truth and the reality. Through outer mind you are attached to unreal and false things of the world that brings sorrow and suffering in your life.

The moral and ethical values that we preach and follow are a social product which each society evolves to maintain discipline in the society. Consequently the moral and the ethical values that come through society are transient and perishable, these die with the death of the mind. Moral and ethical values don't apply everywhere for all time because societies have a changing nature, with the change of society the values also change.

Beyond the world (beyond mind) the moral and the ethical values have no significance because you attain the eternal virtues of spirituality and divinity. Moral and ethical values are cultivated and cultured but the eternal virtues of the divine remain unchanged. The disorder and lawlessness that we experience in the society today is due to lack of understanding and realization of our true nature.

We generally have wrong idea that spirituality means renouncing family and home but it is not so. Spirituality is internal evolvement which can be attained while living at home. Spirituality is not to make life distasteful. It is to make life affirmative, open, lovable, festive and a celebration. Mind always thinks in term of material richness but beyond mind this attitude drops because you become cosmic and spiritual. Mind is not our true nature but it is an acquired and cultivated nature so to remain only mind conscious is a great mistake because mind is the mother of all sorrows and suffering in life.

It is expected that you must maintain balance between polar opposites, avoiding choice of living with either of them. You will confront wise and wicked in this world because of dual nature of the world. It cannot happen that all becomes either wicked or wise. If all becomes wicked human life on earth will perish and if all become wise then life on earth has no meaning. The manifestation works with duality and distinction. By nature we are wise but we become wicked through our mind which contains worldly impurities of negativity. You cannot calibrate all minds to spirituality because everyone has different nature, temperament and tendency as such earnestness differ in every individual to evolve.

The law of pure mind is mainly to evolve internally so that you experience your true nature of the supreme self by dissolving impure mind. Order and peace in the world is possible only when individuals mind are in order and peaceful state. To help the world you yourself have to go beyond the need of help by discovering your inner self. Things will happen in life as they are, you have no control over these happenings. Accept life and flow with it without resistance. It is rightly said that it is joyful when accepted and painful when resisted.

When war is forced on you, you need not sing the song of spirituality to appeal to your adversary to retreat but deal with your enemy by launching a counter strike that is the principle of war. Spirituality is for your inner growth it will not quieten your enemy. Enemy will be quietened by your counter attack that is the language the enemy understands and that is the way to live life in the world of duality. Beyond mind thinking about war is sin because beyond mind you become spiritual and Godly and have deep feeling of love for all. The polar opposites of war and peace are experienced when you are governed by mind.

Aggression, violence and reactions are product of mind, so to expect peace and order in the world through mind is like putting a cart before the horses. To expect a total peace in the world will remain illusory and imaginary because total peace can come only through your true nature of being (supreme). The temporary peace that we experience in the world from time to time is a partial peace which comes through conscious mind. You will face both peace and war alternatively while living in the world of distinction and duality.

Body and mind has close relationship. If body is sick mind is disturbed and when mind is sick it affects the health of the body (indigestion, sleeplessness, loss of hunger etc). Body and mind must remain healthy and pure for a joyful living, these are the two wings of life through which reality is actualized and ecstasy of joy is experienced. Body and mind are only instruments as such these are not sinful but the unwise attitude makes these sinful when you identify events with mind and get attached and involved.

All problems are body's problems food, clothing, family, friends, fame, name, honour, status, achievements, security and survival. Pain is to the body and suffering is to the mind. When mind identifies with the pain of the body suffering happens. Birds and animals only experience pain and feel negligible suffering because their conscious mind is not developed. Pain is natural happening but suffering is created through mind. When mind drops, suffering disappears.

You are divine by nature and your divinity resides in your body as self through consciousness which shines peacefully and endlessly to guide you for right actions as a spiritual teacher (Guru).

Bad habits are both instinctive and social. They reflect ignorance and weak mind. Weak mind picks up bad things sooner because it lacks sense of discrimination and determination. In worst of bad company a strong minded man will never pick up bad things because he understands and realizes the implication of bad habits on mental and physical health. Do not blame anyone for your wrong habits. You alone are responsible for all that you inadvertently pick up as a habit. Bad habits appear mechanically and unconsciously but these dissolve when you become conscious, aware and watchful as a witness.

Witnessing stops nourishment for survival of bad habits which subside when you do not cooperate and patronize through participation. Habits are to the body and mind and not to your real being as you are not the body and mind but beyond these. Bad habits cannot be given up through forced discipline and control but these dissolve automatically when you attain self discipline and self control through spirituality.

Parents, schools can exercise discipline and control over their wards till they remain under their supervision. But once they become independent they continue with their bad habits unmindful of fear of parents, school and society. The forced discipline and control comes through mind as such it ends on surface level and cannot penetrate deeper to transform you internally. Beyond mind habits dissolve at its own because mind becomes pure self realizing and understanding.

The goal of our life is to attain self confidence, self discipline and self control in a natural way through pure mind. These cannot be cultured and cultivated through mind, because mind provided only partial solution. To counter indiscipline you have to attain eternity. Forced and imposed control through mind remains incomplete and imperfect because mind cannot be eternalized. To make a good human being is not in your hand but it is a happening that happens when you evolve internally at your own. For becoming a good human being you discard your governance through mind and be with your being of self (atma). If you can do that then all will fall in line and mind will stop interfering and disturbing you.

If others could transform you then the world would have been free of sin because so many incarnations appeared on earth from time to time but that could not happen because transformation is a personal and individual exercise from within your own self as such none can help you. You can take a horse to a water point but you cannot make it drink unless it is willing.

It is not science where one man invents and the whole humanity is benefitted. This does not happen in the inner world and that is why Gandhi could not produce another Gandhi nor could Buddha produce another Buddha. Christ once said that do not fight evil, he meant evilness of mind (desire, fear, anger, greed etc) because fight invites fight. Also fight becomes nourishment for evil to prosper. Fighting is not the solution to win over evilness of the mind. Solution lies in your awareness of your being. The teachings of enlightened souls are useful as inspiration but these are all meaningless if you do not translate their teaching into personal experience of the inner self.

Body reflects space and mind reflects time and anything that is bound by time and space is transient and perishable because body and mind dies with the death of the body, with that space becomes universal and time becomes indivisive. The nature of mind is to desire, reward and benefit for itself. It always imagines about future happenings which make mind restless, disturb and noisy. When mind becomes peaceful and steady then give it a noble thought for remembrance so that other thoughts do not enter mind and disturb it. The best noble thought that you can give to your mind is the thought of your being (supreme self) which mind should not forget even for a moment otherwise mind will waver and remain disturbed.

Mind is the main cause of corruption and evilness in the society because mind by nature has greed, temptation and craving for grabbing more, regardless of the fact that it commits evilness in the process of grabbing. It happens when mind remains impure and weak. But when you become self disciplined and self controlled through purification of mind then all negativities dissolve.

Man dies as he lives. If you live a happy life, you shall die a happy death. Sinner and saint both die, sinner dies with sorrow and sufferings but the saint dies with joy and peace. Man dies alone and suffers alone, death is inevitable, it can happen any moment. Suffering is your own creation through mind, when you identify physical pain with mind. The problem of humanity is mainly due to misuse of mind. Desire, fear, memory, imagination etc cause misuse of mind. The right use of mind is through self knowledge, self surrender and selfless service. Self knowledge implies understanding, awareness and experiencing of your real being. Self surrender is total surrender of your ego. Selfless action is righteous action to evolve internally for transformation from human nature to divine nature, with a selfless and impersonal attitude. Selfless action also means not to hurt and cheat anyone and doing all actions for the common good of all.

Whatever you perceive through mind is not you and yours as you are the supreme beyond me and mine. These belong to body and mind. The traditions and customs are product of mind. They reflect wisdom of our elders who drafted norms and conventions for the posterity to follow. These do not apply everywhere for all time and keep changing from place to place and time to time.

However some traditions, are corrupt at times and customs cruel. Cruelty and corruption originates through ego which again is the product of mind. Organizing large scale feasts (marriage and death ceremonies), child marriage, untouchability and caste system are corrupt traditions that are prevalent in the society. Slaughtering of animals for sacrifice (yagya), committing 'sati' and 'purdha' system are a few cruel customs that we follow.

Feasting mind is loaded with desire, fear and other contents, but fasting mind is free of these contents. Feasting mind reflects opaqueness of mind and fasting mind reflects transparency of mind. Feasting mind obscures wisdom and understanding that keeps you bound to physical existence, it hampers your spiritual growth. Transformation does not happen by locomotion and transportation from place to place, you can attain transformation sitting at home instead of moving from pillar to post.

Same water is available everywhere, digging pits all over will not fetch water, drill deep at one place for water. Similarly consciousness is all pervading. You can deepen, widen and enrich it while sitting at your home instead of moving to jungles and caves. In life whatever happens happen now, if you miss this present moment without utilizing it then you will repent the whole life. The golden moments of life do not repeat again and again. You should therefore focus your attention in living with the present reality rather than entangling in past memories and future imaginations which make mind disturbed and restless.

Infact there is nothing good or evil because divinity is beyond such dualities but the mind makes it into sin and virtue. There is only necessary and unnecessary, needful and needless. What is right and what is wrong is in relation to these. Needful and necessary are right and rest is wrong. Mind always desires false (worldly things) and fears the true (supreme self). When your stomach is full you do not desire food to eat similarly when you reach eternity you become whole, total, complete and perfect, then you desire nothing because there prevails only silence, peace and joy. Beyond mind you attain eternity where you become desireless, fearless and deathless because there exists, no duality of polar opposites.

Our mind has complex desires to fulfill which are contradictory and confusing as such the society that we create through mind is also complex and contradictory. Mind needs thoughts to survive, heart needs love and feeling and divinity need total silence. Mind dies with thoughtlessness, heart becomes charitable with pure feeling of love. Ecstasy and joy of eternity happens with total silence and peace.

Personality reflects ego which is through mind orientation. It gives you a pseudo entity of a doer but as a mind you are only an instrument which works through the dynamism of consciousness. Consciousness is the real doer and doing is made possible through the light of awareness of the supreme. Individuality is your identity which you attain through inner transformation as Buddha had attained Buddhahood as his individual identity.

Body seeks to live, mind seeks to think and desire, heart seeks to evolve and soul is sought without seeking when all others dissolve (mind and heart). Body does not dissolve as such but you cease caring for it, realizing that you are not the body and mind but the supreme being. Body as it is non interfering, it is mind which interferes when identified with events. Body cooperates and behaves as you desire. Noble desires keep body and mind healthy because with single noble thought other thoughts subside, thereby you save energy which is scattered in other thoughts. But the narrow, selfish and mean desires ruin your health, energy is spent and wasted in petty desires. Without energy your vitality diminishes, making you dull, dry and lazy.

You become nonvibrant and nonenthusiastic making life a drag and a burden. Some are born very simple, commoner, lacking sharp intellect and education but still they have attained Godliness and divinity of the supreme truth. We all have potential and capability to reach our real being provided we are earnest. Attainment of divinity doesn't need extra qualification or higher knowledge, anyone can realize and experience once real nature regardless of the fact that one is literate-illiterate, white-black, sharp-dull, rich-poor etc. Steady faith is stronger than destiny it reflects steadiness of mind and heart through which you attain eternity which is beyond destiny. Destiny exists in duality. Mind is steady when it is clear and empty. Heart is steady when it is pure, loving and charitable.

Destiny is applicable to things which has form of body and mind bound by time and space which appears and disappears. But formless things are beyond destiny like space has no destiny because it exists with totality and perfection. Destiny of body and mind is death, mind dies with the death of the body. Anything that has death and birth denotes destiny. But eternity is beyond death as such it is real where nothing ever changes. Life is not determined by destiny at the time of birth, you can change the dimension of destiny by transforming yourself from human nature to divine nature (form to formlessness).

There are two 'I's one is pure and egoless (pure consciousness) other is impure with ego (conditioned consciousness). Pure 'I' is spiritual, Godly, universal, impersonal and selfless. The conditioned consciousness is 'I' which reflects ego it is physical, local, particular, limited, selfish and personal.

Toiling and torturing your body does not take you to divinity because divinity cannot be attained by unnatural means. Believing is through mind, knowing and realizing is beyond mind. Stop believing which comes through mind because mind has changing nature with that belief also changes as such concentrate on knowing, realizing and experiencing your being by dropping mind.

Mind is the bridge between matter and consciousness. It is a link between gross and subtle. Mind is everywhere either creating an illusory world or discovering the real world. Illusory world is created through impure mind and real world is discovered through pure mind. The mind is like steps of a house which lead you away from the house and also lead you to enter your house the same steps are used both ways (coming in and coming out).

Transformation means changing the direction of energy from physical channel to divine channel. All instincts are part of energy as such these can be transformed from human nature to divine nature. There are two possibilities for man either to fall down below nature or can transcend nature. Man has two polar opposites to experience – negative and positive. Negative aspect reflects violence, fighting and suppression. You fight sex, anger, greed, and jealousy but you do not succeed because fight invites fight. Positivity reflects non violence and non fighting energy is diverted for higher spiritual growth through witnessing where duality of positive and negative dissolves, making energy to move to its source unspent.

Mind has nature to flow through easier and convenient ways. It works in a routine, habitual and mechanical way. To break and encounter minds nature we create inner inconvenience through austerity (tapa). You feel hungry and mind desires food as a routine but exercise restrain and refuse to eat food to break the routine habit. The creation of inner inconvenience leads you to higher growth because you transcend the nature of mind.

The philosophy of fasting has great significance in causing inner inconvenience which gives you upward push ignoring the mind. The only thing that we can offer to 'That' (divine) is our mind (ego) rest all that we offer belongs to the being because all is rooted in the divine. The subconscious mind belongs to us which is cultivated and cultured by society. This is our creation which divides existence into good and bad.

Mind constantly focused towards divine is the right offering and that happens when you attain egolessness by transcending mind. Offering to divine becomes total when you do not divide reality. Mind works with law of reverse effect if you try to control it, it will go out of control. It creates the opposite to move. The more stillness is sought, the more unstill the mind becomes. The more you try to silent, the more noise it creates. This is the foundational law of mind.

To neutralize the reverse effect of mind, you be with your being (divine). Know, feel and realize divine everywhere in everything. Know bad through good and see good through bad. It means good and bad are two aspects of one reality, that mind creates. Even poison contains divinity and saves man's life when used as a medicine after it is chemically treated.

Mind has two things one is content and another is the container. Content means thought, memories, imagination, illusion, expectation, desire, fear and all other negativities. The whole content should be thrown out like garbage, then only it will be true offering to the divine to enter its kingdom.

Mind divides divine light (awareness) into seven colors which you experience during meditation. However divine itself is colorless. White color is created when all colors become one. When no color is present black remains. There is specific significance of colors for different religions. A man deeply rooted in fear will experience yellow color – yellow is the color of death. Buddha chose yellow color signifying death of human nature to attain salvation (nirvana). Hindus have ochre color (red and orange) signifying color of life. Blue color signifies silence like blue sky and inaction. Green color represents silence and action, it is color of Islam. White color means purity, it is color of Jaina religion. Black color signifies egolessness, it is color of Sufi sect.

CHAPTER 9

Trust Your Soul

Self confidence means trust in yourself (atma). All great souls who appeared on this earth lived life through total trust in their own self and that is why they were known and equated to God. Trusting your soul means total and complete faith and trust in yourself without any doubt. When you completely have faith and trust in your soul, only then, it becomes your 'Sat Guru' (spiritual teacher) to guide your life. Trust and faith also means that you do not depend on anything else except your own soul dissolving totally the conscious mind. It can happen only when your mind becomes non-wavering, peaceful and steady.

On attaining your true self you become love, joy and silence, reflecting your true nature. It is so because soul by itself has peace, love and bliss as its nature. Always remember and realize that you are an eternal peaceful soul and not the body and mind which appear and disappear. The goal of life is to reach 'That' (divine self). Man loses his confidence in self (atma) when he is governed by mind, which keeps him bound to his physical entity making him ignorant and unaware about his true being. The confidence that we display in the outer world is a physical confidence which contains duality. It is not spiritual, divine confidence which comes through inner transformation is free of any contamination of duality and distinction.

Inner self (antaratma) is individual self. Universal self is cosmic self. Beyond universal self and individual self is the supreme self. All are one but known differently due to their difference in functioning. Individual self is embodied self, universal self is the self of cosmic and the supreme self is the foundational base of all. Things remain dormant in the supreme self in seed form.

The supreme self is expressed through, pure being, pure knowing and bliss (sat-chit and ananda). Also these are known as pure existence, pure awareness and bliss. Being reflects physical form, knowing reflects consciousness (chetna) and bliss is undisturbed state of being (pure being). The self confidence is an experience from within your own self of your supreme nature. You should concentrate on becoming self conscious so that the inner confidence develops.

The self confidence is a happening through your own inner experience, you cannot create and cultivate through outer factors. The confidence that you display through nonself center of your periphery is false and unreal because the nonself center is the product of the mind. You should negate the nonself, which creates fear in you. Negating means ignoring the events which originate through ego. Nonself needs support of the soul (self) to exist. Self confidence means you become fearless on attaining oneness with the self. In oneness there is no other to fear from.

Duality created through nonself (mind) reflects fears of different nature – fear of the unknown, fear of defeat, losing close ones, losing job, rebuke from boss, sustenance, fear of authority, parents, family, society, religion, disease, murder, insecurity and fear of natural and manmade calamities. To dissolve fear, go beyond mind and be with yourself and become fearless and confident.

Confidence and courage are two aspects of one truth and both are natural happenings of the inner self. Physical courage and confidence are not spiritual and divine and that is why we experience polar opposites in the confidence and courage that we display in the outer world. Sometimes we show courage and next moment we display cowardice. At times you show confidence but the next moment you become shaky and mentally weak to deal with worldly situations.

The real confidence and courage reflects your strength of the inner self. The realization about false and unreal existence will take you to your eternal self from where confidence flowers. When you are guided by your own self then your thoughts, speech, feelings and actions become pure, selfless dissolving human behaviour. You can do no wrong in the world when you become divine, because me and mine dissolve. Your attitude becomes saintly, devotional and righteous.

Wealth can buy death but not life. It means wealth is temporary and transient which disappears as body disappears on death. By nature you are the supreme self as such you remain supreme self always and everywhere. The nonself screens the supreme self through your attachment to false things due to ignorance and unawareness. You must concentrate your attention on the self (atma) and do not forget it even for a moment.

The noble thought of the self in your mind will dissolve other thoughts making you thoughtless, for higher journey to discover your true self. You only discover things which are lost but here your being is not lost it is always with you as such there is nothing to discover. The only thing you have to remove is the screening effect of mind through inner transformation. Once mind is dropped everything become clear and open about yourself (atma). If you want to forget then forget the false, unreal and nonself which is transient and perishable.

On attaining divinity, the remembering and forgetting end as mind dissolves. Remembering and forgetting happens through mind and beyond mind there is no forgetting and remembering. Trusting your self is trusting God. Supreme God (parameshwara), is the absolute and ultimate truth, reaching there you attain enlightenment, salvation and silence. See chapter three for details about God.

God and soul are two aspects of one reality, God is creator and is pure existence and foundational base from where process of manifestation originates. Soul is the light of awareness of God as knower. God is pure being and soul is pure awareness. God can exist without the light of awareness but the light of awareness cannot exist without the God. It is like sun which can exist without its rays but rays of the sun cannot exist without the sun.

It is a matter of reality that God and soul exist together. Where there is God, light of awareness as soul has to be there. It cannot happen that God exist and soul remains unexpressed that is impossible to happen. Anything worth worshipping and caring is your own self which resides inside you as reflection of pure awareness through consciousness. Seek guidance from your own self (atma) and not from the self styled fake gurus roaming in the outer world.

Without body you cannot be killed, without possession you cannot be robbed and without mind you cannot be deceived. All these reflect trust in yourself (atma). Without body you cannot be killed means you are not the body and mind but the soul which has eternal fate but the fate of body and mind is death which can happen any moment through various reasons. You cannot be robbed without possession means when you attain divinity your attachment dissolves with your possessions. In that state whether wealth stays with you or not does not matter much to you because on realizing your true self the significance of wealth in life loses its importance. Without mind you cannot be deceived means when you go beyond mind contradiction, duality and distinctions dissolve and without that there is no scope for your mind to deceive and mislead you about your real self.

Worship of false, unreal and imaginary idols of God kept in temples cannot provide you relief from sorrow and sufferings because such illusory and imaginary Gods are lifeless and non contributory, these are as good as dead. Such Gods have beginning and end because these are created through mind and when mind dies with the death of the body these Gods also disappear, leaving you disappointed and frustrated.

In spite of man's dedicated worship of God's idols, regularly, he lives a miserable and chaotic life without joy, peace and celebration. What he worships is a dead worship through mind and is not a divine worship that happens through your inner self. Unless you worship your own self you cannot transcend sorrow and sufferings, which you experience in life. The self is the most powerful thing in the world which governs our thoughts, feelings and actions.

You may live life and survive through vital breath but without knowingness through consciousness you have no entity of existence. Self confidence develops as you move closer to your inner self. Self confidence is fragmented and is broken when you allow your mind to interfere in your affairs because it is mind which creates sense of insecurity, fear, uncertainty, anxiety, anguish, worry and tension through past memories and future imagination.

Pure feeling is a bridge between thought and self. To attain self confidence you have to pass through pure feeling (pure consciousness-spiritual). Feelings (heart center) are closer to yourself (being). However pure feelings become impure when they are identified with mind. Impure feelings cannot touch your inner self because these become conditioned with the association of mind, thereby you lose confidence in yourself. Impure feelings corrupt purity which breaks the direct links with your being. The feelings have great impact and penetrating appeal and that is how anything which touches your heart can transform and make you self confident.

As mentioned above contaminated impure feelings can ruin your confidence and make you ignorant and indiscriminative. You may be spiritual whole life but if you are not alert and aware then impure feelings can grip you any moment and neutralize your self confidence. However journey to the inner self is undertaken alone with the guidance through your own self as 'sat guru'. Inner courage and self confidence are essential to experience your true being. You can be guided up to the abyss by the wise but jumping into it is your own decision depending on your self confidence, willingness, determination and earnestness.

Going closer to the self does not mean that you become inactive and do nothing. It only means realizing and knowing yourself with that you develop self confidence for a trouble free life. Going closer to the self also means deepening, widening and enriching of consciousness so that the pure reflection of the self is received uninterrupted.

The best way to be with the self is to live in the present reality because it reflects the supreme self as it remains free from any conditioning. Without conditioning (through mind) you are always with yourself (being). You experience no interference and disturbance from past and future contents when you exist with the present reality.

Buddha and Mahavira had expressed through their inner experience of the self (atma) that soul is the most powerful energy center in the world as such we must harness this divine energy through purifying our mind. Trusting yourself reflects that you are a theist (religious) and distrusting yourself reflects non religiousness (atheist). Swami Vivekananda advocated that faith and trust in yourself is a real religiousness and rest all are nonreligious, who disown the reality of the self (atma).

When you have self confidence and trust in your own self then you automatically discard false tradition and customs of society, temples, churches, prayers and worships. Believing and accepting things from others without knowing and experiencing your self is blindness and ignorance. The aim of life is to be successful and live life with peace, love joy and self confidence.

Meera the great devotee of Lord Krishna was poisoned but she survived, this is a historical fact and to ascertain its authenticity is a debatable matter. However the religion of poison is to kill, religion of body is to die and religion of soul is to remain eternal. Meera did not die after consuming poison but in our divine context it means that poison affect the body and not the soul. Our nature is divine self which is deathless, death happens to the body and the mind not to the soul. If you understand in the physical sense then understanding remains partial but if you understand this historical fact through divine aspect then things become different.

The other implication of this historical fact is that when you attain enlightenment you cease caring for your body, losing sense of its existence. When 'Socrates' the great philosopher, was poisoned, he was asked where should he be buried. He told that his soul cannot be caught for burying and as far as body was concerned it would be dead soon. It could be buried at the place of their own choice according to the traditions. It does not concern and matter to him as to what happens to the body after the soul is liberated.

The trust means absence of doubt and it also means willingness to be one with the self. Trusting family, friend, society, conceptual religion, tantra and mantra can belie your faith and trust anytime but such things don't happen when you trust yourself. When you trust others you become puppet in their hands who exploit you for their personal and selfish gain.

Man becomes great and powerful through trust and confidence in one's own self. Buddha and Mahavira had enormous confidence in their own self that both transcended Hindu society, they were born in. It needs inner courage and confidence to deny and ignore customs and traditions of the society. It is a rare feat achieved by great souls. Self confidence reflects freedom and liberation from bondage of nonself (ego).

Trusting others means distrusting your own self. You can, however trust others for their experience regarding worldly affairs but certainly you cannot trust them for your inner transformation which happens from within your own self. It is like understanding is your own affair no one else can sow the seed of understanding in you. Even incarnations could not transform any one because transformation has to be earned at your own, no one else can help you in this regard.

The worldly information, knowledge and reading of scriptures can make you a scholar but not a man of self confidence. A frog which stays inside a well, desires to live under open sky outside but that cannot happen unless the frog comes out of it. Daily many buckets are lowered into the well to fetch water and if the frog is willing to come out it can dive into any one of the buckets to come out and get liberated. Likewise man who is willing to transform from human nature to divine nature can do so through inner transformation by dropping mind.

Mind always works for reward and benefit but a man of self confidence who transcend mind always feel happy to benefit the humanity. Mind is eternalized when it is dropped through purification. You must understand that self confidence, self discipline and self control happen on realizing, knowing and experiencing yourself through total trust and faith.

Evilness in the society is through mind and dissolution of evilness is through the soul. When you are governed by soul then you attain total solution to the evilness of the society but when you try to find solutions through mind then it remains a partial solution which keeps coming up from time to time. That is the reason that good and bad alternate endlessly. When you use iron hand to control and bring order in society, then temporarily the problems of society may subdue but when the iron hand phase ends the evilness cycle starts again.

The other historical aspect which highlights the fight between physical and the divine is known through an incident from an epic 'Mahabharata'. The 'Kaurvas' (deceitful people) wanted to disgrace 'Draupdi', wife of the 'Pandavas' (righteous people) in public view, for her sarcastic comment against 'Durodhana' leader king of the 'Kauravas', when he entered the palace of the 'Pandavas'. 'Dushashana' one of the Kauravas brothers was ordered to unstrip 'Draupdi' in front of the august gathering to take revenge. In spite of 'Dushahana's' effort he could not succeed in his venture as the sari of 'Draupdi' kept extending endlessly. He got tired pulling the sari and got frustrated and disappointed as such gave up the mission to disgrace 'Draupdi'.

In this context understand that nature and God cannot possibly create and manufacture instantly on the spur of the moment, man made things which can save you from disgrace. Miracles and magical stunts are product of mind and not of God. If that could be true, then God could have produced cooked food, clothing, shelter and other needs of man's sustenance but such things remains illusory and imaginary beyond ones understanding.

These are all mythological stories cooked up to make reading interesting. We should not see too much in such stories, which appear illogical and senseless to understand intellectually with logic and reason. Your feelings are corrupted by such false and unreal facts. There is no reason to take support of such stories to convince people, who get more confused and frustrated. But we continue believing and following such stories due to our ignorance and unawareness.

There is no reason as to why such mythical stories are projected to prove a point. We hesitate to ignore such stories because these are reflected in our sacred scriptures which are written by trustworthy people. We follow them blindly as a tradition by elders without verifying there validity.

We have to understand as to what significance the extension of unending length of sari reveal. Logically there appears no sense at physical level, governed by mind. Beyond mind you are spiritual and divine as such, such things do not happen there, because dual existence dissolves. All such happenings happen in the illusory and imaginary world which the mind keeps weaving every moment. But the fact is, why create such false stories to convince people which has no logic and reason. These are illogical, non appealing and most annoying.

One aspect could be concerning ignorant and unaware people who are given a thought that physical is stronger to divine because physical is gross, known and seen but divine is subtle, unseen and unknown as such what is seen through eyes impresses you more than the insight which have the inner vision of the soul. It also means that body and mind are more important than eternal soul. Ignorant people are mind conscious so they imagine false as real and real as false.

The other aspect is to highlight the power of divine which can salvage you from sorrow and suffering, but that can only happen when you attain inner transformation, otherwise you remain at physical level without any improvement. Divine at its own cannot come to your rescue. You have to earn its grace through inner transformation by self improvement from within your own self which reflects self confidence and trusting yourself.

When you trust yourself totally, only then, you will be saved from disgrace. Here 'Dushashana' reflects mind conscious and 'Draupdi' reflects self conscious. It is fight between mind and soul, physical and spiritual and good and evil. Mind being narrow, fearful, limited with form cannot possibly ever win against limitless, fearless and formless eternal soul. Such stories depict both aspects of life through mythical stories which appeal most to the illiterate people but remain meaningless to the wise people.

People question as to why 'Lord Rama' of epic Ramayana disowned 'Sita' when she was pure especially when she had gone through the torturous test of purity by surrendering and throwing herself into burning fire. It again has two aspects – physical and divine. Physical aspect reflects ignorance and attachment. It also means that while living life at physical level you have to follow the religion of the society in term of norms and conventions set by the society. Society creates laws and conventions for the ruler to follow to set right precedence to maintain discipline and order in the society.

Social values which are physical have nothing to do with spiritual and divine aspect where only eternal virtues of soul apply. The conduct of the ruler king must send right message of justice and fairness to public to follow. As such the ruler has to disown and discard things which reflect attachments to false and unreal things. However Lord Rama's action appear wrong from physical point of view. In physical existence we remain calculative about events in term of loss and gain and imagines separation from the divine self.

When we try to understand deeper inner meaning of spirituality and divinity through mind, then we remain confused and ignorant about the reality of the divine. However when you see things from divine point of view then you realize that the same divinity flows between you and all others, there is no division and separation because divinity is oneness and indivisive beyond distinctions.

On attaining divinity you become fearless and can move in jungles alone independently without any fear in the company of wicked. No one can harm your soul. They may attack your body and kill but you are not the body and mind but the soul which remains unaffected by the death of the body as your true nature is deathless. 'Lord Rama' and 'Sita' both were divine so events of physical aspect did not disturb them.

In the physical world you falsely act to remain in step with the norms and conventions of the society but as a soul you remain unconcerned and unperturbed about physical aspects. As physical entity you experience separation and differentiation but as divine soul you reflect unity and oneness. So 'Lord Rama's' action be viewed in these aspects (physical and spiritual). At no stage physical can ever understand the divine without dropping the mind. So far you remain governed by mind you will maintain separation from the reality of your supreme being. We as human beings will always view things through physical aspect and we will continue with confusion and lack of understanding about the reality of life.

The scriptures talk of language of the soul and we try to understand through our mind and that is why inner meaning of scripture remain hidden from our grasping because the inner sense of scriptures are beyond mind. The physical and the spiritual can never match because one is gross and the other is subtle. The self confidence is a powerful virtue which can salvage you from human problems. Trust in others can be belied and breached but trust in soul steers you from sorrow and suffering.

Here is a classical example of self confidence. However this is a physical self confidence which you gain through indepth study, knowledge and information about the subject. It is like when you study hard with sincerity, honestly, dedicatedly with total concentration you become confident to succeed in your exams.

Jagdish Chandra Bose, an Indian scientist was invited by the foreign scientists to prove his research that plants have life. Jagdish Chandra Bose asked for poison called cyanide and a fresh plant to prove his law of life in plants. He picked up the bottle containing cyanide and poured on the plant. Nothing happened to the plant and it remained as fresh as it was. Jagdish Chandra Bose was shocked to see that the plant did not die. He quickly picked up the bottle containing cyanide and gulped the whole poison himself. Nothing happened to him as well. Later it was known that the bottle had contained some other chemical but it was wrongly labeled as cyanide. The total dedication concentration and his thorough study of his research made himself confident although this was a physical confidence and not a divine confidence which happen from within without any physical aspects.

All eternal virtues sprout in you when reality explodes in you. Life is ours as such it depends on us either to make life pleasurable or make it painful. We are answerable to all that happen around us and not anyone else like fate, destiny, God, boss, family, friends, society etc. If you look for someone else to answer for you then it reflects distrust and lack of confidence in your own self.

All our prayers, worship, visit to temple, churches and mosques are fear oriented. There is fear of family, society, religion and God which force us to follow things and false traditions we are not intellectually convinced. Such actions reflect fear and lack of self confidence as you see things through mind and do not trust your own soul.

The trust in yourself make you fearless, self confident and courageous to transcend the society and false tradition and customs. When you become fearless on experiencing your soul you realize that the soul is deathless and death happens to the body and the mind but due to our ignorance and unawareness we forget this reality.

CHAPTER 10

Symplicity

One must be simple and natural in one's living and behaviour so that one enjoys the ecstasy of life. Simple man lives in harmony within and without with nothing to hide and show. He is pure inside outside. He neither suppresses nor does he indulge, as such conserves his energy of consciousness by dissolving its contents, thereby making the consciousness enriched. When you live a contradictory life and try to show outside what you are not inside it becomes a hypocritic and unnatural living.

With the pseudo entity you become a doer whereas the real doer is the consciousness. You acquire doership when you are governed by the mind. The artificial and unnatural living saps energy because consciousness is localized and fragmented in various desires and engagements. You try generally to show what you are not because you want to mislead others for carrying good impression about you. But people can find out the false image that you display outside because you cannot sustain your superficial and artificial image for long. You will be exposed sooner or later.

The eyes reflect truth and reality, your false conduct and behaviour can be seen through your eyes which can indicate falsity of your concealment about your cultivated act. To know the reality look into the eyes of a man as it has direct reflection of the soul. Eyes reflect purity as these are directly linked to the soul. Mind becomes the seer through consciousness, seen is the object and both are linked through pure seeing (pure consciousness), reflecting reality of the soul. Seeing becomes complete when seer and seen are present, infact seer and seen are instruments to actualize the seeing. However, what is reflected by the eyes can be clouded by the mind temporarily by false projection. But you cannot persist your falsity for all time and everywhere, sooner or later you will be identified.

We experience contradictory behaviour outside and that is why, we are anti sex and anti anger on the surface but highly sexual and angry deep inside the center. When you lack inner purity than simplicity cannot be expressed in action because you remain dual on the surface level and whatever you will express in action outside will always remain dual containing polar opposites. We generally hide things which are labeled sinful by society like sex, anger, greed, jealousy etc, nothing is sinful in life but it is your impure mind which makes worldly things sinful.

The sick and the diseased mind misuse the energy of the consciousness through physical channels instead of transforming that energy for higher growth of spirituality. A man who is simple and natural goes beyond higher and lower nature to his abode of the supreme nature, he remains unaffected by the physical and mental event that happens in the outer world through body and mind (see chapter five for higher and lower nature).

Be simple and be with your being for a trouble free life. Living with your being makes you fearless, desireless and egoless, dissolving the false center of nonself on the periphery which mind creates for its temporary survival and sustenance. Man may have born with any nature (temperament and tendency), at the time of birth but he can always transcend his nature because everyman is born with potential and possibility to transform from human nature to divine nature which entails simplicity.

A man with simple and natural living removes all false covering to hide anything and remains open to live life in a state of oneness beyond duality, contradiction and distinction.

Dancing happened to 'Meera' in a natural way she did not create through effort. In fact 'Meera' became dance herself on attaining oneness, through her simplicity with her deity 'Lord Krishna'. 'Meera' did not conceal happening of dance nor did she fear reactions of the society. She remained unmindful of comments and criticism from the surroundings outside, because she had become single minded with total concentration and devotion to her deity 'Lord Krishna'.

She expressed this oneness between devotee and deity through the medium of dance which reflects the state of eternal ecstasy and joy, ignoring the pleasure of sensuous things of the world. 'Meera' attained her true self through the medium of dance. This goes to prove that you can attain your true nature through any medium provided you are earnest, willing and determined. Sufi saint 'Kabir' attained his true nature through the medium of his profession of weaving. What is required for attainment is total concentration, devotion and realization about the oneness of reality between the absolute and the relative.

'Lord Mahavira' attained inner nakedness of purity through simplicity, he presented himself before the world as naturally as he was, dissolving sense of mind conscious. The things start happening at its own when the simplicity touches the point of creation of the pure consciousness. Sufi saint 'Kabir' having touched the point of creation started composing in a natural way the deep meaning divine couplets at its own without cultivation and effort.

The harmony between inside and outside dissolves split personality which helps you to maintain oneness with reality and truth. The scope of distortion and imagination of the truth disappears when you merge with your true being through simplicity. Mind of simple man remains stable, steady and nonwavering, that leads him to spiritual maturity and understanding the significance of universal brotherhood for peaceful living. His mind becomes open, clear, empty, active, and affirmative with a noble and sacred thought of being.

Culmination of simplicity is silence and stillness of mind which becomes like a cinema screen clear and clean, without any stain of confusion and contradiction. Firmness in decision come through simplicity as it dissolves indecisiveness by maintaining purity inside outside. The false image of goodness that you display outside cannot sustain for a long time it will make you tumble in life sooner or later. Artificial living has no independent existence at its own.

If you do not live a simple and honest life then you display contradictory behavior like a weak man tries to pose strong, duffer tries to be wise and dishonest tries to be honest and coward tries to be brave. Hypocrisy enters and remains present when simplicity is absent. We hate the boss but wear a false smile outside. Internally we feel jealous of other people's progress, richness and goodwill etc but externally we show false and fake happiness so that we are not misunderstood and give them the impression that we are always with them in their prosperity in life, which is not the reality inside.

When you attain purity both inside outside through simplicity, your human behaviour dissolve and you stop reacting to comments and criticism that come from people who surround you. 'Tansen' was a famous singer with emperor 'Akbar' (India) he was very close to the emperor and formed part of his coterie being one of his ten ratnas (jewels) but in spite of his closeness to the emperor he always remained simple, pure and natural. He did not gloat over his singing talent, sharp intellect and wisdom.

One day emperor 'Akbar' declared in the assembly of august gathering that no one in his entire empire could match the singing calibre and talent of 'Tansen'. At this 'Tansen' humbly told the emperor that he knew a man who sang better than him. 'Akbar' desired to call that man to sing for him. 'Tansen' then told the emperor that the man sang for the joy of his soul and not for public. When one sings for once own self then singing becomes appealing and fascinating.

Simplicity is a reflection of pure consciousness. You cannot create, cultivate simplicity through effort, it is a happening which happens at its own when mind becomes non-wavering, silent and pure. Simple living awakens the deep feeling of oneness with your being at the center because you are directly linked to it through your simple and natural living. A man who is impure and non simple tries to become and appear what he is not. He may not be a saint but he acts to appear saintly.

Hypocrisy is a product of conscious mind which prompts you to live a contradictory life. Beyond mind you remain simple and natural. We experience sorrow and suffering in life when we live an unnatural living against our nature of being. The man who is simple and natural with purity inside outside become fearless and transcends fall traditions and customs of the society and false religion, which create guilt feeling of sin in us.

We say that everything is divine, then how can there be sin on earth, sin is not natural it is imaginary and is created through mind which learns from society and religion. Mind divides humanity in lower and higher. Beyond mind we are all divine and we should live our life with divinity.

When you live in a natural way without disturbing the flow of energy the energy is centered in your being unspent. When you become unnatural, artificial and unreal in your living then the energy of your consciousness is scattered and loses its power of concentration. Nature uses enormous energy for running its show of manifestation but still there is never any shortage of it and as such there is no dissipation of energy because the energy of nature is never used for negativity of any sort.

Whereas man scatters his energy in non essential things through desire, memory, imagination, anger, fear, greed etc. As a result of this man always feel shortage of energy in running day to day affair. For want of energy man feels disgusted, tired and frustrated and remains inactive, lazy and dull. A man who is simple and natural does not cheat and hurt anyone because he is complete in all respects and he feels no deficiency of anything. Also he transcends his human nature and that is why he refrain from hurting anyone in life because he sees total love and nothing else.

Man hurts and cheats people when he is governed by mind. It is mind and intellect which disintegrates us from natural living. Nature does not cheat and hurt with any evil motive but still natural calamities do happen, where millions of people die, this is a natural phenomenon to maintain balance between creation and destruction, however nature has no evil motive to destroy humanity such things happen through man's mind.

The law of nature is to create, preserve and destroy, no one can escape this phenomenon of nature. It reflects that worldly things are temporary and perishable, nothing stays in the physical world and nothing changes in the divine world. Man is born, stays for some time and then dies, this is the way nature works. Joy, peace, silence and love are experienced when you attain purity and simplicity without that all is sorrow and misery.

Simplicity takes you closer to your inner self (being) and when that happens you develop self confidence, self discipline, self control, fearlessness, trust, wisdom and understanding. Your acts and conduct become selfless and impersonal. Simplicity makes you super sensitive to the sufferings of others and that way simple man suffers more than the sufferer himself that is the real compassion the simple man expresses in his conduct and behaviour.

A man of simplicity is free of any complex because he is governed by self and self is beyond any complex. Simple man remains beyond confusion, competition, comparison and clash because of his oneness and single mindedness of his behaviour. He makes no distinction between superior and inferior.

In nature there is no complex and comparison. Diamond does not claim its superiority over coal nor does coal compare itself with diamond and suffer inferiority. All exist in natural harmony and balance without affecting each other in any way in term of comparison of any sort. Flower does not claim for its beauty and feel proud, it remains as it is because it is beautiful by nature. It is your thinking which makes a thing beautiful or ugly. When you express your opinion about it then the glamour of beauty of the flowers gets corrupted. When you see things through mind, you pass judgment and make things conditioned with your opinion but beyond mind you are universal and see things as they are without passing any judgment for good and bad.

Mind remains absent in things of nature and that is how the things of nature are beautiful, energetic, with full of charm in life because energy is not wasted unnecessarily. A simple man serves all with selfless service and love and expects nothing in return. Welfare of humanity is super most in his heart. His aim is to awaken people around you so that everyone realizes his true nature and experiences a trouble free life.

Christ had rightly said that those who share and give will be filled with the energy. Sharing and giving means sharing of goodness and love for common good of all through pure consciousness and giving implies blessing, good wishes and awakening you from the sleep of ignorance and unawareness.

If you do not share your consciousness shrinks and gets fractured, reducing its power of spiritual energy. Sharing and giving happens through pure heart when you become spiritual and universal through simplicity. With mind you remain non-sharing personal and selfish. You may earn lot of wealth with your effort but wealth does not stay with you forever as wealth has temporary and perishable nature. Either the wealth leaves you before your death or you leave it when you die.

A man of simplicity does not ever regret for things which are not his because he understands and realizes that worldly things are perishable. The simple man always remains nondesiring and egoless because of his pure consciousness which is beyond mind. It is mind which makes you desiring and ego bound. All successful people attained success as a happening and never by desiring.

The law of nature is that whatever we sow so shall we reap. We generally give worry, sorrow and suffering to people and these are reflected back to us manifold. A simple man with natural living emits vibrations of love, joy and peace which sweeten the atmosphere all around. In nature things happen at its own as a natural phenomenon. You put a rose seed on the ground it will sprout and grow into a rose plant in the right season as a natural happening.

However you cannot pull out a flower prematurely from the plant which has not started flowering. You cannot short circuit natures happening. Whatever important that has happened in your life has happened at its own without your planning and desiring. You were not born through your planning but it happened so as a natural phenomenon. You could have born to any other woman like your mother, there is no definite planning in this context, all happens naturally and accidentally. Simplicity does not mean that you become simpleton in the name of simplicity. People will make fool of you because you lack sharp intellect and have poor reflexes.

CHAPTER 11

Wisdom

Wisdom (intelligence) is a natural happening that happens when you attain pure consciousness. It is deep understanding and right action for experiencing your true self. It is discriminative, spiritual and universal. However intellect is totally different to wisdom. Intellect reflects reason and logic, which is a mental product, it is material, particular and is beneficial for worldly living. Wisdom is insight and understanding which is used for inner growth for self transformation. When consciousness is enriched through eliminating contents of mind then wisdom appears.

With intellect you can design weapons of mass destruction but wisdom guides you to exercise restraint in using such weapons. Wisdom contributes for a peaceful and harmonious existence because wisdom reflects universal love and brotherhood. Intellect is sight which is required for outer world but wisdom is insight which helps inner transformation from human to divine.

Through sight you become ignorant, worldly, pervert and non understanding but all these dissolve on attaining wisdom. A sacred and humanitarian work is actualized through wisdom. When you attain wisdom, imagination and distortion disappears as a result you see things as they are (false as false). Intellect (reason and logic) clouds wisdom through conditioning with desire and fear etc.

Wisdom means choosing only needful, necessary, useful and right and discarding selfish and personal actions. The conscious mind (intellect) is contradictory and confusing because of its contents, as such instant and rightful actions cannot be expected from it. It happens only through wisdom which reflects non-wavering mind (non desiring mind). All actions undertaken through mind remain conditioned because mind fragments and localizes the pure consciousness for petty engagements, consequently the wholeness and totality of pure consciousness is divided, diminishing its power and purity.

Wisdom is realization, knowledge and experiencing of the self (atma). It opens the door to reach eternity, dissolving all craving and attachment to nonself ego. With wisdom renunciation happens as a natural phenomenon which you don't have to cultivate by doing and effort.

Understand very clearly that if you want to renounce attachment and craving to sensuous things of the world then you have to transform internally and attain wisdom. We see people dying of hunger and poverty but we remain indifferent and uncaring to their needs. This apathetic attitude, disharmony and chaos that we experience in the world outside is due to lack of wisdom.

We become sharing, loving, caring, giving, and sacrificing with compassion and concern only when wisdom develops. Also you become selfless and impersonal in all your actions and you always work for common good of all and serve everybody with love and service without any distinction, likes and dislikes.

We give lot of importance to false physical prayers that happen through mind but we are least concerned about those who suffer for want of help from you. It is so because you lack wisdom and understanding which is clouded by mind. Wisdom is transformative and liberating but mind is binding and ignorance. True wisdom is when you attain non-wavering mind to experience silence, salvation and bliss.

When you transcend human nature through wisdom you become universal and spiritual, which reflects in your day to day behaviour and conduct. Transformation from ignorance to wisdom can happen suddenly or gradually, it depends on your earnestness. Transformation process is a deep internal phenomenon which continues uninterrupted provided you are willing, determined, honest and truthful for self improvement to attain the divine wisdom.

The process of inner transformation cannot be known and noticed by naked eyes till the spiritual virtues of wisdom start reflecting in your actions outside, however the inner process continues endlessly and relentlessly. It is like a healing process which continues silently inside but remains unseen till wound shows sign of relief outside.

Understand wisdom through a story. Once, three scientists went to jungle for some research. To go deep into the jungle they had to cross a river with a boat but they did not find any boat nearby to take them across the river. They were waiting for some help, suddenly they saw a moving boat at a distance. Seeing the boat they waved and yelled for help. When the boat came closer to them, the scientist requested the young man to take them across the river, he agreed to do so. On reaching the other bank of the river the scientist saw a skeleton of a dead tiger. One of them said that he could join the bones of the dead tiger, the other said that he could put flesh and blood into it and the third scientist said he could put life into it.

The young man who brought them in the boat warned them that if they make tiger alive it would kill all of us but the scientist ignored his warning and were adamant and determined to make the dead tiger alive to prove their foolishness and stupidity. The young man ran quickly a little far away and climbed the top of the tree to see the funny and stupid act of the scientists. The tiger was made alive as planned, it roared and killed all the scientists.

The young man was illiterate but was wise as such escaped death. The scientists were scholarly and had intellectual mind but lacked wisdom (intelligence). It is to prove that wisdom needs no qualification and knowledge, it is a happening which happen on attaining a peaceful and a nonwavering mind. However for intellect you have to load and burden your mind through information, knowledge and learning.

Goodness of wisdom always prevails over evilness of ignorance, because wisdom is universal and ignorance is particular as such universal absorbs particular and make it non-dual. Ignorance is product of mind and wisdom is product of your true being. No one remembers 'Ravana' and 'Hitler' who were gripped by ignorance to commit violence on people destroying human life and property. But people remember till today, the great souls who were governed by their wisdom and always dedicated their life to bless humanity for peaceful existence with their love and selfless attitude.

In the worldly life we are tossed between pleasure and pain (desire and fear) due to our ignorance and unawareness, this is the result of governance through mind. Pleasure and pain, sorrow and suffering disappear when divine wisdom guides us for righteous actions in the world. Wisdom is the expression of the self it is the way to eternity.

Wise man is he who learns from all that exists and lives. Nature does not give you guarantee of a trouble free life at the time of your birth. Striving and struggling are part of life but a man of wisdom accepts life as it comes with pleasure or pain. Wiseman struggles without greed and strives without seeking. Problems and sufferings are part of life no one can escape from these. Even great souls have suffered at the hands of ignorant people who had pervert tendencies.

'Christ' was crucified, 'Kabir' was trampled by elephant, 'Meera' was poisoned, and 'Mahavira' was nailed through his ears by a shepherd. All these happened through unwise people who did not understand the inner realities of these great souls and always viewed their attainment of enlightenment through mind which is narrow, limited and remains ego oriented.

Such people satisfy their ego by clinging to a thought and a concept, consequently take such cruel step to punish and torture great soul who talked contrary to their pervert thinking and concepts designed through there sick and diseased mind.

The ignorant people feel that they have caused cruelty and pain to the great souls but it is not so because pain and cruelty is experienced by those who are governed by mind. Those who have transcended mind goes beyond suffering and pain on attaining divinity. They lose complete sense of body's existence and with that the pain that is caused to body also disappears. The ignorant people cause harm to the body but not to the soul which is eternal and beyond body and mind as such soul remains unaffected by events that are caused through body and mind. The focus of attention of wise people always remains on the self (atma) as such inner transformation happens automatically from ignorance to wisdom.

Wise man always maintains positive and constructive attitude in life because he becomes selfless and impersonal. To know the world is not that important as knowing your own self which is the source of wisdom. Wisdom is anti dot to the darkness of ignorance. You should always remain aware, alert and attentive about your divine nature so that no other thoughts find place in your mind to shake and disturb your wisdom.

Wisdom is the key to maintain inner and outer harmony (balance between physical and spiritual). A small incident in life can transform you provided you have eye of wisdom. It happened with 'Swami Dayanand' who got instantly transformed on seeing a mouse eating a piece of sweet, offered by a devotee in reverence to the idol God kept in the temple. He observed that the dead God could not do anything against the mouse that was pleasurely eating the offering in front of the idol God. Since then 'Swami Dayanand' decided to abandon idol worship. He realized that serving live people is better than following blind traditions which have no scope to transform you internally.

The outer actions of offering and worshipping idol are meaningless, these only remain as dead rituals being of physical nature, which has perishable fate and nothing more than this. 'Buddha' through wisdom transformed instantly when he saw a dead person and realized that fate of body is death as such there is no point for attachment to body which remains temporarily with you. 'Buddha' since then was determined to transform from death to deathlessness by attaining his true divine self and that is how 'Buddha' attained Buddhahood.

Wisdom always chooses reality and facts of life and ignores the false and unreal which have temporary existence. Wise man learns not only from his own experience but also from the experience of others who were trustworthy and wise in life. You cannot stop the flow of pain, sorrow and suffering, it is a natural phenomenon. However you can always change your outlook and attitude through wisdom by shifting your attention from mind conscious to self conscious.

Flowering of wisdom happens when you go beyond mind. Right understanding, right judgment comes through wisdom. Knowing is wisdom and believing is ignorance. Information, knowledge and learning is essential for living in the outer world for earning your living but not for the inner world which need empty, clear and pure mind to know and understand the inner reality through wisdom.

Unless you actualize your wisdom in all your actions, till then all remains talk. Wisdom enriches when humanity is benefited and relieved from pain and suffering. When wisdom awakens in you then all things fall in line dissolving distinctions, division and separation because through wisdom you become one with your reality. No one can make you wise, you alone have to be awakened from within your own self as an individual exercise.

'Ananda' was a favorite disciple of 'Buddha'. He appealed to 'Buddha' to sow seed of understanding in his mind for true knowledge through his blessing. 'Lord Buddha' refused saying that such things do not happen in nature. Everyone has to become his own light through inner transformation by awakening into wisdom, dissolving ignorance. It is so because all of us are born with potential and possibility to grow to the eternity provided one is willing and determined with total earnestness

If others could have helped there would have been unending chain of great souls in this world but such things do not happen at its own but you have to earn it. Truth is known through wisdom. The wise man is he who sees both aspects of life (negative-positive). Wisdom is science of experiment from within and ignorance is darkness of attachment to worldly things.

The man who is ignorant can never understand the inner realities of great souls. 'Devadatta' cousin of 'Lord Buddha' always remained ignorant to understand Buddhahood of 'Lord Buddha', 'Priyadarshani' daughter of 'Lord Mahavira' never understood her father 'Lord Mahavira'. 'Sudhama' and 'Arjuna' of epic Mahabharata (India) did not understand 'Lord Krishna'. Jews did not understand Christ, Pundits of Banaras (India) did not understand 'Kabir', 'Socrates' was not understood by his wife who was nagging and harsh. Ignorant terrorists do not understand charm of peace and love which happens through wisdom.

Wisdom brings along with it firm and instant decision, concentration, dedication devotion, fairness and justice in all actions and doings. Inferiority complex is product of ignorance but when wisdom appears ignorance and inferiority complex disappears. Inferiority complex comes when you do not live your natural life but you show outside what you are not inside.

If you are duffer by nature don't try to become wise against your nature by false covering and false cultivation and acting. The best thing is to transform internally to wisdom, dissolving duffer nature that you posses. Unless you attain total transformation and become wise you will remain duffer and have to continue with that nature till death.

If you are born duffer than be a duffer till you are internally transformed. Life flows without any distinction but you create distinction and duality through your unwise action of your mind. When you become wise your ignorance is replaced by innocence of inner purity where you have nothing to show and nothing to hide, you present yourself before the world as you are without any false and unreal covering.

Wisdom reflects purity inside outside signifying simplicity and natural living. When you attain wisdom you learn, realize and understand how to live and discarding what to live. How to live means divine and spiritual life and what to live reflects worldly life full of sorrow, suffering and misery. Without wisdom your actions remain inhuman and contradictory. On one side you love, care and show compassion and on other side you hate, commit violence and cause pain. You nurse a child and next moment you orphan him, you make friends and exploit, you look after parents but disown them when they need your support and help most.

Hindus believe that the 'Lord Shankra' (Lord of destruction), opens his third eye to destroy the world to maintain balance between creation, preservation and destruction. Likewise when man attains wisdom, his eye of insight (third eye) opens and develops to destroy the wrong, needless and unnecessary things which cause disturbance and make mind diseased and sick. 'Shiva' is pure consciousness, and 'Shankra' is conditioned consciousness. 'Shankra' merges with 'Shiva' when it attains internal purity and transforms to 'Shiva' as pure consciousness. It means conditioned consciousness transforms to pure consciousness (physical to spiritual).

Man governed by conscious mind enjoys (bhoga) first and then renounces (yoga) but wise man prefers first yoga and than bhoga. Wiseman attains deathlessness by inner transformation as such death of body to him does not matter. Deathlessness means you attain divinity, your true eternal nature which is beyond death. He realizes and understands that you die to live, you destroy to build, you melt to shape, you annihilate to create, you sprout to grow, you evolve to transform.

It means life is eternal it never dies only the form appear and disappears. But the ignorant dies with the death of the body because he imagines that he is body and mind and not the eternal life of divine. A wise man avoids rituals, procedures and process of worship and prayers that are followed in the outer world, instead he worships his own divine self as God, as sat guru (spiritual teacher). Wise man weighs all aspects of life and then decides what to do or what to discard. Infact the whole universe is a learning school for a wise man.

CHAPTER 12

Living Life

Life is unknown, uncertain and unpredictable. No one has control over it and no one can shape it. The best way to deal with life and its mystery is to accept it as it comes, whether it brings joy or sorrow. Be in a festive mood and make life a celebration by living with the present reality free of memory and imagination. Existence and living life is combination of light, love and life (awareness, consciousness and vital breath). Love and life are contained by light.

In life things will happen as they happen without any Justification. Life is not logical because it is a mystery beyond analysis. Logic, reason and analysis apply to things that come through mind bound by time and space which make it limited. Beyond mind analysis is not possible. Life is beyond mind which means beyond physical existence reflecting spirituality, which is a matter of own experience from within. Analysis happens through mind, beyond mind is synthesis.

When things are beyond our control, it is better to accept and live life as it comes with right attitude and positive outlook. Right attitude and positive outlook mean, living and accepting life without choice, judgment, distortion and imagination. The world is unreal because it is temporary transient and perishable. The reality, the truth (supreme) is eternal and uncaused. Real and unreal is in relation to eternity and temporary existence. The goal of living life is to attain divinity for peace and joy, renouncing attachment to unreal world which is full of sorrow and chaos. Real never changes and unreal never stays. Two worlds inner and outer originate from real and unreal. With that two cultures come up, material-spiritual, lower-higher, wisdom-ignorance, objective-subjective, sight-insight, outer-inner, tuition-intuition.

Inner life is governed by the truth and outer life is governed by nonself (ego) created by mind. Absolute truth (supreme) is entirely different to the seen world. One is ultimate and absolute and the other is relative. Ice is absolute but steam and water are relative. The internal culture gives love, peace, joy, truth, nonviolence, universality, selflessness, enthusiasm, self confidence, forethought, self discipline and self control.

Evolution is the core essence of living life at physical, mental and spiritual level. One grows from infancy to youth to old age as a process and phenomenon of nature. Mental growth (development) is actualized through learning, information, knowledge and experience (physical-material) and spiritual. Evolution is possible by attaining and enriching consciousness through pure, empty and clear mind. Physical growth is natural, mental growth is doing and effort and spiritual evolvement is a happening, which happens by itself and needs no cultivation, practice and effort.

Digestion, breathing, circulation of blood, heart beating all are happenings and need no effort from you. Mental growth stops if there is no striving and struggle in life. It is true that you cannot shape life because it is formless and unpredictable. But you can endeavour to shape your career which is limited to your doing, training, effort and practice. You remain unaware of the result which happen at its own. That is why it is said that doing is in your hand but happening is in God's hand.

Strive without seeking and struggle without greed is the way to live life joyfully. Learn from nature about living life harmoniously. In nature things are opposite but never in opposition. They do not disturb and interfere in each other's affairs nor they compete, compare and have any instinct of inferiority complex as we have. They live by themselves with no purpose to neither impress anyone nor get impressed by others as we do.

One dies as one lives. One who lives a happy life shall die a happy death. It is not important what to live but important is how to live a balanced life. While dealing with the world outside use logic and reason, but to evolve spiritually then enrich consciousness. The aim of inner growth is to extract virtues of love, pure feeling, concern, cooperation, compassion, understanding, sacrifice, selflessness.

Spirituality does not mean that you disown life. It means living life with universal brotherhood, uniting with all that exists and lives. The goal of living life is to evolve to eternity. We do not expect everyone to attain divinity because if that happens then world cannot function with divine oneness where only silence prevails. For the world to function existence of duality (positive-negative, male-female, self-nonself) is essential. If that does not happen then the process of nature of creation, preservation and destructions stops. With that no manifestation can happen.

Negative-positive is in relation to the purity of your mind. Once you drop mind and transcend it, negative-positive, and good-bad dissolve. If you want to put a stop to the process of alternating good and bad, it is better you grow spiritually and become universal and go beyond duality.

It does not matter whether you attain salvation (eternity) or not, what is important in this world is to live a peaceful and harmonious life. It is understandable that everyone cannot discover his pure being (eternity) and attain salvation. This is neither desirable nor possible. However at the same time no one stops you living life honestly, truthfully with self-confidence, self-discipline, self-control, enthusiasm and understanding, reflecting, sharing, giving and satisfying attitude. You should not hurt and cheat anyone and listen to others point of view with great patience and tolerance, you may find something positive in what others talk and say.

You may not attain salvation but you can certainly transform your human behavior to spiritual behavior. When your human behaviour is transformed then your outlook of living life changes. Consequently you feed before you eat, you produce to distribute, and you give before you take. You can feed before you eat reflects selfless and sacrificing attitude. You produce to distribute reflects sharing temperament. You give before you take means serving others first before serving yourself. This should be an attitude in your life.

You should understand that self (atma) remains unaffected by actions of the body and mind. Everything is sustained on this earth by the sun but the sun is not affected by whatever happens on the earth. Self regard and self respect are foundation to character building. It reflects becoming self conscious, realizing that same self (awareness-atma light) flows through everyone as such all are divine and be regarded and respected as such. It also means dissolving of all distinctions. When reality is translated into seen world, then living life becomes joyful and peaceful. Two important aspects must be kept in mind to live an undisturbed life. One is realizing the falsity of sensuous things and the other is experiencing the reality of your being.

When you become self conscious you go beyond pain and suffering, as mind drops. When you identify pain with mind the suffering is experienced otherwise there is no suffering. When you attain super consciousness then you do not experience pain and suffering because mind's interference stops, with that the sorrow and misery also dissolve. In super consciousness you remain aware throughout about your supreme nature but in unconsciousness you remain ignorant throughout of the reality and become mind oriented.

Life can be lived in three ways. One is living life as human being, second is living life with spirituality and third living life through divinity (Godliness). When you are in the world as human being use reason and logic, be discriminative about right actions and discard wrong actions which bind and cause suffering and sorrow. Right actions take you closer to yourself (atma).

With spirituality you live life with unity and harmony. Divinity (godliness) is beyond both physical and spiritual, merging with your true being. On attaining that silence and salvation happens, mind becomes nonwavering. You become total light of awareness. That state is whole, total, complete and perfect. You become desireless, fearless and always remain blissful. On attaining that state you jump out of the cycle of birth and death, the concept Hindus follow.

Disturbance is to the body and mind and not to the soul. There is nothing wrong in the actions of the body and the mind. Wrong is with your attitude and outlook. Self (light-atma) reflects inaction and body and mind reflects action. The best way to deal with action is to become a total witness without participation. Let actions come and go, you just watch, actions will subside. Actions disturb you when you are involved and take interest in them. When you do not participate, then actions do not make you restless.

When you become self aware and self conscious, you can never do wrong actions. Self is beyond right and wrong, sin and virtue. Right-wrong, sin-virtue are applicable to worldly living (physical). The world is governed by conditioned mind, hence we aspire, strive, seek, imagine, remember, search, accumulate, grab, lose and then cry. It happens because of personal and selfish attitude.

It is up to you as what life you want to live, life of enjoyment or life of joy, peace and love. Enjoyment is temporary it is obtained through sensuous things which originate in impure mind. Joyful living happens when you become self aware. Joy is an eternal thing beyond mind. With mind bondage is experienced and with the self, life of liberation and ecstasy happens.

Saintly persons neither torture their body nor pamper it and accept life as it comes whether it brings glory or defeat, success or failure. They avoid attachment and obsession. Their mind remains non wavering (cool, silent, steady and stable) in the face of torture, sickness and death. They understand that such things happen to body and mind and not to the real nature of self (atma). For living a balanced life you must surrender to your soul, which has total power to salvage you from worldly suffering and sorrows. All sufferings are created through mind which contains unending flow of impure thoughts.

Love, peace, joy and harmony is the message of soul for living life with wisdom, self confidence and enthusiasm. Wickedness, cheating, hurting, violence, killing, disturbance, torture, chaos, conflict, confusion and contradiction result when you remain mind oriented. It is up to you, what kind of life you want to live – trouble free or trouble packed.

Your conduct should be spiritually pure with love for all and selfless service for benefit of humanity. Your actions should be fair and just intellectually with logic and reason. You should be nonhurting and compassionate to the problem of others while living in the outer world. You should follow the customs and traditions which are free of blind faith.

A spiritually mature person does not take long journeys on foot to visit places of pilgrimage and nor does he tortures his body by forced hunger (fasting) and spending sleepless nights for attaining spirituality. All this is false sense of austerity and is meaningless. The real austerity (tapa) is attained through, purification and emptiness of mind which you can achieve, sitting at home by becoming a witness to all that happens around you. When you do that, then events stop disturbing you because you remain detached, noninvolved and unconcerned.

Enlightened souls prefer a simple and natural living and feel fully contended with minimum needs because they attain desirelessness, thoughtlessness by making their mind empty and clear. Bounded soul is man and free soul is God. What is known through love is true knowledge because love comes through heart center (universal consciousness) and heart is a link between matter (body) and soul (navel center-life center). To reach the truth (supreme soul) you have to first attain pure consciousness (universal love) to discover your true nature of pure being (truth) and there ends the search of all worldly knowledge.

The truth and the supreme knowledge is the knowledge of the pure being (supreme God - self). What is done through love is true service because doing through love is selfless and impersonal with a sharing and sacrificing attitude. The right living is which takes you closer to your soul, through enriching of your consciousness, which makes you master of your mind.

Our inner self and outer self must live in harmony to avoid contradictory behaviour and split personality of confusion and chaos. Outer must be controlled by inner purity so that the impurities of the outer are dissolved. The burdened and stuffed mind creates opaqueness and does not let the inner purity (light of awareness) travel to the outer mind, which gives rise to ignorance and delusion.

Action is the tool in the hand of God to reward and rebuke you. This is done through your mind. Pure mind reflects reward and impure mind invites punishment, it means everything revolves around mind so better we concentrate and sincerely and honestly endeavour to keep our mind empty and clear like a mirror which reflects all without staining itself. Mind is like the steps of a house which are used for both moving in and out of the house. Mind is equally used for entering into the inner world (pure mind), also the mind is used for survival in the outer world (conscious mind).

Man suffers for his own doings because his mind always remains in a state of impurity, desiring endlessly something or the other every time. Desire disturbs our inner peace and silence, so we have to attain a desire free mind for living life peacefully. Mind means disturbance and activity whereas self (atma) means peace and silence. Your aim of life should be to sacrifice the imperfect, false and unreal to perfect, true and real for a living life happily. It also reflects transformation of impure and disturbed mind to pure and nonwavering mind.

For living life peacefully actions have to be righteous. Right actions lead to joy and wrong actions brings sorrow and misery. The tide of fortune of good phase comes to one and all in life but only man with 'wisdom' turns this phase in his favour where as the ignorant remains unaware about it and lets the opportunity slip out of his hand and repents with tearless weeping. When the tide of bad phase comes, wise man accepts it as a part of life and remains cool, calm and steady without making any noise, cribbing, commenting, crying and criticizing. He realizes and remains aware that nature of manifestation is such where good and bad alternate endlessly.

The ignorant not being aware of the fact of reality breaks down and curses everybody for his suffering, not realizing and understanding that the suffering is his own creation and none else is to be blamed. Incomplete actions ruin success, house without roof and crop without harvest are incomplete actions which turn success into failure.

In saintly living devotional thought is essential, in human living pure thought is essential, in divine living thoughtlessness is essential. In devotional love deep feeling of oneness happens between the devotee and the deity where ego is totally surrendered. The feeling of oneness dissolves all other thoughts. Pure thought means, pure motive and intention to do an act for good of all with selfless service and attitude. Thoughtless is essential to attain godliness (divinity) through empty and clear mind.

You cannot control your mind through grit and determination like you cannot bridge a flooded river, with determination and hard work. The best way to control the mind is to become a witness to the events of mind and avoid identification with them, by this thought will gradually subside. Without thought mind remains peaceful, steady and under control.

Toiling and torturing to the utmost is neither hard nor a sacred work because it is physical. Anything that is physical remains at surface and cannot go deep down to attain spirituality. Physical cannot become sacred because physical remains selfish and personal but to be sacred you have to be universal with selfless and impersonal attitude beyond duality. Hard work means dedicated, concentrated work with single mindedness to achieve and produce results for the benefit of the humanity and also for your better living of life.

There is no point of talking tall about hidden gold wealth under earth unless that is extracted through effort and hard work for the benefit of humanity. Likewise talking about ethical and moral life is of no use unless you live that way and reflect these values in your conduct and behaviour. We generally follow blindly what majority of people do. This is a deep rooted habit of rut which cannot be leveled easily. In the name of wrong customs and traditions many things are done which bring uneasiness in living life. The false traditions and customs break the universal unity and brotherhood of love. Infact everything is in your hand either to make life blissful or make it miserable.

Running away from responsibilities is immaturity and cowardly and reflects weak mind. All are punished equally by nature for wrong doings because nature is just and fair to all. But you notice your pinch of punishment more, not realizing the harder pinch others experience. We cannot control actions of others but we can certainly control our actions and reactions by maintaining right attitude and outlook.

Life becomes what you think, one can attain good life through noble thoughts or can ruin oneself through evil thoughts. Man's great advantage is that he can choose between heaven and hell. It means he can either continue with miseries and chaos of life or go beyond sorrow and suffering. Life has no purpose except to be. It is so, it is as such. Purpose happens for things of utility like car has utility so has the house. We see purpose in everything through our mind because mind always thinks in term of benefit and reward. Things seen through mind remain partial, for totality and whole seeing surrender to your being (self) to experience the reality. Mind experiences falsity of the world

You should see same consciousness flowing through everything as such your emphasis should focus on consciousness and not on outer structure and appearance of things. When contact between consciousness of the seer and the seen is established then unity happens.

Morality exists with distinction because morality is the product of society. Each society has its own standard of morality which keeps changing from time to time. However true religion is beyond morality because their remains no distinction of polar opposites (sin-virtue, negative-positive).

One becomes deathless (formless) when one grows and evolves. Deathless does not mean that body does not die, body's fate is to die so it dies. Deathless means you attain your true nature (supreme) which is eternal and never dies. Deathlessness means dropping of mind and merging with eternity. You cease caring for body and mind and remain unaffected by their happenings. Deathlessness reflects that soul is eternal but body and mind have death as their fate. You become formless means you focus your concentration to the formless self (atma). What death do you expect to space? It is either bound or free. When space is bound by a pot it becomes a bounded space of a pot but when the pot breaks the bounded space merges with the universal space.

Man has three categories one is intellectual, governed by mind. The second is emotional which is governed by heart and third is man of action who strives and struggle in life. Intellectuals have love for knowledge both worldly and divine. Scientists have love for worldly knowledge of the universe. They use logic and reason for their knowledge. Divine knowledge is the supreme knowledge of your own self (pure being), all worldly knowledge ends there. Great souls like Christ, Buddha, Mahavira had attained this knowledge. Emotional types are governed by love and feeling like 'Meera'-'Chaitanya'. Such people have love for devotion, art, music, dance and poetry. If love does not grow to spirituality (universality) then it remains physical and pervert. The third type of person is one who remains positively active for general good of all like 'Mahatma Gandhi'. Those who are negatively active involve in destruction of humanity and become like 'Hitler'.

Live life with body and soul working in harmony with complete coordination and perfect tuning. Body and soul are two wings of life. All four combined (body-soul-pran-chetna) actualize and sustain life. If you lose contact with soul, you remain spiritually empty and when you lose contact with the body and mind, you remain materially, economically backward and poor. Outer chaos is reflection of inner disharmony and disturbance.

Right living is total living in the present actuality without being influenced by past and future. Right living with totality also means total involvement in work in hand with complete concentration so that no other thoughts disturb you while committed to the work in hand. You can try this while walking, exercising, bathing, eating, sleeping, playing, reading, writing, seeing, listening, feeling, working. All actions can be made into whole action dissolving partial action which separates and divides from the supreme self (whole). Whole is holy because it brings peace, love and joy and part is hell because it brings chaos, misery and suffering

You cannot change anyone. You can only change your attitude and outlook. You will experience polar opposites while living physical life governed by conscious mind (outer impure mind). Polar opposites (duality) dissolve on knowing and experiencing your true nature (pure being). On attaining your pure being, habitual, mechanical and unconscious living (animalistic living) stops.

Inner world is known through meditation and witnessing. Outer world is known through love without distinction which happens on attaining spirituality. To dissolve ego you need effort but to know your true being only self awareness and witnessing are required.

Life's problems are solved by living life and not by thinking and feeling. Animals live with instincts and not through awareness, because they are born with actuality as programmed by nature. They do not have potential and possibility to grow as man has. Man is born with essence and he has to actualize his essence through self knowing, self surrender and selfless service.

In fact man is less of nature and more of culture because man ignores living life according to the temperament that he receives from nature and prefers to live life as cultured by parents, family, society, education, learning. This type of living is hypocrite and contradictory living. Do not choose life between good and bad, sin and virtue. Accept life with both aspects (positive-negative). You have no choice to choose between breathing in and breathing out you have to accept both for living life. If you choose either of these, death is instant.

For living life, acceptance and contentment are two cardinal points which lead you to your inner self. Acceptance means, live life as it comes instead of choosing between polar opposites. Once you choose, your mind wavers which disturbs the silence of acceptance. Right acceptance and contentment is when you stop choosing. Contentment reflects desirelessness which happens when you attain non-wavering mind.

Material growth can give you bigger house and make you rich economically but it cannot give you bigger soul and make you spiritually rich. Evolution of consciousness makes you detached (renounce) free, selfless and impersonal with deep love for humanity. If you find contentment in the beginning, then the end will also bear the contentment.

We talk of contentment but we continue living in discontentment. Our mind talks of spirituality but our heart sings the song of materialism. We are dishonest, irreligious and confused. We suffer because of this combination between false and imagined contentment and real discontentment that we face in life. Effort is needed only when you try for something which you are not.

You need not follow copy and imitate but be what your destiny wants you to be. If the whole wills to be through you then be that way and do not try to be anything else. If the whole wills through you as a rose flower then be that and do not try to become a lotus flower. You can have the whole world without having any soul within, it means non evolvement and non actualization of essence which amounts to not having soul.

You can just be a beggar but still you can have your soul alive and evolved from within to provide you bliss, peace, silence with non wavering mind. Growth of your being is important than anything else. Soul evolvement is essential for happy living, rest all is meaningless. Inner growth cannot be nullified by death, rest all is snatched by death. Outer growth is discontentment and inner growth is contentment because inner growth is a way to reach eternity where everything is dissolved. Achieve something which transcends death, only then you are growing towards your being which is deathless.

Contentment comes through inner self and consolation reflects your ego self. You are poor and you console yourself by declaring that – "I am destined to be so", this is not contentment but consoling yourself to pass time and remain dishonestly and falsely happy temporarily. The whole is with you, within you, you are not a part which separates. You have to realize and understand this that everything is whole and you belong to the organic whole. It is mind which separates and divides.

Total contentment is wisdom which reflects governance through divine self, wisdom is egolessness. Believing in soul and not experiencing is to deceive yourself. Contentment is nondesiring, it is attained through desirelessness, when you are filled with desires discontentment continues, causing contradictory living. Life must be lived spiritually so that peace, love, harmony and understanding are sustained.

There is deep meaning and inner significance of dispersion of mud idols in water. We see it happening traditionally in Hindu religion as rituals. It symbolizes desirelessness, detachment (renouncing) from temporary existence of worldly things. Hindus make mud idols of goddess 'Durga' and God 'Ganesha', worship for specific period of time and disperse them at the end of period preferable in water which signifies pran (vital breath). Dispersion means to uncreate. First create the image and then un-create signifying death of false and unreal existence (desires). God creates world, preserves it and ultimately destroys it. So man creates images, preserve it for some time and then un-create through dispersion. Creation is caused by desire and non-creation reflects desirelessness and non-desiring is contentment.

Buddha says non-desiring is 'nirvan', salvation and total contentment. Attachment bondage is product of desire. You must live your life with total contentment. Dispersed things move back to the source of their element. Three things are important to live a balanced and harmonious life, one is learning to remove ignorance, second is learning but not clinging to it. If you cling to learning you become knowledgeable, but you remain unwise. Third is when you unlearn and empty your mind you become wise because consciousness becomes free of contents. The child is ignorant and the sage is wise. The child has yet to know and the sage has gone beyond knowing. Clinging is bondage, nonclinging is freedom. Living life is to transform from unconscious to conscious and then to super conscious, (ignorance-knowledge-wisdom).

CHAPTER 13

Change of Mindset

General Aspects of Transformation

Man is absolutely free either to actualize his divine essence of divinity or fall below to live an animalistic life. Transformation is his choice, one cannot force. It is not caused or cultivated by anything. It depends entirely on his earnestness. It is a natural happening which reflects freedom and liberation of the self from ego.

Science is a product of causation, where cause may be known or not known but divine self for certain is uncaused. Causation reflects the world whereas beyond it, the eternity is unknown and uncaused. Things which are caused bear the 'why' factor as it happens with science. You cannot cause man to be something.

You have choice to look at the world in a spiritual way or in a materialistic way. Spirituality exists in eternity not in time. You can become spiritual any moment any time. You can attain Buddhahood and Krishnahood in this life itself, provided you are willing and earnest. It may appear difficult but not impossible.

When you experience your inner self, transformation happens. Unless that is attained, total solution to the problems of the world is not possible. Whatever solutions that we find remain only partial and a patch work. They provide temporary relief for some time, but do not dissolve our sorrows and sufferings eternally.

We are habitual of accepting such partial solutions which bring more problems in future than the relief it provides. Mind set reflects fixed thinking, thought, concepts, ideas, doctrines, beliefs, ego that is cultivated through outer world. This is cultural aspect of mind set. The other aspect of mind set is natural attributes of harmony-passion-pervert (satva-rajas-tamas) that come to us through nature at the time of birth, as temperament (swabhava). These are natural and accidental beyond man's control. There is no possible way for man to analyze the process and happening of nature and reach definite solution and that is why it is called accidental.

When there are no definite answers to the happenings of the nature, it is called mysterious. We link all our present sufferings to actions of the past life which is not reality. Concentrate on transformation more than knowing about concepts and doctrines. Let concepts exist and die, you should not identify with them, these are of no help except burdening and loading your mind.

You need an empty and clear mind for changing your mind set (transformation). To believe or not to believe in concepts is a matter of realization and understanding which comes through wisdom. You should not base your living life on concepts but live life with reality and actuality which you can experience while living with the present. No one till date has attained Godhood based on concepts. Mind set can transform only by growing from within at your own. No one else can transform you, it is your own individual exercise.

Enriched consciousness neutralizes your habitual, mechanical and unconscious way of routine working. You become totally aware and enlightened to accept only reality and reject all that which comes through conditioned mind set which is always unreal and false. However if you are not attentive, alert and aware then things will happen habitually, hardening your mind set and psyche. Evilness from rigid psyche becomes difficult to dissolve.

Existence (physical living) without change of mind set is no better than animalistic living, where you lose sense of discrimination. Terror, rape, violence all are caused by man who has animalistic mentality. All this happens because he is spiritually empty inside and remains unaware about his Godly nature. However he can attain it, get absolved of all sins and evil mindedness. This chapter is exclusively dedicated to change of mind set (transform) from evilness to goodness, from physical to spiritual, from ego to egolessness, from nonself to self and from mind to no mind stage.

We all by and large live a habitual life and do not understand the value and importance of inner spiritual life. To be spiritual does not mean stopping worldly dealings and working or renouncing world to live an ascetic life. It only means extracting inner eternal virtues of selflessness, universal love, cooperation, compassion, sacrifice, self confidence, self discipline, self control etc. The eternal inner virtues in your behaviour and conduct outside make you a man of trust, goodwill, reputation and integrity. You become sensitive to problems of others with non-hurting and non-cheating attitude.

Physical problems of human nature (rape, violence, terror, murder, smuggling, robbery, theft etc) should be dealt with an iron hand because you cannot make people spiritual over night by imposed control and discipline. China has controlled social evilness through hard and strong actions. Physical control means installing fear of authority. Such strong measures may not eliminate evilness from the society completely but the situation will improve greatly.

Strong government which has the will can always improve the situation, these again are partial and temporary solution because at the end of strong government social evils crop up again. For total solution, individual mind set must change and unless that happens there will be no reduction of social evils. People can be made aware and awakened to improve individually. We have tendency to take pride in the glories achieved by our elders in different fields, not realizing that their glories have become a history. These can inspire but cannot transform you.

It is known fact and reality that all that exists and live is divine. Anything that originates from divine source has to be divine. From pure water source, pure water flows and it remains pure till it is contaminated by man due to his ignorance and stupidity. We must think, feel and realize that same divinity flows in all of us through consciousness. Now question comes up that when we all are divine and holy then why do we behave undivinely? It is because of the fact that divinity is corrupted by distortion and false imagination through our mind set. We believe that we are the body and mind, separate from the soul. It happens because our mind creates a separate nonself (ego) center at the surface which blocks our wisdom, and journey to our inner self (atma).

It is the opaqueness of our mind that pollutes divinity. Actually divinity cannot ever be polluted, it remains pure always regardless of any medium, it flows through. It is your diseased and sick mind which imagines and thinks that it has polluted divinity. Water remains water regardless of the container. It is contaminated only if the container contains sediments. It is not the divinity that becomes negative but it is the perception of mind that becomes negative and identifies things as such.

Negativeness of mind comes through both natural attributes and cultural cultivation by society and others. Once negativity of mind set is dissolved through empty, clear and pure mind you transcend duality of human nature and become divine, in your action. With mind you are devil and without mind you are divine. Divinity is best revealed when it is received as whole through pure mind without being conditioned by thought, feeling, desire and fear etc. Things of nature are beautiful, attractive and charming because these do not lose their wholeness of divinity, as they remain unpolluted by mind.

The blessing and grace of 'sat guru' (spiritual teacher) as self inside you comes only when you present yourself to him with empty and egoless mind. The divine message of Krishna, Christ and Buddha is for all to transform and not for selected few. But only those transform who are willing and earnest.

Changing of mind set entails, going beyond mind, making mind empty, clear and transparent free from all negativities. It means without identifying with negativities. No transformation can happen without this. Body and mind which has form and are limited cannot take you to the formless and limitless reality.

The process of change of mind set remains hidden and unknown till you reflect change outside in your action, attitude and outlook. You must know that internal happenings remain unseen until matured and appear outside in your conduct and behaviour. Spouting of seed remains hidden till it comes out of earth as a plant, but internal process continues.

Transformation of mind set should be gradual and natural. Sudden and instant transformation is like an explosion which you cannot withstand, you may collapse and die. Instant is preceded by long preparation, fruit falls suddenly but ripening takes time. You cannot extract a flower from a plant prematurely because flower comes out of a plant gradually and naturally as programmed by nature. In the same way do not rush to reach the ultimate, let it happen gradually in a natural way, for which you just accept life and keep flowing with it as explained.

Transformation Infact is death of ego. Death is a process of growth as seed dies before it sprouts. Transformation is a happening and it happens naturally without effort, when mind becomes pure. Transformation is inner phenomenon and change is an outer phenomenon which is attained through effort.

A thief can become a monk, a criminal can become a saint. This is only an outer change to appear different than what is actually hidden inside. This happens to be a physical change externally without change of heart and soul. As such one experiences polar opposites (sinner and saint) till one attains divinity through total transformation.

Energy is neutral, you can direct and transform energy of consciousness towards any stream, positive or negative. Negativity reflects indulgence and suppression in which energy gets wasted, as such you should avoid both. The best way is to recycle energy to its source, through witnessing so that it is not wasted and is used for transformation of mind set. Recycling means you attain pure consciousness. With that impure mind set subsides. Real transformation is when your mind becomes innocent and non-wavering reflecting purity inside and outside. Mind set means keeping balance and harmony between negative and positive.

Science can give you moon and planets through intellect but it cannot give you spiritual wisdom of universal brotherhood and compassion to change your mind set. Like outer polar opposites there are inner polar opposites also known as feminine and masculine (sun and moon). Sun remains hot at periphery and cool at the center, moon is hot in the center and cool on the periphery. This is a natural phenomenon. Feminine does not reflect mind of a woman but it is a state of mind (nature, tendency and attitude) which can belong to man as well, it means the inner nature of human being which could be possessed by either of these. Feminine mind is cool, stable and passive outside but hot inside reflecting instability and activeness. Masculine mind is hot outside and cool inside. There are examples in the history about women who had masculine mind and ruled their country with iron hand. Queen Victoria, Margaret Thatcher, Golda Meir and Indira Gandhi are examples of such woman. When you attain divinity, masculine and feminine dissolves then you are governed totally by your divine nature.

Techniques

Now we will deal with various ways to drop mind (going beyond mind) to make it empty and clear of thought, desire-fear (pleasure and pain), memory, imagination, concept, idea, attachment, craving, social culturing and conditioning). There are over hundred techniques to make mind pure, but we will deal with a selected few. You can choose any one technique that suits your temperament and nature.

You must practice the selected technique at least for forty five minutes daily for a period of six to eight weeks. Initially, do not do it for forty five minutes at a stretch but improve the timings gradually so that it becomes easy and comfortable. The essence of all techniques is aimed at reducing of thoughts which disturb mind and make you restless. Different techniques are given as under:-

Witnessing

Witnessing is mother of all techniques and it is the best technique for centering to your being. Centering is the authentic way to exist with the reality because centering entails pure action. Activity on the periphery (surface) reflects reaction and not action, which you do in response to something done to you. Somebody insults you and you promptly respond by your reaction. Once you are centered, you do not react because you realize that reaction happens through false center (peripheral body) and not through your real self which is abode of peace, love and silence. Insult and abuse touches the periphery (body) and not the center (self).

Action comes from you and reaction is forced upon you. Reaction contains duality but action is cosmic and beyond distinction. When you begin to act from the center, every act becomes total and atomic. When you see a flower you say 'it is beautiful', you have imposed your opinion on the flower, distorting the originality and virginity of the flower. You have corrupted the fact by your judgment thereby breaking the link with your soul through witnessing. Your opinion about flower is based on past learning and experience.

Anything which is past is dead and not alive. Thinking means bringing your past to the present, witnessing means no past just the present. Cessation of thinking is witnessing. Be non thinking in all your activities, so that you remain linked to your soul through your witnessing. Every act becomes total if you are nonthinking, this is necessary for inner evolvement. In witnessing there is no sense of 'I' but in thinking, the sense of 'I' persists. More thought, more ego. Witnessing means egolessness. Witnessing is state of no mind no thinking.

The world of reality is reached through witnessing. Witnessing is indivisive because it is the direct reflection of the divinity. You can have different thoughts through which you are categorize into Hindu, Muslims and Christians etc but you cannot have Christian soul, Hindu soul and Muslim soul separately because witnessing reflects oneness and universality but thoughts are many and different which divides whole witnessing into parts. Witnessing is a technique which is simple, easy and practical to follow. It is culmination of meditation, and direct reflection of awareness through pure consciousness, free of contents.

In witnessing you watch things without participation, opinion, judgment, likes and dislikes. You do not condition and localize them. True, total and complete seeing, listening, doing, working, serving, thinking and feeling happen through whole witnessing. When you do whole witnessing thoughts automatically subside, nourishment to them stops as there is no participation and interest to sustain them, and consequently thoughts dissolve. When thoughts subside mind becomes empty, clear and pure for higher spiritual growth.

With whole and total witnessing thoughts do not find space to play. You should bring all your activities (breathing, walking, bathing, eating, playing, working, travelling, meeting etc) under the domain of pure witnessing so that your activities become total and productive and a direct link is reflected with the self (atma) which will lead you to the supreme self (aram atma), your true nature (pure being).

Pure witnessing does not mean that you stop working but it means to work freely with pure and open mind, free of conscious mind which binds and conditions the whole into part. Let witnessing happen in a natural way effortlessly without thinking and feeling. Thoughts and feelings are required while dealing with the world but these become meaningless for inner virtues of spiritual growth. Use logic and reason while you are with the world but be with yourself (atma) for inner evolvement.

When you become self (atma) conscious, the eternal virtues of love, peace, joy selflessness, sharing, sacrifice, self discipline and control will be reflected in all your actions including logic and reason which will have touch of reality, truth and purity.

When you pass through a crowded street you witness all that passes by without involvement and identification, continuing your journey without interference and disturbance. Witnessing should be total and complete and not partial and fractured. Fractured witnessing is partial and is a conditioned witnessing, which blocks the light of reflection of the self (atma), consequently nonself is created by the conscious mind opposite to self (atma), causing duality between real (self) and unreal (nonself).

Infact, witnessing is the master key to open the door of wisdom and understanding. Witnessing is a method of centering on work in hand so that other thoughts are avoided, resulting into strong relationship between the work and the self, only then work becomes worship. In centering there is direct reflection of the light of the self. It makes thoughts and feelings noble and pure because light of self burns the impurities of the mind. Witnessing operates only in the present because present reflects the reality (self), past and future (memory-imagination) reflect conscious mind. Present actuality is spaceless because the whole space is filled by the light of the soul, beyond time and space.

In the absence of witnessing your mind set cannot be transformed. Meditation is the process and witnessing is the goal. The crunch of the whole thing is that you be a witness every moment to a wandering mind to dissolve its impurities

Meditation

The word 'Aum' is a significant sound symbol as a secret key. Aum has five steps. The first three steps (AUM) are gross. The fourth is half step which happens when we utter 'aum' and in the end lingering resound of mmm is experienced only when you are alert and aware. The fifth step of resound is just never heard. The fifth is soundlessness, this happens when vibration of sound 'aum' disappears in the infinite cosmic space.

These five steps indicate many things. Human consciousness has five steps. Waking, dream and deep sleep are gross, it reflects 'aum' ('a' for waking 'u' for dream and 'm' for deep sleep). The fourth step is turiya (pure consciousness) reflecting witnessing. The fifth step is when witnessing dissolves transcending consciousness and reaching the source. The 'aum' is a cosmic sign symbol. The symbol reflects soundlessness of the source which is attained when you are silent, thoughtless, desireless and without feeling. When you reach the source (being) the soundlessness you experience, resembles 'aum'.

Sound and electricity are convertible. Science says electricity is the basic for manifestation. Religion say all is through sound which is based on soundless source (being) and that sound is 'aum'. One should not mistake symbol for the real. 'AUM' is a symbol of something (source) it resembles. A photograph can resemble but that is not real. You should not stop at the symbol but go beyond through it to the source of soundlessness.

First create the sound of 'aum' in yourself through mind. Next step is to use the sound of 'aum' inwardly. Then even stop that to let the sound echo itself without distortion, in an original and natural way without effort. Lastly drop the feeling of 'aum' as well which was a barrier to reach the source. The 'aum' is a method to drop into the oceanic (source). The meditation is a constant contemplation of 'That' (whole). The 'I' and 'Thou' should not become barrier. If you can remember 'That' (real world) continuously, then you are in meditation.

Whenever you are with things and persons, remember 'That'. Never see the limited feel the unlimited. Never see form, look deep and see the formless in it. Never see any person superficially through his personality (outer-bearing). Penetrate deep and feel which goes beyond to the governing unifying power of total reality. The contemplation should be with awareness avoiding routine, habit and mechanical remembrance that may lead to sleep and make you unconscious (ignorant) about your source.

If you can constantly contemplate 'That' in everything, in all events with awareness, then consciousness expands. The expansion of consciousness is true meditation, which makes you thoughtless that leads you to silence. Whatever you do, do it totally as if divine has willed to do through you. The doing with totality becomes meditation. Do not touch a thing without feeling 'That', do not love anyone without feeling 'That'. Do not impose, just be a witness with awareness of 'That'. Silence is meditation. Silence comes when mind dissolves. Physical and outer silence which is cultivated and forced is superficial silence. Real silence comes through inner awareness.

Sound becomes noise when you do not like but it becomes music when you like it. Noise and music belong to outer sound, soundless sound is inner sound of the eternal source. Sound is outside, silence is inside. We are identified with our possessions, thoughts, ideas, concepts, emotion and many other things except our own being. Noise, conflict, anguish and tension are product of identification.

Your (being) is silence and everything else is sound, you are the temple and your divine self is the God inside you, reaching that you attain silence. Silence is achieved through understanding your mind. Do not leave the world but leave the mind because mind is the world when you identify with the mind. Meditation is antidote to mind. You stop thinking, mind will evaporate. Withdraw cooperation with mind it will dissolve. Accept the existence of mind, be aware of it and live in this world from your center of the being which you reach through meditation.

Remain in the center and do not be bothered about the activities, on the periphery. You are the center (soul) and not the surface (body). If you attain the inner silence, the inner center and you lose the whole world, even then it is worth attaining. Body reflects space and mind reflects time Movement of mind (inner space) stops through meditation.

There is no movement in the present as it reflects reality where only stillness prevails. Live in the present through meditation to attain stillness. Mind moves in past and future due to desire. Kill desire through meditation, to make mind nonwavering. With meditation silence comes against sound, stillness comes against movement and nonbeing (egolessness) comes against ego.

The mind which lives in meditation transforms all work into play. It is work which exhausts you not the play. If you do work with playful attitude, work becomes worship because attitude of play is meditative, subsiding thoughts. Meditation helps in transformation of mind set from bondage to freedom, as it is a process of subsiding thoughts. Thereby making mind empty and clear.

Meditation is an earlier stage and witnessing the final. Meditation is initially practiced as a discipline on fixed hours in the morning and evening and later it becomes a happening to witness every moment. When you mature in meditation, the fixed hour meditation dissolves and witnessing happens. Meditation is an act of attention to one thought so that other thoughts find no place in the mind.

You can meditate on one noble thought that you are the supreme. Be aware of this thought during your meditation. You can also meditate on gap between two breaths or meditate on sound symbol of 'AUM'. One who is not aware of the reality can meditate on an imagined deity of one's choice but remember one thing, be totally meditative to the thought you choose. The best way of meditation is to watch the flow of thoughts without involving yourself with the thoughts, gradually thoughts will subside. When thoughts subside then you can choose one single thought to meditate on.

You can choose any way of meditation that suits your temperament and nature. The whole concentration should be aimed at reducing the thoughts from the mind to make it empty and clear for spiritual growth. When mind becomes quiet through meditation, witnessing happens. Meditation is the only way to stop disturbances and restlessness of the mind and make it quiet.

The cause of disturbance is the multiple thoughts. One should not aim at achieving or seeking results in meditations. Let things happen naturally without imagining achievement. Aiming to achieve in meditation, disturbs meditation as achieving makes you bound and conditioned. Shift your attention from achievement to meditation.

In meditation be a spectator not an actor. Through meditation consciousness becomes pure which can lead you to eternity or salvation (nirvana). Knowledge of the supreme self comes through meditation. The best time to meditate is in the morning and the evening because you remain least agitated at these timings. In the morning you remain cool before you start your days work and again you are at peace in the evening when you come back home after day's hard work.

However, if your mind is matured and steady, you may do meditation any time. Every moment is auspicious, it is your mind which imagines inauspiciousness at its own. Meditation is like your breathing, it should continue in all your doings. When you mature in meditation, make all your doings meditative giving full attention to the work in hand, dissolving all other thoughts.

Meditation is inner breathing, whereas outer breathing is physical breathing. You cannot miss your breathing for a moment likewise you should not miss meditation for a moment. It only means whatever you do, it must be done meditatively with total attention. You can enter meditation from anywhere. A poet through poetry, painter through painting, singer through singing, dancer through dancing, worker through working, professional through his profession, actor through acting and so on. All can succeed in their respective fields through meditation because they can project their interest meditatively with total attention, rejecting all other thoughts which may interfere or disturb.

As mentioned earlier Sufi mystic 'Kabir' entered meditation through weaving and got enlightened. He was deeply involved in weaving and that became meditation. 'Meera' entered meditation through dance, 'Christ through love and service, 'Mahavira' through nonviolence, 'Buddha' through silence, 'Mohammad' through brotherhood and simplicity (pure inside and outside). Meditation is a way to realize the presence of self through thoughtlessness. Meditation is doing initially but doing disappears in deep meditation.

Breathing

Yogic way of breathing improves health. It cannot transform your mind set because physical breathing remains away from inner depth of the spiritual aspect. Inner transformation is only possible when you breathe with awareness meditatively. When you breathe consciously your attention is focused on breathing, stopping other thoughts to enter and disturb. When breathing is done with total awareness, the other thoughts subside and mind becomes clear and empty for spiritual growth. In this technique watch the gap between two breaths. You will notice there is no breathing between gaps of two breathing.

Concentrate on these gaps while breathing in and breathing out. Two gaps are created, one when breath turns for outward journey and the other when breath turns for inward journey. The gap is silence, emptiness, void, nothingness, self, reality, truth, present existence and stillness and salvation.

Navel center is the life center, (center of self). To activate this center deep and slow breathing touching the navel center must happen. While doing this be aware and be a witness to dropping, thinking (mind center) and feeling (heart center) and transcending to navel center (center of being). Navel center is beyond duality of thinking and feeling so to reach there, mind and heart have to be dropped to maintain purity and oneness of the self (pure being). Do not let techniques become habitual and mechanical.

You must breathe from abdomen and not from chest. A newly born child breaths from abdomen because it is innocent, pure and away from mind but closer to soul. Soul is located around navel center. You must have noticed that when child breathes his abdomen rises and falls reflecting breathing through the abdomen.

Vital breath (pran) is cosmic energy. Air is only vehicle to carry pran and is gross and physical. Pran (vital breath) is the real thing that vitalizes the body. You must understand that whichever technique you may choose to follow, you must do it for at least forty five minutes at a stretch and for a period of six to eight weeks. Do not jump to achieve the target of forty five minutes on the first day itself. Gradually you can increase the timings. Do not do meditation with grit and determination, it should be done naturally without aiming at achieving the target.

Awareness

The unconscious (ignorant) can only be transformed through awareness. For awareness you have to concentrate not on the cause outside but on the source inside. Science is more concerned with the cause and religion is more concerned with the source. Cause reflects environment outside and the source is connected with your own being. Use your own body as a device for awareness, when you walk, walk consciously, do all actions consciously.

Breathe consciously, be in and be out with the breath. Do not allow any breath to be in or out without consciousness. When you focus on breathing, thoughts stop automatically and you are then linked to your source (being). Continuous awareness of breathing will stop mind, dissolving anguish and anxiety.

'Mantra' is another way of awareness. Be aware fully while reciting a 'Mantra'. Do it without thinking and feeling. Don't try to understand 'Mantra' intellectually, it should not be done in a mechanical manner otherwise it will induce sleep. Be aware every moment of 'Mantra' and make a circle of energy by becoming speaker and listener through witnessing and awakeness. When you recite a mantra you remain on the periphery but when you listen to the sound inside you get linked to the center through awareness.

When your surrender is total (conscious mind- ego is dissolved) you automatically become aware and attain super consciousness to win over darkness of unconsciousness. Awareness first throws you out of ignorance and later takes you beyond worldly knowledge to your being. Empty and clear mind is needed for knowing yourself and not a knowledgeable mind. We are aware of worldly things and surroundings very much but we remain unaware of our being. Awareness implies remembrance of the self. Whatever you do outside do it totally, continuously remembering your being inside. This process will help you in centering to your inner self. When you are totally centered you are exploded into the reality, completely transformed (you are enlightened), you become blissful and silent.

When this happens presence of your being is experienced in all your doings. Working through the false center of periphery (surface), you confront anger, greed and jealousy. But when you start working through your center (being-divine self) all your vices get dissolved and you become free and liberated.

There are two ways to become whole and perfect, one is to become totally unconscious (animalistic) and be governed by instincts which nature provides, and the other is to transcend unconsciousness through awareness. Becoming totally unconsciousness is not possible because whatever part of mind that becomes conscious remains with you as awareness for knowing worldly things through senses controlled by the conscious mind. You cannot move back totally to unconsciousness, you progress but you cannot regress.

If you live life knowingly (with awareness of your being) then you do not waste energy and time, and can attain your inner self in one life. If you move unknowingly (unconsciously) then you cannot reach your divine self even in million lives. Unknowingness reflects ignorance and unconsciousness. You have to bring awareness to every cell of the body, to your total being so that gap between conscious and unconscious is eliminated. Man cannot transform unless inner cells are changed through total awareness.

Some feel that without changing the chemical structure of the body nothing can be changed. When anger strikes you, some glands release chemicals into the blood which make you angry. If Buddha was silent, peaceful and did not show anger, it only means that such chemicals were lacking which created disturbance and anger. So the only need is to change chemicals, there is no need of meditation and there is no need of becoming more aware.

The above concept is dangerously negative, destructive and unnatural because it can destroy and dissipate the natural energy flow which maintains balance of hormones in the body. Body becomes diseased when hormones are disturbed. If you control hormones through artificial means you will become impotent, losing potency of sex energy which can be utilize for evolvement and growth to your being.

It is only when you are totally centered to your being, your consciousness awakens every cell of sex energy to become active for attaining divinity. Now sex cells cannot behave independently to flow through physical channel unless center orders them to act, they cannot act. They will remain inactive preserving their energy power. The center utilizes sex energy cells for divine growth. If the sex cells are not potensized through awareness then these work independently at physical level destroying the energy power. Emphasis of religion is always on transformation of consciousness, to create greater force of awareness inside, so that awareness can spread to every cell of the body. All cells get centered to your inner being from the outer periphery through awareness.

The physical body that is born dies one day but the enlightened body that you attain through awareness remains centered eternally. You must create an inner center of awareness through breathing method which Buddha advocated. It entails breathing in and out with awareness, and not breathing unconsciously and unknowingly. When you breathe consciously and knowingly with awareness, your mind drops and with that thoughts dissolve. This is called going beyond mind and moving to your inner self, with fully spread consciousness that penetrates every cell of your body, this happening is the real transformation from known to unknown.

Mahavira used hunger, fasting as a method of awareness. When the body is totally hungry, you remain knowingly conscious of hunger, a stage will come that you will automatically be centered.

But remain pure witness throughout to hunger without any thinking and feeling. Awareness has two aspects. One is to be aware of the false, discard and negate it without identifying. The second aspect is that you remain aware every moment that you are the supreme self (pure being) and then you remain unaffected by the happenings of the body and the mind, as you realize that you are not body and mind but beyond these.

Awareness has larger scope of application, it is universal. You remain aware of many things. While walking you hear various noises, sounds, see passerby and different kinds of vehicles. But do you identify yourself with these, certainly not. You only concentrate on your walking. Similarly, awareness is indivisible, it reveals but does not identify and without identification it cannot be conditioned, localized and fragmented. It is the reflection of the supreme self (atma).

Consciousness which originates from awareness when centered in the mind gets localized and becomes bondage. It is consciousness only which perceives and cognizes (knowing) things through mind. This means it has the nature of knowing, which is actualized through mind, but it is awareness which makes it possible by revealing things through its light. Dust particles are seen in the light of the sun, but the sun remains unaware of these. Awareness is our nature (soul) and witnessing is the process

Awakeness

Awakening is alertness and aliveness to control and save consciousness from being made localized and fragmented, by the mind which is continuously engaged in various activities like desiring, thinking, imagining, memorizing. Mind stops you from living in the present. The contamination of consciousness through mind divides and separates consciousness from the whole.

Consciousness is enriched when free of contents because the mind cannot then condition and localize consciousness.

With contents of thought, consciousness shrinks and loses its power and effect. Alertness and aliveness cautions us and stop thoughts which contaminate consciousness. Awakeness saves you from routine and habitual working through mind and keeps reminding us about our real nature of being. Awakening can stop minds wanderings because awakening can check and reject thoughts which are irrelevant and unnecessary. Alertness and aliveness bring you back to the present reality stopping you from living between past and future. The present reflects living with the soul (self).

Attention

In attention you give attention to one particular thing only. Attention is particular, awareness is universal, and as such it is thoughtlessness. When you become your being, dissolving all thoughts you attain oneness with your supreme self. Be attentive in all your doings. If you look at a flower attentively without any conditioning (thinking, feeling and opinion) then you will notice that after due course, flower will disappear and a direct link gets established between your consciousness and the reflected consciousness of the flower.

So see things as they are without expressing opinion, likes and dislikes. When you do so the whole seeing is actualized and then you come in direct contact with yourself (atma). The best way to attain attention is to shift your attention between the eye brows. Close your eyes focus both eyes in the middle of the two eye brows. Do not squint your focusing? Focus on the tip of your nose without staining your eyes. Do it in a natural and easy way to avoid headache. If you cannot manage then seek guidance from an expert.

Pay total attention to focusing and nothing else. Gradually thoughts will start subsiding, reflecting dropping of mind. The point between two eye brows is known as the point of wisdom (third eye). When you are centered in the third eye, the door of wisdom opens dropping human nature and attaining spiritual nature. The third eye is not physical but a subtle body part, which on opening does not see the other man's physical structure but only his soul. Seeing soul to soul is unity and seeing only outer body (form) is separation.

Reaching your Being (Life center)

If you become aware of your center, of the self (life center), then you realize actuality of life. Navel center is the center of your being, which reflects oneness beyond duality. When you encounter danger your thinking and feeling stop and you react intuitively. Like when you see a snake you react and jump away suddenly without thinking and feeling. Such physical reactions happen through conditioned thinking and feelings, which are unreal, unnatural, cultured and cultivated, breaking the contact with your being.

When you face danger you are thrown to your life center (navel center), transcending thinking and feeling. When you confront a tiger in a jungle some breakdown and collapse, some run away and some try to face the tiger. Those people who collapse and runaway seeing a tiger are those who take support of thinking and feeling conditioned by past experiences. Their reaction is unnatural and cultivated. Whereas the man who spontaneously at the spur of the moment, decides to fight out the tiger is not through coached psyche but a reaction which happens through your being.

Such things happen instantaneously, free of thinking and feeling and beyond cultivation. Cultivated response is physical and natural reaction is from your being. Navel center is touched in accidental happenings. The best way to touch your life center is through awareness and witnessing which establishes oneness with your being.

Concentration

Concentration means uninterrupted flow of focusing at one point, without thinking and feeling and without blinking your eyes. Period of concentration can be extended gradually from five to forty five minutes as per your ease and comfort. Select any point on a wall for concentration or put a bold dot on a wall and concentrate with eyes open, gradually the point of concentration will dissolve which means the mind which identifies the dot will drop. Without the mind the dot cannot be recognized and as such it becomes invisible or disappears, because contact of object is broken without the mind. When the mind drops then contact with your pure being is established. The aim of this technique is to transform mind from nonself (unreal) to the self (real).

Contemplation

Contemplation means directing your thinking to a particular thought and not a point. Scientists, philosophers, poets, painters, singers, dancers, sculptors and devotees contemplate on a single thought dedicatedly and devotionally, not allowing other thoughts to disturb when they are deeply contemplating. Similarly to make your contemplation divine, keep noble thought of your pure being (supreme self) in your contemplation every moment, so that no other thoughts find space to disturb you. Mind drops automatically opening way for you to reach your being.

Actualization

Actualization means to translate the possibility and potential inside you to grow and evolve for discovering your pure being. Animals are born actualized according to the programs set by nature. They have no possibility and potential to grow beyond their animalistic limit. However man is born with potential and possibility to grow but he has to actualize his essence of pure being by dropping mind. He cannot become divine automatically but has to earn and attain divinity.

Full man is better than a great man. Full man is complete, perfect and whole as divine being, who has actualized his essence of inner self. But great man is an outer phenomenon (physical) so he may be spiritually empty inside. I will like to be a full man than a great man. A great man is body and mind conscious but a full man is governed by his soul (pure being). You may lack talent to be a great man but you have all the potential to attain Buddhahood.

Developing Sense of Feeling

Heart center is base of love, feelings, emotions, surrender and faith. Mind center reflects reason and logic. Mind first looks for reason in love but heart sees love first. Mind thinks of past and future but heart exists in the present. Heart is a link between navel center and mind center. Heart center comparatively remains pure being closer to the soul (navel center), but it gets impure when identified with the happenings of the mind.

Things coming through heart have more appeal and impact. You may convince a man with logic and reason but you cannot convert a man. Transformation only happens through the change of heart. The best way of centering to your being (navel center) is to develop feelings in the heart without thinking.

When you have total feeling or whole feeling it reflects pure love transferring between person who sees and what is seen. When that happens, only seeing remains and seen is dissolved. Only pure love and feeling remains, object of love disappears. Whatever you do, just feel deeply (universally). Try this while seeing, hearing, reading, working, walking, playing, bathing, eating etc. Feeling by nature is spiritual, pure and universal but when conditioned and identified by mind, these become limited, physical and impure.

So drop mind completely, to attain universal feeling (pure consciousness). With pure feeling consciousness becomes the center point and not the physical form that appears outside.

Moving energy to the Source

The subtlest of the subtle is divine energy. Consciousness (spiritual) is super subtle energy, vital breath is 'pran' energy (subtle energy) and matter (physical energy), gross energy. In the present context, we will deal with energy of consciousness (chetna) because this is the basic energy through which the process of creations begins.

Once it is known everything will fall in line. Consciousness is a link between divine and physical. Moving energy to source means, keeping consciousness pure, free of contents and beyond duality and nonself (mind). Energy by nature is neutral, you can direct it in any direction, towards positive or towards negative.

Manifestation is actualized through the combination of both positive and negative energy. Without creation energy remains pure, positive and divine. Energy becomes negative when you identify energy with the happenings of the mind which creates nonself (ego).

Moving energy to the source also means moving it to the life center (navel center) of the soul (self). It automatically happens when consciousness becomes free of contents. So concentrate on keeping your consciousness pure always and every time. When it is used consciously with awareness without involving with the happenings of the mind, it becomes universal free of mind's bondage, it can then lead us to the divine source of energy.

To move the energy to the source we should neither suppress nor indulge, as both sap energy. Suppression is worst than indulgence because suppression needs more effort to suppress which eats away lot of energy. We suppress the flow of energy to look different then what we actually are. A dishonest man suppresses his dishonesty and acts as an honest man outside, he lives with a split personality. You wear false smile in front of your boss to please him but inside you may be burning and screaming against his behavior which has been annoying and hurting.

When you suppress energy it hangs between source and indulgence and keeps appearing. In suppression energy (consciousness) becomes polluted (negative). It gets engaged and localized in suppression. Indulgence is therefore better than suppression relatively, for physical existence because it creates inner complexities which is not so in indulgence. However both indulgence and suppression are damaging.

Will and Surrender

There are two paths to reach your being, one is surrendering and another is willing. Path of willingness aims at awakening your inner self through awareness that you are the soul and not the body. Path of surrender is concerned with ego, it entails forgetting that you are a separate entity of non self ego. The total and complete surrender reflects egolessness. When you surrender your ego, you are left with your pure and eternal self that means you are awakened into your inner self.

There are various ways to remain awakened about your being. 'Mahavira' used fasting as the device, to awaken his self. When body demands food, do nothing, don't think, don't feel, just witness totally that will awaken you to your inner self. Witnessing will create more awareness in yourself. The present life which we are living is a life full of sleep (ignorance).

Surrender is concerned with your ego and not with yourself. In surrender you have to give up your physical self (ego). Ego is not a part of your being and that is how it can be surrendered because that is your own creation. You can only surrender what belongs to you. You can surrender either to a spiritual teacher or to the divine God of your being because you need some medium to surrender to, you cannot surrender in a vacuum space. Surrender means being lost in something.

Yogi follows the path of 'Will', negating everything till he attains eternity. Devotee follows the path of surrender. In the path of 'Will' there is no God according to 'Mahvira' because on reaching your inner self you attain the status of God. Surrendering means, now I am not - now you are. Surrender is total trust.

Meditative Working

Meditative working means doing work with total concentration, devotion, dedication and complete involvement like meditation, avoiding all thoughts except the thought concerning your work. When other thoughts subside, mind becomes clear and empty. Try this in all your doings, in your whole day's working schedule (walking, playing, bathing etc). In meditation, you watch flow of thoughts without involvement and interest, mere watching thoughts subside. In meditative working you totally concentrate on single thought, concerning the work in hand, leaving no space for other thoughts to enter your mind.

Remember, you have to remain totally single minded while doing the work only then the work becomes meditative and productive. If you fragment your concentration and let consciousness move in different directions for local engagements then the working becomes seeking and selfish and not selfless. When meditative working is attained in your daily doings then it equals to meditation. If you follow this technique earnestly, you will very soon experience transformation from non self to self.

Pure Imagination

Imagination that we are talking about here is not the imagination that comes through conscious mind. It is the imagination which is beyond mind, spiritual and divine.

The real imagination is desirelessness and fearlessness. Imagination through mind ruins you and imagination beyond mind makes you discover your supreme nature (pure being). Imagination is an attitude and becomes reality. Imagine that you are running, and you will notice that deep breathing happens, you start perspiring, and your pulse rate also increases. Imaginative exercise equals to physical exercise but imagination must be real and deep. It should be total without conditioned thought and feeling.

It is pure energy which makes mind and body pure to move in the imagined direction for actualization. Impure mind generates impure imagination which retards your inner evolvement. Close eyes and imagine deeply that spiritual force, cosmic (pure consciousness) is present everywhere, within and without (inside-outside). When every cell of your body is potensized by deep feeling of spiritual presence everywhere then all distinctions disappear and the universe becomes an ocean of energy.

Dropping mind

Dropping mind is not a technique but a consequence of cumulative effort of all techniques. Mind automatically drops when you follow any one technique sincerely and honestly suiting your temperament (swabhava). Dropping of mind means, dissolving, the conscious mind (outer mind). This happens when mind is made empty and clear of thoughts. Thoughtlessness is the key to drop mind. Flow of thoughts does not stop at its own nor can they be stopped through grit and determination. You cannot bridge a river when in flood. The journey to spirituality cannot be actualized unless thoughts subside because you need a cool, steady, mature and pure mind for higher spiritual growth.

You need an empty and fasting mind and not a loaded and feasting mind. Burdening the mind with thoughts, concepts, ideas learning, information and knowledge be useful for earning and living life in the outer world but meaningless for inner growth.

All techniques are aimed at dropping mind (going beyond mind) so that your journey to spiritual attainment becomes smooth and loving. While dealing with the world you need conscious mind (logic and reason) for your existence and living life. Even when you attain spirituality thoughts persists according to minds nature but the only difference would be that you will cease caring for them by erasing memory and rejecting thoughts instantly without getting engaged and involved.

Dropping of mind also means disidentifying with the events that happen through the conscious mind (outer mind). This can happen when you realize through understanding the falsity of worldly things. Understanding comes through pure consciousness (spirituality). The other way is to be aware of your supreme self (true nature) and know that you are not body and mind but the pure being, as such you remain unaffected by events that affect and happen to body and mind.

Our true nature is pure being and not the nonself created by mind. So the nonself has to disappear for transformation to discover your own self. When you see world through mind you see ego, nonself, matter and physical aspects, but when you see world beyond mind you see your real nature (pure being) of divinity. When you see world through mind, you experience pain, suffering and sorrow and beyond mind you experience eternity, silence, salvation, joy, peace and love.

CHAPTER 14

Answers to Important Questions

Answers and questions originate within the doubting mind and beyond mind these end because we become one with the reality. In reality distinction and difference dissolves because you become perfect, complete and total. Mind being imperfect and limited will always have endless questions till it attains purity and stability. The purpose of making a separate chapter of questions and answers is to bring clarity and understanding to reader's mind which will facilitate grasping with ease and comfort.

However answers to important questions are given as under:-

Q-1. When all are born with equal possibility and opportunity to actualize their divine nature, then why only very few have attained their true nature and rest remain ignorant and unwise in their mission of enlightenment?

A-1. We all are divine by nature and the goal of life is to actualize the essence of our divinity. Animals are born actualized and live life as programmed by nature. Animals have no choice to evolve and attain divinity. They continue living there life in the cycle of birth and death. For them there is no way out to jump out of this cycle.

No doubt that all are born with equal capability and are entitled to attain divinity but all have different temperament, tendency and attitude which affect willingness, earnestness, determination, zeal and enthusiasm to attain. Man brings three attributes (harmony-passion and pervert) at the time of birth through nature as an accidental phenomenon. When things happen unpredictably and unexpectedly at its own beyond our control, such events are called accidental happenings.

With intense earnestness one can go beyond nature and can transcend these attributes which form man's nature, tendency and temperament. It happens when you identify false as false and understand your real nature through clear and empty mind.

Culturing, cultivation, learning and knowledge make mind opaque to reflect the reality. The attainment is a natural happening and not an effort, doing and practicing. Happening means smooth flow of life without any outer interference. Happening is an internal phenomenon beyond our understanding like digestion, sleep and hunger, these happens at their own and we cannot create these through our choice. Happening is natural and universal without distinction, but becoming and doing is unnatural because these need outer effort and practice to achieve something for personal gain by being particular.

Q-2. The great incarnations and spiritual teachers have appeared in the world from time to time but still the world is full of sin, sorrow and suffering. Why it is so?

A-2. The objective world (physical) is neither virtuous nor sinful. It is the mind which makes it so by creating distinction between good and bad. Separation and division are created by ego oriented mind. Separation reflects imperfection and incompleteness. Separation from the true self gives you an idea through nonself ego (mind) that you are only body and mind and not divine. Consequently you remain attached and involved with worldly things and face misery and chaos.

The objective world is not the problem but the subjective world which you project through imagination and illusion with your mind endlessly, causes disturbance and restlessness. It is your diseased mind which needs healing to bring peace, order and harmony in the world. The world projected through mind is a dream world which keeps changing moment to moment. Dream disappears on waking up. Dreaming is not the factual reality but only an imaginary entity. Similarly when you become aware of your true nature you go beyond mind dissolving the imaginary world (unreal world) that you create through mind. The sin, sorrow and suffering are your own creation to disturbed mind.

Mind is healed and purified when its contents are dropped by deepening and widening of the consciousness free of all negativities of the mind. Evolving from within your own self is an individual exercise and no one can help including the enlightened souls and spiritual teachers. They can guide and take you to the bank by inspiring you but crossing over to the other bank is your own wisdom and action. Individuals make society and when individuals improve society improves automatically. Improving of individuals mean curing of the diseased mind, which is the essence of all problems. The spiritual teachers cannot transfer their wisdom to others, they can only inspire and awake you about your true nature. If enlightened souls could transmit wisdom then the world would have been free of all sins.

Man is innocent in ignorance, guilty in action being unwise, sins without knowing and suffers without understanding. However the great incarnating souls sweeten the worldly atmosphere. One Christ, one Krishna, one Mohammad and one Buddha transformed the religious atmosphere which inspired people and attracted tremendous following. But inspite of all this none of us could attain Buddhahood because people remained only followers to a concept given by the great souls. Without experiencing from within, all remains a belief which cannot transform you internally. Unless there is inner transformation you will continue committing sins and face miseries in life.

Q-3. When we all are divine then why do we commit sins of all kinds including striving to seek, struggling for greed and grabbing to possess?

A-3. All is divine in the world of duality and distinctions. It is reflected in everything as stability, peace, joy, love, harmony, purity, power and wisdom. Everything contains reality in the center. Sin has virtue in the center, death has life in the center and poison contains nectar in the center. Nothing in the world can exist independently without the center support of the reality (divinity).

The outer world reflects the body of the inner world (reality). Reality remains motionless and stable inside but its reflection outside remains full of activities like waves and ocean relationship. Waves rise and subside outside but deep down in the ocean there is total inaction and silence. The reality is beyond sin and virtue because in reality only oneness of being exists.

Anything which is universal and spiritual (pure consciousness) do not commit sin or virtue like all five elements which make no distinction between right and wrong, sinner and saint. Sin is committed when you become personal and particular reflecting selfishness. Universality reflects ocean of love beyond any distinction and description. Universality reflects living life integrally with all with selfless and impersonal attitude. When you become personal and particular you remain mind oriented which leads you to ignorance and attachment to worldly things. Consequently your power of wisdom to discriminate between real and unreal is lost forever. You see unreal as real and real as unreal, it reinforces your ego, attachment and involvement with the outer world causing disturbance and restlessness in the mind. These make mind sick and diseased.

Desire and fear as such do not interfere but it is your thinking which makes them right and wrong depending on the quality of psyche you reflect. The quality of psyche is influenced by three attributes (harmony-passion-pervert) which we receive from nature at the time of birth, also learning culturing and cultivation by the society greatly contribute to the quality of the psyche.

People commit sin without wisdom and suffer without understanding the reality and are attached and involved with the events which mind projects. Your real nature is pure peaceful and lovable as such it cannot commit sin but when you become mind conscious then contradiction, conflict and confusion set's in blinding you about the right and truthful action. Activities happen through mind and silence happens through knowing your divinity.

Once you know that you are not the body and mind but the soul then you will go beyond sin because sin is the product of mind. Within mind sin survives and beyond mind it dissolves. The pain and suffering is to the body and mind and not to the soul.

When you see things through conditioned mind, your thoughts and feelings are corrupted and become impure. Things seen through created impressions of past experience distort the reality. You should focus your attention totally on your soul and not to the false and unreal events which mind projects.

Q-4. How do you realize and attain the experience of your true nature? Do techniques in any way help discovering the real nature?

A-4. You attain and discover a thing which you do not have or you have lost but in your case you have not lost your divine nature, it is always with you present so there is nothing to discover or attain. Once you refuse to identify with false and perishable things of the illusory world created by mind then wisdom, realization and understanding will flow at its own as a natural and normal happening which will lead you to your divine nature.

You cannot create happening through doing and effort. However doing and effort are necessary to achieve something specific in the outer world but in the inner world things happen at their own, like growing of nails and hair etc. Happening remains pure and natural when there is no interference by mind. Empty and clear mind becomes transparent to reflect the light of soul in its totality without staining.

The reflected light of the soul strengthens your mind with peace love, wisdom, self-confidence, enthusiasm, zeal and understanding.

The wrong focusing of attention brings misery, sorrow and suffering. It is so because wherever you focus your attention the energy flows towards the thought of attention. Transformation happens when attention is focused totally on the soul. If the attention is focused to the negativities of the mind then only ignorance can happen and there will be no transformation from within. The energy that radiates from the soul remains eternally pure as such you should always endeavor to maintain the purity of the divine energy in all your actions, by maintaining purity of the mind. The actions through impure mind turn the pure energy into impurity which brings sorrow and suffering in life.

No doubt worldly thoughts have definite role to earn the living and also discharging the social responsibility. Thoughts create problem and interfere only when you are emotionally involved and attached. Keep mind free of contents to be free of thoughts. To keep mind true think true. Once you become aware of your true nature then whatever you do becomes a blessing to humanity because your behavior and conduct start reflecting love, peace, joy, compassion, harmony, wisdom and power.

The best way to become soul conscious is to develop witnessing attitude to events which happen in the outer world. You only watch and observe without participation and emotional attachment. When mind does not interfere then no impressions of event is created because mind becomes pure dissolving all stains of memory and imagination. When mind attains purity the consciousness deepens and widens. Pure consciousness is a bridge between the spirit and the matter (mind-subtle matter). Consequently to be with your divine nature you must keep and maintain the purity of consciousness every moment. It is the consciousness which illumines the mind for right thought, speech and action.

In a day to day working clear mind and pure heart denotes selflessness, impersonality, devotion and service to all with love. There are two belief systems, one is that you suffer for sins of your past life and other is that all happens through will of God. You should dissolve these belief systems by becoming self (Atma) conscious. Concentrate on self improvement so that you are transformed from human nature to divine nature.

Techniques are useful for initial beginning but you must discard these when you come on the right track of spirituality because then things start happening smoothly at its own. It is like taking one step forward to the elevator step and then rest happens automatically to take you up to the next floor without effort. Use and utilize things wisely but do not cling and get emotionally attached. It is like using a water boat for crossing a river. You must discard the boat on reaching to the other bank. You cannot afford to carry it along with you wherever you go that may become a burden and hindrance to your journey. Ignorance is succeeded by wisdom and wisdom is succeeded by salvation (enlightenment).

Experience is possible in duality. Experience is essential to grow mature and achieve. Experience has three aspects knower, knowing and known. Without these experience remains incomplete. Knower is mind (subjective), known is objective things and knowing is the reality of awareness which links knower and known. Knower and known disappear with death of the body and reappear when new body is formed. Knowing is light of awareness which is eternal and can be actualized through knower and known when these appear.

There is no experience of your true being (divinity) because there is only oneness, wholeness, totality, perfection and completeness. For your true being you have to be total and whole, for experiencing your divine nature you have to be by living that way and there is no other way out.

Q-5. How do destiny, karma (action), will of God, chance and accidental factors affect our living life?

A-5. karma has three components, thought, speech and action. Pure thoughts make speech and action pure. However without pure thought you may act to be decent in your speech and action but in reality it is hypocrisy. Evil thoughts, intention and motive make the other two aspect of karma (speech and action) corrupt, contradictory and confusing. Pure thoughts liberate you from ego but impure thoughts bound you to sensuous things which cause sorrow and suffering. You are linked to your soul through pure thoughts. You should concentrate on purifying your thoughts so that speech and action fall in line through spiritual maturity with inner evolvement.

Destiny is what you make yourself through negative reactions to the actions of others. Reactions create negative impressions in the mind. These narrows thinking, feeling, action and hardens destiny. The main reason of your suffering is due to your belief system which you have learnt through society. Culturing and cultivation is the product of the society. The formation of destiny stops when you realize and experience your true nature. Divine nature is beyond destiny because it is total, complete and perfect. Destiny happens through mind which remains always impure, incomplete and imperfect. Destiny dissolves when you go beyond mind and become one with your divinity.

Life is a mystery, it is unpredictable beyond our control. You cannot shape life like service career because things happen in life at its own as a natural phenomenon and process. Consequently you live and accept life as it comes. You have no choice to reject but accept it without any resistance. It is joyful when accepted and painful when resisted. You need to change your attitude and outlook. You must realize that your real nature is divine which remains unaffected by events projected by mind. However events affect those who remain body and mind conscious. However nature has not given you guarantee of a trouble free life at the time of your birth. Striving and struggling are part of life.

Infact destiny, karma, will of God and accidental factors are blanket words to cover up ignorance. When you lack wisdom you find escape to blame others for whatever happens around you. You do not accept responsibility for your own wrong doings, this is mainly to shield your weakness reflecting lack of trust and self confidence in the soul. Destiny is a temporary and perishable phenomenon which is linked with the body and mind. Beyond mind when you become formless and changeless, destiny dissolves. You can shape your destiny by transforming from human to divine (form to formless). Come out of the belief that you are born with designed destiny and you have to live your life accordingly. It is not true because making of destiny is totally in your hand and it is not a natural phenomenon which happens at its own. You can ruin your life by believing in destiny. Transcend destiny by experiencing your true nature.

Karma and destiny are interlinked and are inter dependent. Action shapes destiny provided your actions are sacred, right and pure which can lead you closer to your soul. Your true nature is beyond action, there only inaction and stability prevails with total silence. Your true nature is the foundational source which makes all actions possible. Within mind you have many beliefs to follow and beyond mind all beliefs dissolve. When you are with earth you will experience days and nights but when with the sun you will experience no darkness. Ignorance and darkness are the birth place of beliefs and concepts. Wisdom is the tool to destroy ignorance. Ignorance means becoming body and mind conscious and wisdom means becoming soul conscious.

The visit to sacred places is considered a noble act. Visiting such places with desire contained mind brings no transformation from within. Desires reinforce your ego and belief. Transformation happens when mind attains purity and stop interfering, desiring, imagining and memorizing. Mind can be purified sitting at home without visiting sacred places. Transformation happens from within and not through outer rituals and procedures. The sacred places visited with evil mind bring back evilness only without any transformation. When mind becomes pure every place becomes sacred regardless where you stay and go. You should concentrate on unloading and emptying of evilness rather than blindly following a belief system in the name of false tradition and custom.

The will of God is a misnomer. The God has no will of its own to express. Things happen in nature according to phenomenon and process the nature projects. At source the God is supreme which cannot be mentalised and verbalized in the absence of consciousness. When consciousness is born as motion from the motionless supreme, then the world is manifested and is expressed through the instruments of body and mind. Source remains one and eternal but its expression through consciousness makes differentiation and distinction.

God is a form of energy (divine-spiritual-physical). The energy does not interfere because it is neutral, it is neither virtuous nor sinful but the mind makes it so. It entirely depends on you as to how best you can utilize the different aspects of energy in reaching your divine self. It is said that God helps those who help themselves it means it is your wisdom and dexterity as to how you channelize the energy for transformation. God has no role and will, he is beyond duality of sin and virtue, pleasure and pain. It is the quality and strength of your mind which has the capability to transform you through wisdom, insight and understanding. No one else can help you. God remains helpless in this context. Utilization of nature's energy is an individual phenomenon.

Sun sustains life on earth but sun is not responsible for whatever happens on earth because things happen according to different nature things and individuals have. You cannot shortcut nature's process and phenomenon. You cannot stop growing of crop nor can you pull out a flower prematurely from a bud. You cannot produce a child within a week. You cannot interfere with nature if you do you will be punished.

If you continue with your ignorance, believing in concepts and blaming situations and others then you will remain unwise accepting mind as your master. The fact is that you are responsible for suffering and sorrow as such accept this reality and do not find pretext of any nature to link it to karma, destiny and will of God.

Q-6. Why do we feel that we are not the body and mind but we are divine?

A-6. As a matter of fact whatever exists and live is divine. Man can actualize his divinity but others remain deprived as they are born actualized according to plan and program by nature. All existence survives on the support of divine source which remains independent and eternal. However existence as such has no independent survival. Anything which depends on the support of eternity remains false, unreal and perishable. We are divine by our real nature as such we are eternal and a foundational base to all that exist in the universe. However our body and mind are temporary and false as these are born and die, these appear and disappear.

In life you will like to choose things which give you permanent peace, love, joy, power, purity and wisdom, these flow through your own soul as such you will like to be governed by the soul and not by the body and mind which are perishable. Consequently you belong to the divine entity as your true identity and not to the body and mind which needs support from your divine power to sustain it-self. Body and mind are sustained by divine energy that flows inside in the form of soul. Our focus should be on the divine energy that flows inside and not on the outer structure of body and mind that appear. Anything which is perishable has no eternal identity, as such we should not attach importance to body and mind.

Q-7. What do we gain by attaining our true nature of divinity?

A-7. We do not gain extra power and status by knowing our true nature but we certainly recognize and discard false and unreal which hinders our journey in experiencing the reality. You gain immense peace and boundless love, joy, power, purity, wisdom and harmony between inner and outer, these strengthen our mind with self confidence, enthusiasm, zeal, determination, devotion and selfless service which makes us desireless, fearless, sharing, sacrificing, ego-less. With these traits we transcend sorrow and suffering and live a trouble free life.

When you attain divinity you become self disciplined and self controlled at your own. Things in the world improve when man of power, will and wisdom appear, but when their period ends the cycle of misery starts again as such these measures are temporary. When you experience your true nature then chaos and misery will dissolve forever. The dissolution of miseries become the highest gain, status and an asset in our life in term of divine power which is the ultimate and absolute truth, we all should aim to attain.

Q-8. We are conscious of body and mind as such obsessed and governed by memory and imagination prompted by desire for pleasure and fear from pain. The cycle of pleasure and pain is unending. How do we jump out of this cycle?

A-8. The simple and easiest way to jump out of this cycle of pain and pleasure is to shift your focus of attention from mind conscious to soul conscious so that you go beyond mind. It is mind which creates pain and pleasure through desire and fear. When you are governed by mind you are involved and attached to petty and perishable pleasure which you seek from things of the outer world and fear pain when you get detached. Pain and pleasure dissolve when wisdom enters your mind because wisdom reflects a no mind state.

Q-9. Evil exists in the mind which makes it diseased, how to heal the diseased mind so that everything is set right to live a trouble free life?

A-9. The evilness of mind are desire fear, anger, greed, jealousy, memory and expectation. It is caused by ignorance about your real nature and attachment to false things of the world. The diseased mind reflects wrong use of mind which happens through the contents of evilness. Right use of mind happens through wisdom and understanding.

The evilness of mind troubles those who become slave to mind but those who are masters of mind remain unaffected by the actions of the mind. To bring mind in order and to make it quiet you should not fight evilness of the mind because fight invites fight. You cannot control mind with grit and determination. Mind revolts because it is governed by the law of reverse effect, it means when you force mind to be quiet it will become more noisy and restless.

The only way to dissolve evilness of mind is to become a total witness without participation and involvement, the evil thoughts will gradually subside at its own in a natural and normal way. When you do not participate in the play you remain out of it.

The wrong use of mind is seeking, grabbing, striving, holding, losing and crying. It also means selfishness, non-sharing, non-sacrificing, hurting, cheating, depending, fear, attachment, restlessness, perversion and ego orientation. The right use of mind is clarity, purity, peace, love, joy, compassion, selfless service, impersonality, self discipline, self confidence, detachment, fearlessness, desirelessness, self realizing, wisdom, enthusiasm and zeal, forethought sharing, sacrificing and welfare of the humanity. The right use of mind heals the diseased and sick mind. Misuse of mind brings sorrow, suffering, chaos and misery in life.

It is the state of mind which makes all the difference to bring either bondage to sensuous things or liberation and freedom from these. You must concentrate on refining and purifying your mind according to techniques given in chapter thirteen.

Q-10. There is an eternal changeless source behind all change that we experience in the outer world. However change cannot take you to the changeless being as such how do we reach to the source?

A-10. In this context answer of question four covers many aspects however some important aspects are amplified and elaborated as under:-

There are two aspects of one reality. Real-unreal, true-false, eternal-temporary, formless-form, causeless-cause, desireless-desire, fearless-fear, changeless-change, lifeless-life, light-darkness, wisdom-ignorance, inaction-action, spirit-matter, motionless-motion, intuition-tuition and inner-outer etc. The existence and living life in the world depends on these aspects. There can be no creation in oneness, perfection, completeness, whole and total. Duality becomes the mother of creation. Motionless stability is essential for motion to cause creation like river bed is essential for river to flow.

Stability is real, eternal and causeless but motion and mobility are unreal and false as these are temporary and perishable. All that appears is outer structure and has a changing nature. It is like our body which has nature of birth and death but our soul is birth-less and deathless signifying eternity. Stability reflects peace, love, silence, inaction and non wavering mind but when motion happens passion, disturbance, restlessness, perversion, anxiety, anxiousness, imperfection result which cause narrowness, bondage, selfishness and indifference. These are reflected through body and mind and are created through the process of motion. As it is there is no problem with the body and mind but problem arises when you become conscious of these and identify with physical and mental events ignoring your divine and peaceful soul.

To reach your divine nature the changing nature of body and mind cannot help because change cannot take you to changeless. To reach the divine truth you have to refine, purify and make your mind divine so that light of soul is reflected fully negating all negativities of mind. Pure mind is equated to divinity. If you want to reach to changeless then change the nature of mind and make it pure.

Q-11. What is the grand plan and purpose of creating such a world which is full of disorder, restlessness and chaos? Will there ever be relief and peace in this world?

A-11. There is no plan and purpose of creating the world. It is there, it is so because the process and phenomenon of nature is such that things happen as it happens beyond any one's control and analysis.

Accept the reality of the world without distortion and imagination and stop finding purpose in the creation of the world.

There is no purpose for a flower to be beautiful, it is beautiful by nature. Flower does not aim at beauty. The purpose is seen in the nature's created things by man in the outer world for his own utilization and comfort but such things do not happen in nature because nature is cosmic and beyond particular with no purpose to please any one. It is man who seeks purpose for his survival and sustenance.

When you see things of nature with purpose then your seeing becomes fractured, impure, imperfect, distorted and particular. Consequently your focus of attention remains on outer appearance and structure and not on the inner divine energy which flows in all equally. Seeing only outer appearance reflects disunity, division and separation which cause sorrow and suffering. Total and whole seeing reflects oneness, unity, peace, love, joy, harmony, purity and wisdom.

When you see a flower see it as it is without expressing judgment of ugly and beautiful then seeing becomes whole and perfect free from mind's participation. When you appreciate and condemn flower then seeing becomes distorted and imagined. Your focus should remain on the consciousness inside which flows between you and the flower alike, after a while you will experience that you and the flower have become one through consciousness because by seeing this way the outer structure of flower disappears at its own and only pure consciousness remains.

Things of nature be seen and felt as suggested above so that division and separation dissolves and only unity prevails. Our culturing (sanskar) has become so strong and hard that we have learnt to focus attention on outer appearances only ignoring the consciousness flowing inside. Consequently we must treat all with divine attitude without hurting anyone.

However we should continue working relentlessly in the world according to our nature and temperament but always keep in mind that we all are one as a reality and not different as we imagine. This way of thinking, feeling and attitude will make living peaceful and harmonious without any ill will for anybody. You will stop comparing with others and you will compete only through fair means avoiding conflict, clash and contradiction. You will be able to transcend your born nature and you will become one with the reality. Your whole focus will shift to serve all with love and selfless attitude. You will strive for common good of all.

There is no chaos and disorder in the outer world. The chaos and restlessness is in your mind which you project in the outer world. Outer chaos reflects inner disharmony. You want peace in the world but where are peaceful people. To bring order in the world set your mind in order. You can help the world by going beyond the need of help yourself, it can happen when mind becomes empty, clear, steady and pure. The objective world is neither pleasurable nor painful it remains as it is. It is your mind with impurities which create disturbance and disorder in the world. it is entirely in your hands to either suffer or transcend suffering. No one else is responsible except you.

Q-12. How will one sustain his family and others who depends on him for sustenance and survival because after attaining true nature one ceases to care for worldly things?

A-12. The divinity does not tell you to disown and disassociate from the world. It is neither possible nor desirable. In fact divinity turns and transforms you from particular to universal making you the ocean of love to live integrally in unity with all without any distinction. Disowning, division and separation tendencies are experienced when you become body and mind orientated. Beyond mind you become Godly and bless humanity with love, peace and compassion.

Lord Buddha did not disown the reality which flowed between him and his family. He disowned the outer structure and appearance of the family which is deemed false and perishable. Lord Krishna, Lord Rama and Mohammad always lived with their families with an affectionate detachment attitude, discharging all social responsibilities. These great souls did not find any difference in living with the family because they realized that the same reality flows between them and the family. When you attain divinity you are transformed from human nature to divine nature and then the whole humanity becomes your family.

Q-13. How have the body and mind come into existence, bound by time and space. These trap us in bondage? How do we attain freedom and liberation?

A-13. Reality is beyond time and space as such it is eternal and changeless. Anything which is bound by time and space (forms of all nature) exists with the support of timeless and spaceless reality. Forms die after completion of its span of time of existence. The body reflects space and mind reflects time. Anything bound by time and space is temporary and transient as such has no real identity as the soul has. The space bound by pot is called pot space and when pot breaks the pot space merges with the universal space. Space is gross and physical but time is subtle and spiritual. Space and energy (time) are interlinked. Both remain bound in the form, energy sustains the form. When form disappears both become universal as universal space and cosmic energy.

The span of existence differs widely from an insect to a planet as planned and designed by nature. Why and how it happens remains beyond our knowing and understanding. We have to just accept this reality and concentrate on self transformation which is under our control.

The body and mind come into existence through combination of many factors, no single factor is responsible for producing these. It begins from the motionless source of divine being which give birth to consciousness as motion, all happens through consciousness. Gross form of consciousness is vital breath (pran) which vitalizes the body with life force. Consciousness illumines mind and make it aware of worldly things. The dense form of consciousness is matter which produces five elements and three attributes, harmony-passion-pervert (satva-rajas-tamas). The totality of all these factors contributes in manifesting the body and mind.

The bondage happens when you are governed by body and mind and identify with events which mind projects every moment. Ignorance does not mean lack of learning and knowledge of worldly things but it means ignorance about your soul. When you become soul conscious all negativities of mind dissolve. Purified mind liberates and makes you free from bondage of attachment and involvement, because you go beyond mind with soul awareness and cease caring for falsity of worldly things.

Q-14. In spite of our divine nature why do we behave in a contradictory manner and conduct un-divinely?

A-14. Divinity is beyond the traits of duality of good and bad. The combination of good and bad happens through the conditioned mind which sees separation from the soul. Duality, distinction and separation are product of mind. Mind cannot exist without these and beyond mind all dissolves only divinity remains. Mind is a thought, memory and imagination content prompted by desire and fear. These blind the mind in the wake of absence of divine light which remains dim due to opaqueness of mind.

Mind has tendency to see false as real and real as false because of its confused state in the absence of wisdom. Mind is an instrument to express and actualize the divinity but if you keep the mind in an impure state then it will reflect only negativities which cause contradictory and un-divinely behavior. When mind becomes pure you see things objectively as they are without any distortion and imagination.

It is the mind which makes you believe and behave un-divinely. Infact we are divine by nature regardless of our evilness and contradictory behavior, these do not affect in any way the identity of divinity. Water remains water regardless of any container. The sun sustains life on earth but it remains unaffected by happenings on the earth because things happen according to their nature. The mother nature produces potential seeds of different types containing everything to grow and sustain according to plan and program carved by it but the divinity remains unchanged and remains beyond the affect of things produced by mother nature.

Q-15. How has the world come into existence?

A-15. There are various concepts and beliefs which are prevalent about the manifestation of the world. Only concepts are known but actual reality about the world remains unknown and beyond our understanding. Concepts do not reflect truth these are only idea, thought, theory and opinion about truth as pointers and indicators.

Some say world is uncaused, some say the world is affect of causation, world exists as it is and will continue existing unendingly with a law of alternating appearance and disappearance, according to phenomena and process of nature. The other aspects are that the world is governed by eternal laws and is the result of big bang. The world is imploding and exploding every moment beyond our knowing as billions of cells in our body are formed and destroyed every moment.

The Vedic concept of existence of the world is based on the combination, coordination and interplay of sixteen basic elements. These are grouped in three parts, each part has five aspects which makes total of fifteen elements and the sixteenth element is the supreme divine source which remains eternal and uncaused, however it contains everything in seed form. This foundational source is known as "Paratpar (divine truth-supreme)." These three groups work with the support of the supreme, and these cannot exist independently. The first group is known "Avavya (unending)" it reflects consciousness which illumines awareness about worldly things through mind. Next group is "Akshar (non-perishable)." It denotes vital breath (pran) which vitalizes matter (body and mind). The last group is "Khar (perishable)" reflecting matter, it is physical aspect of creation.

All the sixteen elements are found in all seeds of different kind which exist and live in the universe regardless of an insect, saint or a planet. Without these sixteen elements creation remains incomplete and un-manifested. However do not get entangled with various concepts about creation of the world but accept life as it is and concentrate on self improvement so that you are transformed from human to divine.

However there are two worlds, one is the physical and objective world outside which exists for some time and then perish according to nature's law of creation, preservation and destruction. Nothing in this world has eternal entity. It is has a character of beginning-ending, birth-death, coming-going, appearing-disappearing, exploding-imploding.

However the span of existence and life may differ vastly between things of different entity and nature but regardless of span of life, all perish at the end of their period of existence. The outer world is transient and perishable as such it is unreal and false. The thing which remains eternal and unchanged is real and true (supreme-divinity-truth). The outer world being transient is equated with dream which disappears on waking up as such the changing outer world is known as dream world, which dissolves when you are awake and become aware of your reality.

The other world is mental world which is subjective, personal and private. It keeps projecting an imaginary and illusory world like a dream every moment. The imaginary world which mind projects is due to past memories and future expectations which are prompted by desire for pleasure and fear from pain. The outer world is not the problem but the problem originates through the mental world, when you perceive things with likes and dislikes and see false as real and real as false according to your mindset.

Q-16. Feelings have more appeal and impact then thoughts. Thoughts can convince but cannot convert (transform) why is it so?

A-16. There are three main centers in the body. Mind center which deals with logic and reason. Heart center which deals with emotion, feeling and love. Navel center represents life center of our being (soul). The locations of the center in our body are self evident by their names. Mind center is gross and physical. It works on surface only. Heart center is universal and spiritual and is a link between mind and spirit (life center-navel center). The link is established through pure consciousness as such heart center denotes that. The navel center is divine center the source of other two centers.

We are governed by three worlds. The world of being (reality), the world of feelings (bhava jagat) and the world of thoughts (vichar jagat). The process of governance of life should be that feelings be governed by the soul and mind be governed by the feelings, only then pure thought, pure speech and pure action will make karma (action) of right nature. However if you govern your feelings through mind then feelings get contaminated and will hamper your journey to link you to your divine soul. Feelings always remain pure, being spiritual and pure consciousness reflecting universal love, consequently feelings have deeper penetration to appeal and create deeper impact being closer to soul (navel center). The feeling carry the purity of soul and links it with the mind (thought). However if thoughts are polluted then pure feelings cannot transform your thoughts as such to receive purity of the soul through pure feelings, you have to clear, empty and make your mind pure.

Q-17. How do meditation, witnessing and awareness help in knowing your true being (divine soul)?

A-17. All these are methods and techniques which you follow initially to purify your mind and make it free from content of desire and fear etc. Once you come on the spiritual track through these techniques then you need not do effort and practice in this context because then things start happening automatically which will lead you to divinity (eternity). It is like putting seed in the ground which sprouts at its own when right season comes.

Meditation is aimed to bringing harmony between inner and outer by making your mind thoughtless through the process of meditation. When thoughts subside through meditation then your mind becomes quiet, steady and non wavering dissolving disturbance and restlessness. It happens when you place a seed of noble thought (I am a peaceful soul) in the mind. When your total attention is concentrated on the noble thought the other thoughts dissolve and mind becomes free to reflect the light of soul because it is the law of nature that energy (divine-spiritual-physical) flows in the direction of attention. When divine energy starts flowing through your mind then your actions become sacred and righteous. Remembrance is through mind and understanding comes through awareness. You should go beyond mind to avoid remembrance which works only in the outer world. However awareness reflects the light of divinity which enters the mind when it is pure and clear, consequently your understanding develops through wisdom.

Witnessing is the culmination of meditation. When you mature in meditation and feel light by unloading your mind with its content then you automatically develop a witnessing attitude. In witnessing you become an observer of mental and physical events without involvement, participation and attachment there by you deny entry of thoughts into your mind. When you only observe and don't cling to thoughts then thoughts subside making your mind pure, empty and clear for receiving the light of awareness fully. Through witnessing you are directly linked with your soul because pure mind becomes non interfering. Witnessing becomes a medium for divine light to move freely from the supreme self and reflects its purity through non wavering mind.

Awareness is the light of the supreme which when reflected through refined and pure mind make us wise and understanding so that our thoughts become pure and clear, heart becomes charitable and actions become sanctified. Awareness makes us aware about our true nature so that we are able to discard false things of the external world. We are very much conscious of worldly things but remain unaware of our real nature. In view of this remain fully aware about your divine nature every moment so that your focus of attention to body and mind dissolves.

Q-18. What is the implication of religion, rituals and prayers in living life?

A-18. The religion has two aspects one is true religion which you actualize by experiencing your divine nature. Actualization means being to be what you are in reality (supreme truth-divine soul). It is a happening which happens at its own when false and unreal externals are recognized and discarded through deepening and widening of consciousness (purity of mind). The great souls Krishna, Christ, Mohammad, Buddha and Mahvira always lived with true religion as such they were equated to God.

The other aspect of religion is that we follow and practice in the outer world as a belief and a concept which is false and unreal. It is unreal because it is not your experience but you only follow a thought, idea and concept given to you by the enlightened souls. Different religions in the world are prevalent due to such concepts given by the great souls (Hinduism, Christianity, Islam, Buddhism and Jainism). Anything which is not your experience remains a concept which is distortion and imagination of the truth (reality). The true religion reflects divine soul and the false religion becomes its body. It is up to you to either concentrate and be aware of your center reality or remain body and mind conscious and continue suffering.

The philosophy of rituals is that you believe that the outer actions will bring inner transformation but it can never happen that way because outer is gross and particular like our body which work on the surface level only. The inner is subtle and universal reflecting pure feeling of love. Transformation happens when you maintain the purity of your feeling by becoming spiritual through pure consciousness. Inspiration always happen through inner feelings as such when anything touches feeling it creates greater impact in transforming you internally. Waves on the surface of the ocean cannot bring any change to the silence of ocean deep down.

Worship and prayers that we follow as routine habit signifies adoration of created Gods, Goddesses and deities. We generally pray and worship to demand and seek favours, such prayers are hippocratic, superficial and cannot bring peace, love and joy in life. Such prayers remain physical and work only on the outer surface making no impact inside, consequently you remain unchanged. Instead of concentrating on idols of God and Goddesses outside you should focus on purifying your mind so that you receive the divine light of the supreme fully. As a matter of fact prayer in the real sense is culmination of love where devotee and deity become one dissolving all distinctions and duality. The real prayer means merging with your divine being. The real prayer happens when you attain pure consciousness. When you can reach the highest God (supreme) through pure consciousness reflecting in the pure mind then what is the point serving designed Gods through conditioned mind (impure mind).

Q-19. Are morality and conscience real, created or cultured? What is there link with religion?

A-19. Morality has nothing to do with your true religion (divine nature). Morality is the product of society and the true religion is your real nature. Morality makes distinction between good and bad but true religion is beyond these distinctions, because in real nature your being remain undisturbed as one entity beyond duality. Morality is cultivated and cultured through learning and knowledge to maintain order, discipline and harmony according to the norms and conventions of the society. Morality is not natural and normal it doesn't happen at its own but it is acquired through social training, effort and practice as such it has temporary nature of coming and going. You may show morality outside to keep image of your goodness but inside you may be full of evilness, which you manifest at times to take advantage for personal gain.

It is not necessary that you can transform internally through goodness because goodness is only for social conduct and behavior which is useful in the outer world but it has no significance in the inner world where only silence and the bliss prevail. When you spiritually mature by inner evolvement and become cosmic then the aspects of good and bad dissolve because you become the ocean of love dissolving all distinctions and descriptions. On attaining universality you become virtuous and saintly to bless the whole humanity with compassion, love, purity, peace, power and wisdom, which spreads all around as a positive divine energy which can be received by those who have pure mind. Those who have impure mind will not be benefited by such blessings because impure mind is not strong enough due to contents of negativity to receive the energy which radiates from saintly people as a blessing. When your mind is strengthened with purity and wisdom then your actions automatically becomes righteous and sacred because the divine light passing through pure mind transforms you totally for right action.

Conscience is different to consciousness. Conscience (goodness) is outer self and consciousness (chetna) is inner self and beyond these both is supreme self. Conscience and consciousness are two aspects of one reality. At times we say that my conscience does not allow, it means that my behavior must match to the expectations of my society, beside this my conscience must be in line with the norms and conventions which the society has evolved for my conduct and behavior. Consequently it is deduced that the conscience is the product of society as such it is temporary and perishable, it disappears with the death of the body and reappears when new body is formed.

Anything which comes through culturing and cultivation by society changes with the change of society and that is why the values set by society do not apply always and everywhere for all time, these keep changing from time to time and place to place. Conscience becomes your second nature to survive and exist in the society. Conscience and morality are interlinked because both belong to outer self which are affected by the society. To maintain morality under testing pressure of temptation is a matter of your own conscience. You may show morality under fear, force and threat but you remain immoral otherwise because basically evilness is hidden inside all of us which can prompt for greed and grab if not controlled. Control brings temporary relief. To dissolve evilness permanently drop mind and go beyond because evilness originates through mind which contains evilness of past life and stores evilness of the present life.

Q-20. Compassion is granted by enlightened souls and not by normal human beings, who remains disturbed and restless. Why it is so?

A-20. Compassion is refusing to accept suffering of people. Suffering is a creation of impure mind. It happens when you remain ignorant about your real nature of divinity and get attached and involved with sensuous things of the outer world. Suffering dissolves when you become aware of your true nature. It is like a dream which disappears on waking up. Man of compassion is always concerned and considerate to awake people from body and mind conscious and make them aware about their divine soul so that suffering ends.

Compassion means concern and sympathy for humanity which suffers unnecessarily in the absence of wisdom. You are liberated from suffering when understanding comes to your pure mind through the divine light. The aim of saintly people is to inspire you to transform from human nature to divine nature so that suffering does not disturb you ever for living a peaceful and harmonious life. Compassion reflects universal love for all, so that the humanity improves and moves smoothly on the spiritual track without any interference by sorrow and suffering.

Compassion happens automatically and spontaneously when you go beyond the need of help yourself by experiencing your divine nature, only then you can bless and help others, otherwise you remain entangled with your own problems and will have no time to attend to the problems of others. The physical help that we render to others and show sympathy out worldly is not compassion because physical help gives only temporary relief and can come up again at the end of relief. But compassion aims at permanent relief through inner transformation.

Compassion is granted by enlightened souls who have transformed their mind from human nature to divine nature because only such people can generate positive divine energy to inspire people under grief. However translating inspiration into action is your own doing. Enlightened souls can only inspire and motivate you by their own examples so that you concentrate on self improvement for total transformation to divinity.

Q-21. What is the reality about the concept of rebirth and how does it affect our life?

A-21. It is believed that unfulfilled desires trap energy in the subtle body (memory body). Man has five bodies but only three bodies are important to understand the concept of rebirth, gross body(physical) subtle body (memory) and casual body (consciousness) beyond these there is pure light of awareness which originates from the divine source (pure being).

Memory body does not die with the death of the physical body. The physical body dies once for all and does not return but memory body exists along with consciousness, awareness and pure being which reappear in the new body when formed. The new body is born with fresh brain free of any impressions as such does not remember anything of the past life. However some incidents have come to light where persons do remember events of past life, it is a concept which is unknown and beyond understanding as such accidental. Many abnormal things happen at times in nature accidentally like a women giving birth to seven children at one time contradictory to normal process of nature.

Memory body as believed prompts desire, fear and imagination etc. The memory body is dissolved only when you attain your true nature of divinity. There is no rebirth of the body but there is a concept of reappearance of the memory body. Concepts are not the reality but the distortion and imagination of the reality. However following the concept of rebirth in no way can help you for inner transformation. It can only burden your mind and make it impure of obscuring the reality. In view of this focus mainly on inner transformation rather than believing in concepts which are beyond reason and logic, these be left to people who are governed by body and mind and remain ignorant about their divine entity.

Where there is mind concepts and beliefs will exists but beyond mind these dissolve. Concepts reinforce your belief system through memory body which makes your thoughts impure and polluted and when thoughts become contaminated the charm of living life is ruined because the speech and action are linked to your thought. Pure thoughts are the governing factors to live life with harmony and peace.

Q-22. What we desire we never get, why it is so?

A-22. It is so because we concentrate more on desire to achieve pleasurable petty things of the outer world which consumes and scatters the spiritual and divine energy, thereby energy required to translate into action is reduced making you weak, dull and ignorant. However when we have single burning desire to know our real nature of divinity than all other petty desires which consume energy are dissolved. Consequently we become the power house of conserved energy to materialize the noble desire. Worldly desires are endless which cannot be fulfilled because we waste our energy in the negativities which are of no use to us in inner evolvement and transformation. Needs can be met but not the unending desires which are self and personal orientated as such we fail to achieve what we desire. Noble and sacred desires can be fulfilled but not the worldly desires which are confusing and contradicting.

When we scatter our energy flow to fulfill meaningless desires then it reduces our self confidence, enthusiasm, zeal and determination with that the wisdom is also obscured by remaining ignorant and unaware about right desires. Right desires are those which bring happiness and wrong desires bring sorrow and suffering. Desire orientated mind always compare, compete and suffer from complex, thereby you develop a habit of criticism, commenting, condemning, conflicting, contradictory, clashing, worrying and crying in the end when desires are left unfulfilled.

You may be talented and skilled even then there is no certainty that you will succeed in life because you do not put your soul into action and stop at desiring and thinking level. Desiring and thinking will not help you but translating these into pure and righteous action will make you successful in life. People first want success to become peaceful but it does not happen that way because it is against the law of nature. Success can never make a disturbed mind peaceful. To be successful in life you have to be peaceful first by purifying your mind. Peace of mind can dissolve disturbance and make it quiet and non-wavering.

In self evolvement and inner transformation mind becomes divine and non-interfering. In life inspite of your best capabilities, talent and skill it is not necessary that you will succeed because there are many outer factors beyond our control which adversely interferes and affect your success. When you do not succeed you think, feel and believe that you are not destined to succeed. Linking success to destiny is a word to cover up the failures. You are not destined to suffer but you are destined to dissolve suffering by realizing your divine nature. Desires aimed for common good of all are fulfilled because the energy from others flows to meet your desires which are beneficial to humanity.

Q-23. How do we win over anger, greed and jealousy?

A-23. All these vices have come through belief system which influences our thinking and feeling. These become our habits which are expressed in our actions as such accept these as normal and natural. Anger, greed and jealousy reflect our past karmic accounts (past actions). These do not belong to our real nature but are acquired and cultivated habits of the past life and the present actions which reinforce these vices. These can be dissolved when you realize and experience your true nature. The wisdom and the awareness about your true nature are the treatment to win over all the negativities of the mind.

Anything which is created and acquired through mind is false and unreal because these keep changing from moment to moment. No one has ever taught us that we are a peaceful soul, all teaching and learning has been around mind orientation which produces contradictory and confusing thoughts blocking the light of soul which generates wisdom, understanding and insight. The light of soul when passes through pure mind strengthens it with self confidence, self respect, self discipline, enthusiasm, zeal and determination which are deemed essential for living a trouble free life.

The belief system be replaced by living with our true nature so that you become master of your mind rather than living life as slave to the mind.